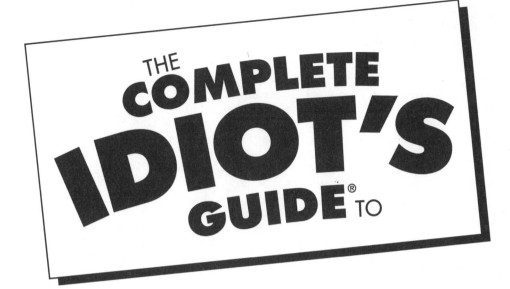

THE COMPLETE IDIOT'S GUIDE® TO

Trouble-Free Car Care

Second Edition

by Dan Ramsey

alpha books

A Division of Macmillan General Reference
A Pearson Education Macmillan Company
1633 Broadway, New York, NY 10019-6785

This book is dedicated to three young ladies: Judy, Heather and Ashley. May your roads be smooth and your journey trouble-free. God bless.

Copyright © 1999 by Dan Ramsey

Macmillan Publishing books may be purchased for business or sales promotional use. For information please write: Special Markets Department, Macmillan Publishing USA, 1633 Broadway, New York, NY 10019.

International Standard Book Number: 0-02863583-3
Library of Congress Catalog Card Number: 99-65262

02 01 00 99   4 3 2 1

Interpretation of the printing code: the rightmost number of the first series of numbers is the year of the book's printing; the rightmost number of the second series of numbers is the number of the book's printing. For example, a printing code of 99-1 shows that the first printing occurred in 1999.

Printed in the United States of America

Car Care Card

About Your Car

Year _____

Make _____

Model _____

Body style _____

Vehicle identification
    number (VIN) _____

Family _____

License plate number _____

Engine displacement _____

Engine number of cylinders _____

Cylinder firing order _____

Engine oil type _____

Engine oil capacity (with filter) _____

Carburetion or fuel injection _____

Recommended fuel octane _____

Fuel tank capacity _____

Spark plug type _____

Spark plug gap _____

Ignition timing _____

Distributor parts numbers _____

Air filter part number _____

Fuel filter part number _____

Oil filter part number _____

Drivebelt part numbers _____

Radiator capacity _____

Manual transmission
    lubricant type _____

Manual transmission
    lubricant capacity _____

Automatic transmission
    fluid type _____

Automatic transmission
    fluid capacity _____

Power steering fluid type _____

Battery size group _____

Battery CCA (cold crank amps) _____

Tire size _____

Tire pressure _____

Car Maintenance Schedule

H=under the hood; U=under the car; B=beside the car

Weekly or every _____ miles:
- ➤ Check oil level (H)
- ➤ Check coolant level (H)
- ➤ Check windshield-washer fluid level (H)
- ➤ Check power steering fluid level (H)
- ➤ Check brake fluid levels (H)
- ➤ Check tires and pressure (B)

Every three months or every _____ miles:
- ➤ Check battery and charging system (H)
- ➤ Check hoses (H)
- ➤ Check cooling system (H)
- ➤ Check transmission fluid (H/U)
- ➤ Check differential lubricant level (U)
- ➤ Check suspension and steering (U)
- ➤ Check exhaust system (U)
- ➤ Check windshield-wiper blades (B)

Dates done:
_____
_____

Every six months or every _____ miles:
- ➤ Change oil and filter (H/U)
- ➤ Adjust throttle linkage (H)
- ➤ Adjust carburetor (H)
- ➤ Adjust brakes (U)
- ➤ Adjust tire rotation (B)

Dates done:
_____
_____

Once a year or every _____ miles:
- ➤ Adjust the ignition timing (H)
- ➤ Replace engine drivebelts (H)
- ➤ Replace chassis lubricant (U)

Dates done:
_____
_____

Every two years or every _____ miles:
- ➤ Replace radiator coolant, cap, and hoses (H)
- ➤ Replace fuel filter (H)
- ➤ Replace air filter (H)
- ➤ Replace spark plugs (H)
- ➤ Replace spark-plug wires (H)
- ➤ Replace other ignition parts (H)
- ➤ Replace PCV, EEC, EGR parts (H/U)
- ➤ Replace automatic transmission filter and fluid (U)
- ➤ Replace manual transmission/ transaxle lubricant (U)
- ➤ Replace differential lubricant (U)
- ➤ Replace wheel-bearing lubricant (B)

Dates done:
_____
_____

alpha
books

Handling Common Automotive Emergencies

To safely jump a dead battery using another vehicle's battery:

1. Use a jumper cable to connect the dead battery's positive terminal to the helper car's positive terminal.

2. Connect the helper car's negative terminal to a bolthead on the disabled car's engine.

3. Start the helper car's engine, and then the disabled car.

4. Once started, remove the jumper cable in reverse order of how it was installed.

To change a flat tire:

1. Turn on your emergency flashers and raise the trunk lid to signal to others that you are having a problem.

2. Use the flat edge of a tire tool or screwdriver to pry the hubcap off the wheel rim. Use a tire tool to loosen but not remove the four or five lug nuts holding the wheel to the axle.

3. Place a block behind a wheel on the other axle. Then place the car jack under the car frame or on the bumper as described in the owner's manual. Stop raising the jack when the wheel is high enough to rotate the tire without touching the ground.

4. Remove the lug nuts and place them in the hubcap so they don't get lost. Remove the tire and set it out of the way.

5. Install the spare tire on the car. Screw the lug nuts on the car by hand, making sure that the tapered side of each nut faces the wheel.

6. Lower the jack until the tire firmly touches the ground but isn't supporting the car. Use the tire tool to tighten the lug nuts in a criss-cross pattern.

7. When all lug nuts are tight, lower the jack until it can be removed. Replace the wheel cover by pressing it against the wheel rim. Don't drive a space-saver spare tire at highway speeds for more than 50 miles.

If your car overheats:

1. Carefully lift the lever on top of the radiator cap to release pressure, being cautious of escaping steam and coolant.

2. After a minute or two, place a folded cloth over the cap and twist the cap counter-clockwise one-quarter turn to relieve more pressure. Remove the cloth to keep it from becoming soaked with hot coolant.

3. When the cap stops spewing liquid, place the cloth over the cap again and twist it counter-clockwise further to remove the cap.

4. Allow the engine to cool down for at least 20 minutes before replacing spilled coolant.

Emergency telephone numbers:

_____

_____

_____

_____

Contents at a Glance

Contents

Foreword

When you hear the word kingpin, do you quickly think of a mob boss? If someone mentions a valve guide do you focus on heart surgery? And who is this guy MacPherson and why does he always strut? Actually, all of these are automotive terms and they mean important things to people who know the ins and outs of automotive repair. But many of us, car enthusiasts or not, are a bit short of expert when it comes to repairing automobiles, whether new or old.

Author Dan Ramsey has done a masterful job with *The Complete Idiot's Guide to Trouble-Free Car Care*. It is chock full of insights, definitions, handy tips, how-to-instructions and more—all presented in the most non-threatening, easy-to-use manner. I've been around cars all my life and have skinned my knuckles on everything from a 1929 Model A Ford to a 1992 Mercedes-Benz 4000E, and I can tell you this book is a delight.

If things mechanical intimidate you or someone you know and love, Dan Ramsey is your guru. He tells you clearly and simply how to remove a radiator (reminding me of the time I had to do this job on a beach in Baja California, Mexico, then wade out through the surf to clamber into a small boat to go find someone with a solder gun!), or how to rebuild your car's brakes, or any of a hundred other jobs. He also outlines those things you can do quarterly, semi-annually and yearly to keep your automobile in tip-top condition.

And, for those who really have limited mechanical knowledge, Dan discusses the sounds that cars make and what they usually indicate. Following that, he tells you how to use this information at the repair shop so that you don't get ripped off. There truly is something for everyone in the pages of this book.

In this, the second edition, Ramsey has brought some valuable enhancements to the book on such subjects as "Cars on the Internet" (Chapter 4) and the "Non-Nerd's Guide to Understanding Your Car's Computer" (Chapter 16). These and other additions and modifications make this second edition a very valuable resource for anyone who owns and drives a car. It's certainly a book that I will keep very close at hand.

Thos. L. Bryant
Editor-in-Chief
Road & Track

Introduction

Americans have been in love with their cars for about a hundred years now.

That love affair has been chronicled and fed in many ways. The clearest example of this true love was offered in a classic love story movie, *American Graffiti*. It illustrated the role that cars play in our growing up. Steve courts Laurie with his Chevy. Terry courts Debbie with the same Chevy. Curt, who drives a tinny foreign car, craves meeting the blonde in the Thunderbird. John and Falfa duel it out in a drag race at sunrise. It's all there: love, lust, bravado, insecurity, and the acceptance that youth struggles with. And it's all greased with 30-weight oil. Cars are part of the love process. For some, they are the love objects until something more human comes along.

American Graffiti was the top-grossing film of 1973. You might also remember 1973 as the year of the first large-scale gasoline shortage. Or you might not. Cars waited in line for hours to fill up with fuel at any price. Real or contrived, the gas shortage was a wake-up call to the American motorist whose thirst for gas-guzzlers was getting out of hand. Luxury cars of the '50s and '60s were getting single-digit miles per gallon. They weighed up to 5,000 pounds—that's two-and-a-half tons, folks. They were born in an era of 19-cents-a-gallon-and-a-free-glass gas, but they quickly were speeding to an era of dollar-plus-gas-and-you're-lucky-if-they-clean-your-windshield.

Our love—and progressive need—for cars is also reflected in other areas of our society. There is hardly an aspect of our daily life that has not changed dramatically because of the automobile. Without cars, there would be no Burger King, freeways, or opportunities to "see the USA in your Chevrolet." Nor would there be a Gulf War or Exxon Valdez.

Cars have changed our language as well. A hood used to be something Robin or Red Riding wore. Today's hood covers the engine, or is where you live. A trunk was a real steamer trunk mounted on the rear bumper into which you stuffed clothes for travel. Today's trunk includes a spare tire, a jack, and little room for a suitcase. A muffler was something you wrapped around your neck when it got cold. Today's muffler reduces engine noise but produces obnoxious television commercials. (Read this book and you won't pay a lot for that muffler, either!)

The British, who invented the English language and then had it taken from them, developed their own language for their cars. A *hood* is a *bonnet*. A *trunk* is a *boot*. A *muffler* is a *silencer*. Don't ask what the underskuttle is. No wonder we're called "two countries separated by a common language." The car illustrates this difference.

Nowhere is our dependency on the car so clear as in the American pastime called *the commute*. Because of the car, we live beyond walking distance of our jobs and recreations. In many parts of the country, we must pile one to five people into an automobile designed for two to four people, and then join what is euphemistically called *the rush hour*. In most cases, it is neither a rush nor just an hour. Worst of all, some driver who has deferred automotive maintenance decides that it can no longer be delayed—and stops in the center lane! (Give this book to that driver as you slowly drive by, instead of editorializing on his parentage.) The wonderful invention that gets us to and from work also keeps us from doing so.

The commute also gives work to others: cab drivers, police officers, disc jockeys, billboard makers, road builders, and, of course, gas station attendants. They are no longer *service stations* but *gas stations*. They don't have to like you anymore. You need them—and they know it.

The car is also how many of us express our personality—or at least the image we want others to see. The banker drives a Cadillac to work. The young salesman (or the older dentist) glides to work in a Corvette. The yuppie telephones clients from a Beemer. The broke-but-still-proud driver chugs along in a rust bucket held together with Bondo and bumper stickers. The office worker drives a Toyota with $200 in extra trim options to differentiate it from the 200 other Toyotas in the parking lot. The 50ish man drives a '50s car to say, "I'm not old; I'm a classic."

And what would life today be without the power of ground transportation? An airplane carries your package to Minneapolis overnight, but it is a van (big brother to the car) that picks it up and delivers it. Other vans deliver fresh bread to that little Italian restaurant you like so well. Taxis carry the automotively disadvantaged to and fro. Buses vie for passengers and the right of way. They are all related to the wondrous invention we call the *car*.

In the Beginning...

Before the automobile was invented a century ago, people moved from here to there and back using a variety of vehicles. Before the horseless carriage was the horse. The horse is a wondrous invention that God gave us so we would have something to feed oats to (and something to fertilize the oats with). First we rode the horse, and then we attached wheeled vehicles to it. Then, when the car came along that went faster than a horse, we drove to the racetrack to bet on slow horses.

Two centuries ago, the first carriage without a horse was built. It was powered by steam and could run for only about 15 minutes without running out of the same. Top speed was slower than a walk. If these vehicles had caught on, today's rush hour would be three days long!

A century later and a century ago, the internal combustion engine was invented. It was installed on a carriage previously pulled by a now-unemployed horse. Top speed was faster than a walk—except in England, where a person waving a red flag was required by law to precede any such contraption. Within 10 years, Karl Benz, Henry Ford, Ransom Olds, the Duryea brothers, and many others had successfully built and even sold a few auto (self) mobiles (movers). They weren't very auto or very mobile by today's standards, but they moved people from point A to point B. They were a curiosity. Nobody expected that they would replace the horse.

It wasn't that the cars didn't run well. They did. It was that the roads of the day were made for beings with flat feet, not round tires. Winter and spring turned roads to ice or mud. Horses did okay with these elements, but cars got stuck up to their axles or slid completely off the so-called road. A horse could pull a wagon out of the mud, but a horseless carriage could not. Many farmers helped buy the farm by pulling these early inventions from the mud with their mudders.

Things got better, though. Cars were built with more power. Roads were graded. Some roads were even covered with asphalt to keep them smoother longer. And cars got cheaper. The assembly process developed in manufacturing horse-drawn carriages were soon applied to horseless carriages. In fact, a few of the earliest car manufacturers—including Studebaker—were wagon manufacturers first. If you can't beat them...

Henry Ford did much to bring the early automobile to the average person. While most manufacturers were building larger and more complicated cars, Henry kept it simple. He also made it efficient. By standardizing parts so that they were interchangeable, Ford was able to build cars in a progressive assembly line. This method brought down costs. A standardized car could be built for less than $1,000. At one point, a new Model T was priced at less than $300. Henry made it up in volume, producing as many as 10,000 cars a day! Ford did for cars what McDonald's did for hamburgers.

Historical Footnote: The Model T was built to be maintained and repaired by the owner. It may have been the first and last automobile to be so designed.

But the Model T, or "Tin Lizzy," wasn't for everyone. Cadillac offered luxury cars with the latest feature: a self-starter. The driver (or chauffeur) didn't have to use a hand crank to start the car and then jump in before it quit. The car could be started from the driver's seat. Other car designers offered larger engines, more seating, more colors, and more design options. The simple car was becoming more complex.

The Great Depression didn't change car designs much. There was the luxury car (Duesenberg, Packard, or Chrysler) for the rich, and the common car (Ford Model A, Chevrolet, or Plymouth) for everybody else. The Depression did help the auto industry, however, because the unemployed were put to work extending the American road system as part of the public works program.

Then World War II came along and the auto industry put its manufacturing skills to work in the war effort. Gas and rubber tires were rationed, and money was spent on war bonds and keeping the old car on the road. The first new postwar cars looked exactly like the prewar cars because they were. But the auto race was renewed quickly as returning GIs started new jobs and families. They had seen the world, had brushes with death, and were ready for new brushes with death on the open road. The auto industry was geared up to give it to them.

The 1950s was a great decade for the American car. Motors developed more power. Cars became an art form with chrome and fins and aerodynamic lines. They had names like Champion, Deluxe, Customline, Golden Hawk, and Bel Air. Cars of the '50s also had an easier road to travel than their ancestors. The interstate highway system was expanded with the help of the federal government, which saw it as a tool of defense. Most families saw it as a way to visit more places faster. As they got hungry along the way, they stopped in at The Colonel's or stayed at Howard Johnson's. The more widely people traveled, the more they depended on familiar names. Franchises were a byproduct of the popularity of the automobile.

The 1960s brought muscle to the American automobile. The '50s started with engines of 200 cubic inches in size and ended with those of 300 ci. The '60s bumped the size up to 400 ci and beyond. We were hungry for power.

But power corrupts. It also guzzles gasoline. Although some cars of the 1960s became more efficient to conserve gas, it was the 1970s that forced everyone to make one acronym the most talked-about feature on new cars: *MPG—miles per gallon*. The American car manufacturers didn't hear the warning in time, so the auto-buying public went to foreigners.

By the 1980s, names previously unheard in American garages now were spoken of as the best built, most efficient cars: Honda, Datsun, and Toyota. Some American car manufacturers joined in with these foreigners. Others faced them bumper-to-bumper. This was war!

Along the way, however, cars became more complex. Engines that had two valves per cylinder now had three or even four. Engines with one camshaft (you'll learn these terms later) now had two. Fuel was no longer dumped into the engine; it was injected. And it took a computer to make it all run smoothly.

Unfortunately, this complexity took the do-it-yourself element out of car maintenance and repair. You seemingly need an engineering degree—and a politician's salary—to keep your car maintained and repaired.

We're going to fix that!

This book demystifies the common car, clearly describing how it works, what you can do to keep it working, and what you can do when it doesn't work. It might not put any professional mechanics out of a job, but it certainly will reduce the number of unprofessional mechanics who take advantage of car owners they consider "complete idiots."

Ready?

The Dirty-Hands Test

First, let's determine how you want to participate in making your car trouble-free. Let's take a test. Please answer the following questions as appropriate:

1. When it comes to working on my car:
    A. I prefer to pull out my checkbook.
    B. I probably could change the oil, but please don't ask me how.
    C. I don't mind getting my hands a little dirty, as long as I can save a few bucks.
    D. Gimme a wrench and get out of my way!

2. The best description of my mechanical aptitude is:

   A. I've never successfully taken anything apart and put it back together.

   B. I've fixed things before, but I usually have a couple of parts left over.

   C. I've occasionally brought life back to things I was going to throw away.

   D. If it ain't broke, break it and fix it!

3. I would like to learn how to:

   A. Reduce the costs of owning my car.

   B. Understand what the heck the mechanic is talking about.

   C. Maintain my car but leave the repairs up to someone else.

   D. Do all of my car's maintenance and repairs.

4. Who should read this book?

   A. All of the above!

How to Use This Book

Whether you're someone who wants to do all your car's maintenance and repairs or someone who just wants to know more about how cars work, this book will help.

To make the task easier, this book is offered in three parts to help you understand, maintain, and repair your car. Read it from cover to cover, even if all you want to do is understand your car better. First, because you will get a clearer understanding of your car as you read how specific maintenance and repairs are made. Second, because you might realize that you can do more of your own maintenance and repair than you think you can.

Part 1, "Understanding Your Car," includes valuable information on how cars run, how to learn about your specific car, and how to read and use service manuals. These are the basics. With this information, you can drive more confidently and talk to your mechanic more knowledgeably. Whether or not you decide to do your own automotive maintenance and repair, this section will help you become a more informed consumer.

Part 2, "Maintaining Your Car," shows you how to make your car last longer, drive better, and cost less through regular maintenance. You may or may not decide to do it yourself, but understanding the requirements of regular car maintenance will help keep money in your pocket. You'll learn what maintenance you can do without tools, how to select parts and tools, and how to work safely and without getting dirty.

You'll also be introduced to the CAR Maintenance System, an easy-to-remember method of ensuring that regular maintenance is performed on your car. You'll also learn how to find a mechanic who won't take advantage of your plastic.

Part 3, "Repairing Your Car," is a must-read for every car owner—whether or not the owner will actually do the repairs. It clearly explains how to find out what's wrong with your car, and then offers step-by-step instructions for making the needed repairs. You might decide to do the repairs yourself, or you might decide to hire someone else to do them. In either case, you will know what's involved and have a pretty good idea of how much it should cost.

Repairs covered in this section range from simple parts replacements to complete engine repair. Knowledge is power!

Do you know what an exhaust gas recirculation system is? If not, you will! As you read such terms in the text of this book, you can quickly look them up in the glossary—everything from Advance to Zerk fitting.

The front of this book includes an easy-to-use maintenance card for keeping track of all the maintenance and repairs on your car. It also offers information you can use to confidently handle most common automotive emergencies. Keep this card in your car's glove compartment. Better yet, when you're done reading it, keep this entire book in your car. (This book probably won't fit in the glove box—especially if you keep anything more than gloves in it!)

Extras

Along the way, you'll see little boxes that include special information you can use.

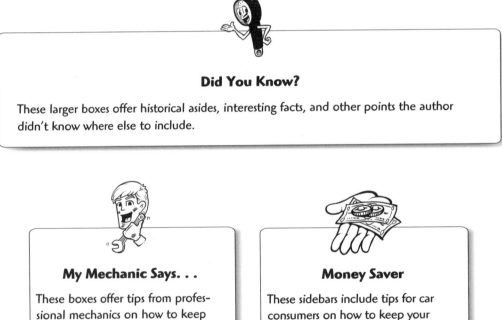

Did You Know?

These larger boxes offer historical asides, interesting facts, and other points the author didn't know where else to include.

My Mechanic Says. . .

These boxes offer tips from professional mechanics on how to keep out of their shop. Nice of them!

Money Saver

These sidebars include tips for car consumers on how to keep your wallet from needing frequent repairs.

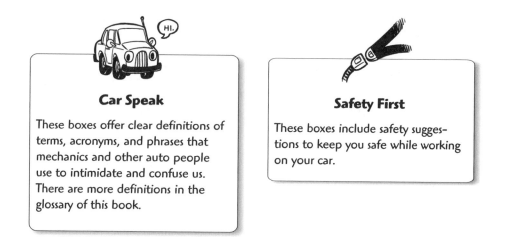

Car Speak

These boxes offer clear definitions of terms, acronyms, and phrases that mechanics and other auto people use to intimidate and confuse us. There are more definitions in the glossary of this book.

Safety First

These boxes include safety suggestions to keep you safe while working on your car.

Acknowledgments

There's no way I can list all the people who have contributed to my understanding of cars. However, maybe I can start with a list of those who directly contributed to this book. Here goes.

Thanks to Harvey Kelm of Lane Community College, Gil Hensen of Hensen's Texaco, Dennis McQuire of Coast Auto Electric, Martin Lawson of Automotive Service Excellence, Monica Buchholz of the Automotive Service Association, and Mary Norton and Betsy Martinelli of the Steel Recycling Institute. Thanks also to Christopher Finch for his enjoyable autobiography of the American automobile, *Highways to Heaven* (Harper Collins, 1992), which poetically expresses our love affair with cars. Thanks to Mike Michelsen, who shared his Mark II with us. Thanks to Jonathan Quitevis of Honda World, who helped us adopt Li'l Red. Thanks to Richard Day, automotive author and friend. And thanks to Floyd Clymer, who wrote the first books I read about these fascinating machines.

Editorially, thanks to Judy Ramsey, Theresa Murtha, Jake Elwell, George Wieser, Lisa Bucki, Fran Blauw, Richard Stepler, Denise Hawkins, and illustrators Tina Trettin and Jeff Yesh. Thanks to Powell's City of Books, Portland, Oregon, for amassing such a diversity of research materials.

Automotively, thanks to Honda, Ford, Lincoln, Chevrolet, GMC, Pontiac, Jeep, International, Plymouth, Dodge, and Studebaker for cars that showed me what trouble is—and taught me how to fix them.

Special Thanks from the Publisher to the Technical Reviewer...

The Complete Idiot's Guide to Trouble-Free Car Care was reviewed by an expert who checked the technical accuracy of what you'll learn here, to help us ensure that this book gives you everything you need to know to begin your expeditions under the hood. Special thanks are extended to Richard L. Stepler.

Richard Stepler is currently a freelance writer for *Popular Mechanics*. He joined *Popular Science* in 1973 as assistant editor. In 1994, he was promoted to editor of the 124-year-old magazine. During his career as editor and writer, he has covered many subjects, including science and technology, building technology and design, automotive technology, and computers and electronics, helping to establish the magazine as a recognized authority in these fields. Representing *Popular Science* at trade shows throughout the country, he has done interviews on television and radio. Most recently, he directed the efforts of the magazine in developing an online site on the Internet. Before joining *Popular Science*, he served as chief editor of several trade magazines, including *Reprographics* and *Government Data Systems*. He has also served as technical editor at the Institute of Electrical and Electronics Engineers. Stepler is a member of the American Society of Magazine Editors, the National Association of Science Writers, and the International Motor Press Association, where he has served as vice president.

Part 1
Understanding Your Car

Have you ever learned how a card trick or a magic trick was done? Something that was a mystifying puzzle suddenly becomes easy. In fact, it becomes fun! That's what's going to happen in the first part of this book. You're going to learn how your car does its magic. You're going to understand how your car starts, moves, and stops. Not just cars in general, but *your* car!

You're going to discover things about your car that you never knew before. You're going to see its innards without even getting your hands dirty. You're also going to graduate into the elite group that mechanics cannot intimidate: those who actually understand how their cars work.

So get ready! Prepare your mind for a leap that exchanges faith for facts. You once had faith that it all somehow worked logically, that it wasn't just black magic. You will soon have the facts. If you have dreaded the mechanic more than the dentist, if you consider yourself to be automotively dysfunctional, if you are intimidated by goblins living beneath the hood, turn the page and enter the world of automotive magic tricks.

It's going to be fun!

Chapter 1

How Cars Run: What Makes Them Go?

In This Chapter

➤ How your car runs

➤ How the engine works

➤ How other parts of your car work

➤ The differences between cars

"Yeah, it looks like the steebenfelz is shot," says the mechanic with the straightest face he can muster. "It'll cost a thousand bucks."

No reaction from the car's dumbfounded owner.

"That's just for parts. Labor will add another fifteen hundred," the mechanic adds and then watches for a reaction.

The car's owner grabs for a nearby wall to brace himself, but doesn't speak.

"Of course, if you want the job guaranteed, you'll need better quality parts—another grand."

Finally, as the car's owner sees his life savings being wiped out by a steebensome-thingerother, his wife steps in to the conversation.

"Look, a steebenfelz has nothing to do with the frammerammer acting up. Besides, a new steebenfelz is about 60 bucks, and labor should be little more than an hour. Who are you trying to rip off? Get up, honey, and let's leave this crook!"

"Yes, dear."

Knowing how your car runs can make the difference between a fair repair and a royal rip-off. Mechanics have been known to take advantage of a customer's lack of knowledge, inventing expensive solutions where there is no problem. Finding a qualified and honest mechanic doesn't require luck; it requires a basic understanding of how cars run.

You know you've been ripped off when you see your mechanic on "60 Minutes."

How Your Car Runs—Assuming That It Does!

Three cars occupy my driveway right now. One is a 1995 Honda del Sol, another is a 1984 Honda Accord, and the third is a 1956 Continental Mark II. As different as these cars are (you could make the two Hondas from the metal in the Continental), they all run using the same laws of nature. They use many of the same functional parts. The parts may not look the same, but they do the same things.

In fact, the first cars of a century ago and the latest cars have much in common. They both create and control power. My Hondas do it. My Continental does it. Your car does it. Everybody's car does it: creates and controls power.

How?

Cars create power in the engine.

Cars control power with everything else.

Actually, the engine doesn't "create" power. I lied! What happens is the engine changes chemical power into mechanical power. Where does it get all this chemical power? Why, from chemicals, of course.

Money Saver

Which gasoline should you buy? Check your car's owner's manual for the recommended octane rating. Then check the rating posted on pumps at gas stations. Using gas with a rating higher than the recommended one will not make your car run better, and they are more expensive. Instead, look for additives that keep your engine cleaner.

Explosions happen thousands of times a minute in your car's engine. Fortunately, they are controlled explosions; otherwise, you wouldn't get very far before you had to replace your car's engine. Gasoline igniting inside the engine causes these explosions.

Knowing that, think back to your science class in high school (the one you slept through, right?). Between snoozes, you learned that a fire requires fuel, air, and a spark for ignition. Sounds about right. But what does this have to do with your car?

Your car's engine changes chemical power into mechanical power by igniting fuel and air, and then using the power from the resulting explosion to move something. Obviously, these little explosions can't directly turn the car's wheels. Other things have to happen first. And it takes a bunch of explosions to produce enough power to pull away from a stoplight.

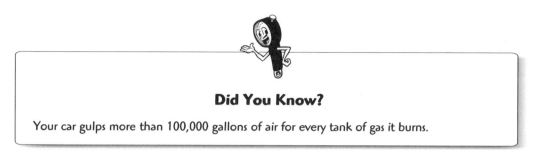

Did You Know?

Your car gulps more than 100,000 gallons of air for every tank of gas it burns.

So an engine must produce a number of explosions to develop much power—and it must do so in a controlled way so the explosions don't blow up the engine.

We're getting there!

An engine is built so that the explosions are orderly. Your car may have four, six, or eight cylinders. Each cylinder offers a place where controlled explosions can occur. Each cylinder (shaped somewhat like an upside-down can) has a solid top and sides, but a movable bottom, called the piston (see the illustration of a cylinder). So guess what happens when the explosion occurs? The piston moves.

An engine cylinder.

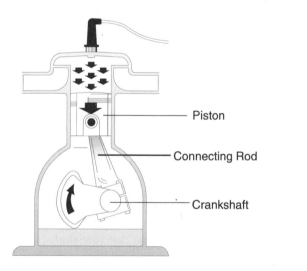

Piston

Connecting Rod

Crankshaft

Each explosion pushes the piston downward in the cylinder. A connecting rod at the base of the piston transfers this power to the crankshaft. If you can produce enough controlled explosions in the cylinders, you have rotating power that can (eventually) be used to turn your car's wheels.

Okay, okay. There's a lot more to engine operation than spinning a crankshaft. But that's what happens. That's what gave power to the first cars, and that's what powers your car.

So let's talk about control.

The rest of your car controls the power your car's engine produces. One part of your car starts the engine. Another turns the car in the direction you want it to go. Yet another stops your car when you want it to stop.

Yes, your car has many more parts. The body holds the parts and the people in place. The air-conditioning system keeps people from getting grumpy on long trips (not always successfully). And the radio keeps teenagers' hands busy changing channels. But everything else simply supports the two functions of your car: to create and control power.

Did You Know?

The Steel Recycling Institute reports that today's car bodies are made with more than 25% recycled steel. This recycled steel comes from older cars, old appliances, soda pop cans, and other resources. Even used oil filters are recycled. For more information, contact the Steel Recycling Institute (680 Andersen Drive, Pittsburgh, PA 15220) at 800/876-7274.

Salvage yards also efficiently recycle many cars by dismantling retired cars and selling off the usable parts. This service saves resources needed to replace perfectly good parts. For more information, see your local telephone book's yellow pages under "Automobile Wrecking."

If you want, you can stop reading right here and know more than most people know about how their cars run. Or you can keep going and have some more fun learning about your car.

The Infernal Combustion Automobile

Good choice!

Something with as many parts as your car has must do more than create and control power, right? Not much—in fact, once power is created in the engine, *control* is the operable term. Nobody wants to ride in a car that's out of control!

Let's take a simplified look at the many automotive systems common to all cars. Automotive systems are simply groups of parts that serve related functions. The rest of this section explains each system and how it works with the others in your car.

The next two figures show how systems are arranged in a left-handed and a right-handed—oops, a rear-wheel-drive car and a front-wheel-drive car, respectively. These terms refer to which set of wheels delivers the car's power to the road—rear or front. More on this later.

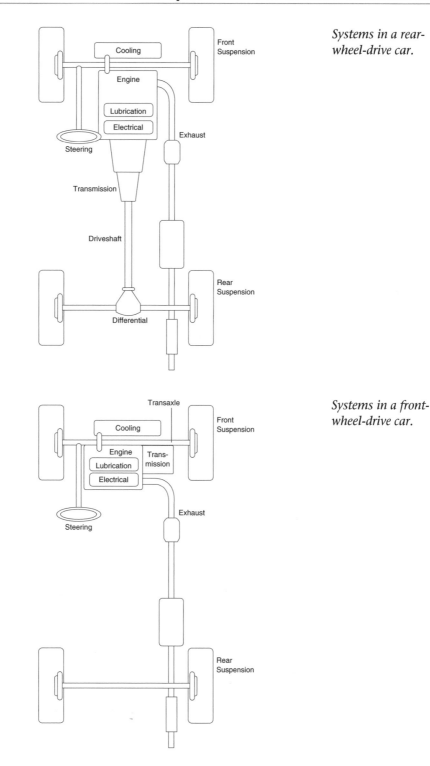

Systems in a rear-wheel-drive car.

Systems in a front-wheel-drive car.

Fuel System: How Your Car Digests Gas

As you've already seen, an engine needs fuel and air to run. What kind of fuel? Gasoline for most cars, diesel for a few, propane, and natural gas for even fewer. Most cars run on gasoline, so that's what we'll explore.

Car Speak

Your car's *carburetor* dumps a stream of fuel into passing air; this is then distributed to the engine's cylinders for burning. A car with *fuel injection* doesn't have a carburetor; the fuel injector injects metered fuel into the intake *manifold* (a holding reservoir) at each cylinder for burning.

Gasoline doesn't burn well as a liquid. It must be mixed with air into a vapor that burns easily when ignited. So your fuel system stores the gas in a tank and then pumps it, as needed, to a carburetor. The carburetor mixes the fuel with the right amount of air and then sends the fuel/air mixture on to the engine to be ignited in the combustion chamber.

Your car's fuel system includes the fuel tank, the fuel line, the fuel pump, the carburetor, and filters (see the figure showing the fuel system). Instead of a carburetor, your car may use a fuel-injection system to mix and deliver gas to your engine more efficiently. Some fuel injection systems replace the carburetor, while others use injectors at each cylinder. Most cars that are less than 10 years old have fuel-injection systems.

The fuel system.

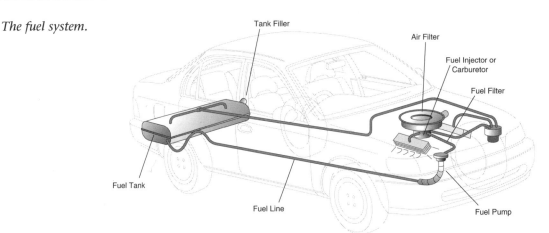

Ignition System: Keep the Spark in Your Life

Did I mention ignition?

To ignite the fuel/air mixture in the engine's cylinders, an electrical spark must be delivered to the cylinder at the exact second it's needed.

The battery and alternator provide the electricity, the ignition coil transforms low voltage into high voltage, and the distributor sends the spark to the cylinders (see the figure illustrating the ignition system). Older cars use a mechanical system, called a distributor, to distribute the spark. Newer cars use computers to help manage the ignition in what's called a *distributorless* or *computerized* ignition system.

Don't worry. There won't be a quiz. For now, just picture how all these systems work and interact.

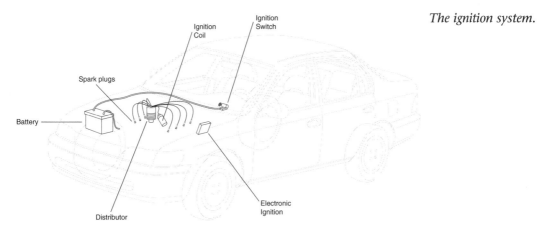

The ignition system.

Cooling System: Cool It!

With all these explosions happening inside your engine, you'd imagine that it would get hot as…well, you know where. It does. In fact, without a cooling system, your engine would soon self-destruct.

Air-cooled engines are designed to be cooled by air flow. But most automobile engines today are water-cooled. Actually, they use a mixture of water and other *coolant* chemicals to keep the engine's temperature within a safe operating range.

The coolant cools the engine by capturing heat from the cylinders without actually entering the cylinders (see the figure showing the cooling system). It does so by flowing through an adjoining chamber called a *water jacket*. Heat transfers to the coolant, which is pumped to the radiator through hoses. A fan blows air on the radiator to cool the liquid. The rotation of the engine drives the water pump. On older cars, the engine drives the fan; newer cars use electrical fans.

When it's cold enough to freeze your backside off, cars can also circulate some of that heated coolant through a heater core to warm up the inside of the passenger compartment.

Pretty cool (or warm), eh?

Car Speak

The ignition system's *spark plugs* are metal and ceramic parts that use electricity to ignite the fuel/air mixture in the cylinder. You need one spark plug per cylinder when you change them.

The cooling system.

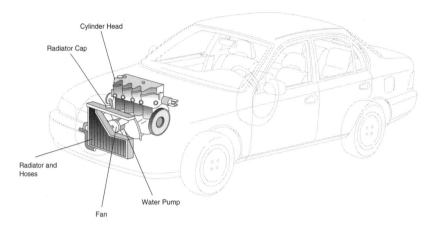

Lubrication System: It's Not Just Snake Oil

Rub two objects together for a few seconds and you'll see the results of friction: wear. To reduce wear, put some oil or grease between the two objects.

That's how to keep your car's engine from wearing out: Lubricate it well. Inside your car's engine is a system to store, pump, and filter oil that lubricates moving parts.

There are moving parts outside your car's engine as well: wheels, axles, and so on. These parts need a thicker lubricant, called *grease*.

Car Speak

Coolant, a mixture of water and ethylene glycol (named for a famous jazz singer of the '30s) placed in a car's radiator, helps transfer the engine's heat to the air.

Did You Know?

Which beauty oil should you use in your car? First, check the label; it should tell you that the oil "meets" or "exceeds" API (American Petroleum Institute) standards. You'll also see other letters on the label, such as SG or SH, which are the current standards for gas-engine oils. CD is the current standard for diesel-engine oils. Second, check the label for the acronym SAE (Society of Automotive Engineers) for the viscosity or weight of the oil, such as 5W-30. Then follow the car manufacturer's recommendations as printed in the owner's manual. If you don't have a manual to follow, select a 5W-30 for use in colder climates or a 10W-30 for use in moderate climates for year-round protection. Lower weight (thinner) oil allows cars to start more easily in cold weather.

More cars die prematurely due to poor lubrication than probably any other cause. Save a life: Lube a car! You'll learn how in Chapter 12, "CAR: Biannual Replacements."

Exhaust System: Why Your Car Burps and Belches

The controlled explosions inside your car's engine produce gases that must be removed to make way for more fuel/air mixture. The exhaust system does this job.

The engine pushes these gases out through a manifold that collects them from all the cylinders and then pipes them to mix with the outside air. Exhaust gases transmit the noise created by all these explosions, so the gases must be muffled (hence, the muffler).

Emission-Control System: Smog Gets in Your Eyes

Nobody likes to smell stinky exhaust air, nor does anyone want to live with the unburned fuel emissions from cars. So today's cars have an emission-control system that reduces stinky exhaust and emissions before they pollute the air (most of them, anyway).

The catalytic converter is the most famous member of the emission-control family, but there are others. You'll learn who they are and what they do later in this book. You'll also learn how to maintain and even repair slackers.

Transmission System: Getting That Power to Work for You

All that power from the engine must be transmitted to the wheels. In part, the transmission system handles this job.

Without a transmission, your car probably would have a top speed of about 20 miles an hour. Although that would reduce the number of speeding tickets issued, you might barely make it home in time for breakfast rather than dinner.

If you've ever ridden a more-than-one-speed bicycle, you know how gears work. The largest gear gets you going. Then the chain moves to a smaller gear as momentum builds. A car's transmission works in a similar way.

A car's transmission consists of a box of gears that transmit the engine's power to the driving axle (see the figure displaying the transmission system). It works like this: First gear transmits the engine's power to move the car from 0 mph to 20 mph. When shifted to the smaller second gear, the transmission helps the car go from about 20 mph to 40 mph. Third gear, even smaller, moves the car from 40 mph to 60 mph. Fourth gear takes it to as fast as it will go—oops, 65 mph. Some cars have a fifth gear for economical high-speed cruising.

A manual transmission.

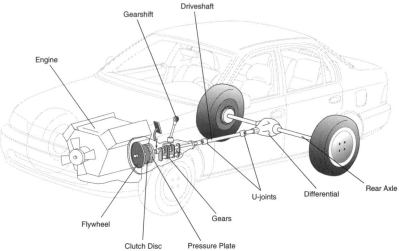

A manual transmission requires that the driver press a clutch pedal and move a gear-shift each time a new gear is needed. Engaging the clutch helps mesh the rotation of the engine and transmission.

An automatic transmission selects and uses the correct gears as needed with no help from the driver. A torque converter transfers the power smoothly to the driving axle.

The driveshaft and differential send this power to a rear-wheel-drive car. Front-wheel-drive cars use a transaxle unit to serve the same function, combining the transmission and differential into a single unit.

Yes, that's a pretty simplified description of how an automotive transmission system works. There will be time for more details later. For now, that's all you need to know.

Electrical System: Battery Powered!

Your car's electrical system is actually a couple of related systems. The starting system starts your car using a battery and starter. The charging system uses the engine's power to drive an alternator, to recharge the battery, and to power accessories. Many other systems within your car then use the battery's electrical energy to operate.

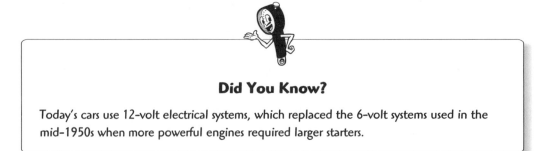

Did You Know?

Today's cars use 12-volt electrical systems, which replaced the 6-volt systems used in the mid-1950s when more powerful engines required larger starters.

Steering and Suspension System: Keeping Control!

Imagine a world without left turns! Or with no turns at all!

Nowhere on a car is control seemingly more important than in the steering system. Without a steering system, cars can only move straight ahead. The steering system transfers movement of the steering wheel to movement of the tires, kind of like monkey see, monkey do (see the figure illustrating the steering and suspension systems).

The suspension system plays a supporting role. It absorbs the up-and-down and side-to-side movement of the car as it glides or sputters down the road. Without a suspension system, the road you travel is rough.

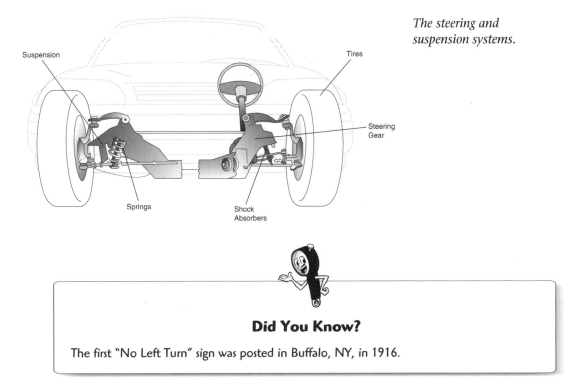

The steering and suspension systems.

Did You Know?

The first "No Left Turn" sign was posted in Buffalo, NY, in 1916.

Brake System: Stopping Without Bumps

Look out for that tree! Imagine a world without brakes. Commuting would be a world of bumper cars. Travel would be limited by the speed at which you could drag your feet to stop your car. You would have to wear a pair of brake shoes!

Fortunately, every car has a brake system—and a pretty efficient one at that. Each wheel has a brake controlled by a hydraulic controller called the *master cylinder*.

Power brakes use a booster to make stopping easier. Anti-lock brake systems (ABS) make braking smooth and efficient. The emergency or parking brake holds the car in place when parked, as long as you remember to put it on.

Other Systems: All the Other Junk You Need

Several other systems and components help your car run. Wheels and tires apply the engine's power to the road. Passenger-restraint systems keep people from becoming projectiles. Entertainment systems, well, entertain. Each system helps make driving cars more efficient, safe, and fun.

Rocky Road, Maple Nut, or Vanilla?

If cars are so much alike, why do they look—and act—so different?

Because there are thousands of variations on the basic car design to meet the needs, tastes, and budgets of the auto-buying public. An overview of the basic car "flavors" you might encounter follows.

Modern Home-Grown Cars

Cars built in the United States during the past 20 years—since the so-called Gas Shortage—have much in common with each other. They tend to be smaller and more fuel-efficient than their predecessors. They also feature more safety equipment, and they typically require less frequent maintenance and fewer repairs than older domestic cars.

All these features make for complex cars. As in many other areas, computers control an increasing number of decisions in modern domestic cars. They also keep owners from doing some of the repairs. Even so, you can participate in the maintenance, trouble-shooting, and repair of your modern domesticated car as you learn how it works.

Note that the frequency of maintenance on modern domestic cars varies greatly, depending on when the car was built, its design, and its equipment. Domestic cars of the 1970s may require an oil change, for example, every 3,000 to 5,000 miles; newer cars can safely go 7,500 or even 10,000 miles between regular service.

Immigrant Cars

The Europeans and the Asians long ago figured out that cars should be smaller rather than larger, so they built cars according to this rule. Some foreign cars emphasize quality whereas others promote efficiency, but most were smaller than those made in the United States.

This efficiency of size has given foreign cars a reputation of being difficult to maintain. That's not necessarily so. They are different, but usually not more difficult. With "foreign" cars being made in Ohio and U.S.-built cars being designed by international joint ventures, the differences are becoming blurred. The process of driving, maintaining, and repairing these cars is nearly identical to the process used for domestic cars.

The frequency of maintenance on foreign cars also varies, depending on the manufacturer, the design, and other factors. Oil changes, for example, are suggested at between 5,000 and 7,500 miles for most cars. A few require even less service. You'll learn about your car's maintenance frequency from the owner's manual or service manual, as well as from Chapter 6, "Do-It-Yourself Maintenance: Getting Your Hands Dirty."

Senior Citizen Cars

There are those who say that the "old cars" should be scrapped to save gas for more fuel-efficient vehicles. That makes as much sense as turning the Gettysburg Battlefield into an efficient high-rise condo.

Older cars (those built before 1975) are both historical and efficient. They might not get 30 miles to the gallon, but most get 15 to 25 miles per gallon (mpg). After being rebuilt with modern parts, they can burn unleaded gasoline. They're typically driven fewer miles than today's cars, and they often get more frequent tune-ups by owners who fuss over their cars.

Elderly cars offer another advantage: Most are easier to work on than newer cars. It takes a rocket scientist to rebuild a modern fuel-injection system. A rock dweller can rebuild the carburetor on an older Ford or Plymouth. Parts are cheaper, too.

Money Saver

To calculate your car's fuel economy, write down the odometer readings at two consecutive fill-ups. Subtract the first reading from the second reading. Divide the miles driven by the number of gallons used. Example: odometer reading at first fill-up: 28,718. Odometer reading at second fill-up: 29,130. Gallons purchased for second fill-up: 12.8. Miles driven: 29,130 − 28,718 = 412. 412 divided by 12.8 gallons equals 32.2 miles per gallon.

Keeping an older car trouble-free takes more time than for newer cars but is relatively easier. Older cars require more frequent maintenance. Cars of the 1930s through 1950s usually require lubrication and oil changes every 2,000 to 4,000 miles. Those of the 1960s could often go 5,000 or more between regular maintenance. Your car's manuals will help determine the frequency.

No matter how it has been restored or maintained, an old car is still old. It needs more repairs and more frequent service than a newer car.

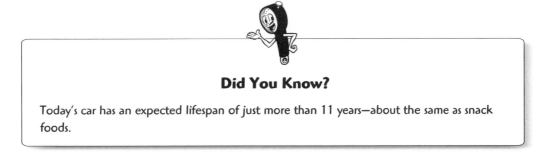

Did You Know?

Today's car has an expected lifespan of just more than 11 years—about the same as snack foods.

The Least You Need to Know

➤ The automotive engine changes chemical power into mechanical power by igniting a fuel/air mixture and using the resulting explosion to move something.

➤ All other systems on your car—fuel, ignition, cooling, lubrication, exhaust, transmission, electrical, steering, suspension, and brakes—control something.

➤ There is a diminishing difference between modern foreign and domestic cars and how they work.

➤ It's healthy to love your car!

Chapter 2

Learning About Your Car: What Does What

In This Chapter

➤ Identify your own car

➤ Fill out your Car Care card

➤ Learn how to easily track your car's maintenance

You've seen how cars run, in theory. Now you're going to start applying all this theory to your own car. You're going to learn some things about the make and model, the specifications, and how they all relate to keeping your car trouble-free.

First, let me say something about your car(s). You may have just one car or you might have more. I'm not going to call it/them car(s). I'll refer to it/them as an it and to car(s) as a car. Much simpler. And a whole lot less confusing. I've only included space on the Car Care card at the front of the book for recording info about one vehicle because you're going to keep it in that car. Feel free to copy the card (or, better yet, buy additional copies of this book) to record information on other cars.

Where was I? Oh, yes…

Just One Big Happy Family

Like people, cars are born into families. And the more you know about the family, the more you'll understand your own car. It's true in spouse candidates as well as cars.

A Pontiac Grand Am is the Grand Am *model* built by the Pontiac (*make* or *marquee*) division of General Motors or GM (*family*), for example. A Ford Escort is the Escort model built by the Ford (make or marquee) of Ford Motor Co. (family).

What does this family relationship mean to you? Parts are frequently interchangeable within makes and sometimes even families of cars. Some parts that fit the Pontiac also fit a Chevrolet (also made by GM) of the same year. In fact, makes within the same family might use the same engine or transmission. The total difference between a Dodge and a Plymouth minivan, for example, usually includes the spelling of their names and a couple of cosmetic differences.

Parts have families, too. Many cars within the General Motors family, for example, use parts manufactured by GM's Delco division. Cars manufactured in Germany may use more parts from Bosch, a German automotive parts manufacturer, rather than Autolite, an American company.

You can pretty well figure out who's related to whom by driving past the family reunion known as Auto Row, the street in your town where all the new car dealers congregate. The signs will tell you:

➤ Buick is a member of the GM family.

➤ So are Chevrolet, Pontiac, Oldsmobile, and GMC.

➤ Cadillac is the Rich Uncle and Geo the poor cousin in the GM family, rarely seen together.

➤ Lincoln and Mercury are somehow related to Ford.

➤ Chrysler, Dodge, and Plymouth are a close-knit family.

➤ Jeep and Eagle wear the Chrysler emblem, so they must be adopted.

➤ Honda makes Acura, Toyota produces Lexus, and Nissan birthed Infiniti as upscale cars.

➤ The independent Mercedes and BMW live alone.

➤ Nobody sells Yugos anymore.

Seeing these relationships can help you when you need parts or service. The Chevy dealer can often find a part for your Olds. A Plymouth part is a part for your Dodge. But don't even ask the Mercedes-Benz parts person for anything but an M-B part!

Did You Know?

Chevrolet was named for a racecar driver. Pontiac used to be called Oakland. Dodge was originally Dodge Brothers. General Motors was not named for a military leader.

Blood Brothers and Kissing Cousins

Cars have model names as well: Integra, Golf, Sentra, Protege, Prizm, LeMans, ad infinitum. However, they are sometimes just aliases for feature and trim packages. A Geo Metro is still a Geo.

Learning your car's model is important in identifying the engine, its maintenance requirements, and its replacement parts.

Is your car a sedan, a coupe, or a hatchback?

➤ **Sedan:** An enclosed car with two or four doors and seating for four or more. So there are two-door sedans and four-door sedans.

➤ **Hatchback:** A three- or five-door sedan. It adds a door at the back that serves as an entry for people or, more commonly, cargo.

➤ **Coupe:** A home for chickens. No, that's not right. A shortened version of a two-door sedan.

➤ **Hardtop:** Somewhat like a hard-head. A sedan that doesn't have a support post between the side windows.

➤ **Convertible:** A car with a removable top. It can be a hardtop convertible or a softtop (*ragtop*) convertible. During the late 1950s, Ford even made a retractable hardtop convertible that withdrew into the trunk. My del Sol has a targa top, a partial top that lifts off and fits in the trunk.

➤ **Family vans and small trucks:** These vehicles have their own nomenclature based on the purpose, size, and seating.

Did You Know?

By 1930, only 20 states required people to have driver's licenses to operate a vehicle.

Playing the Numbers

It's time to pull out the paperwork. Your car's registration and certificate of title will tell you more about the car. You'll need these facts to better identify its needs.

When you purchased your car, the state took some money from you and gave you a slip of paper. Then the mail carrier brought you some more papers from them. One of those papers is probably the certificate of title and the other is the registration certificate or card.

Go find one or more of them, please. Hints: The registration card is probably (should be) in your car's glove compartment, along with the car's insurance card, and the title is probably put away with your other important papers.

These documents are going to tell you lots of things: the license plate number, the names of the owner and *lienholder* (the institution to which you owe money on the loan you secured to buy the car), and maybe even the odometer reading when it was purchased or last registered. Ignore all this stuff. What you're looking for is this:

➤ Year

➤ Make

➤ Model

➤ Body style

➤ Vehicle identification number (VIN)

Remove the Car Care card from the front of this book and record this information on the card for your primary car in the "About Your Car" section of the card.

Okay, maybe you already knew the year and make of your car, but this gives you a chance to verify that it's correct. You'd be surprised how many people learn from the registration that their car is older than they thought. And, believe it or not, the state might have made a mistake in registering your car.

While you're here, verify the name and address of the owner(s) (probably you) and security interest holder or lessor (probably the lender or lease company). If anything has changed (such as, heaven forbid, you paid off the loan), take the papers to your lender and your local motor vehicle office to get them updated.

The year, make, and style of your car are important facts you'll be asked as you order parts or service on your car. And the parts store and mechanics don't care if you own a Super-Duper Sport Special with the Elongated Trim Package. They want name, rank, and serial number—er, year, model, make, and style.

Actually, they want more than that. The parts and service folks also ask about the engine and, maybe, the transmission. For transmission, they ask, "Manual or automatic?" which you'll quickly answer. But you might not know the size of the engine.

How can you determine the size of your car's engine? Take out your tape measure and measure from top to bottom, and then from side to side. Now, add the numbers together and ignore the answer. The car's owner's manual tells you the correct answer. It's measured in cubic centimeters (cc), liters (L), or *cubic inches (ci) of displacement*. That's the amount of space inside each cylinder times the number of cylinders. It takes 1000 ccs to make a liter. (You knew that!) So a 2-liter, 4-cylinder engine has a half-liter (about 500 cc) of space in each cylinder. That's enough math for now!

Some engines have their displacement size written right on them, and others note the engine size on a sticker under the hood. For some cars, you have to read the owner's manual to figure out which engine you have.

Did You Know?

To translate engine size in liters to cubic inches, multiply liters by 61 (a 5-liter engine is 305 cubic inches in size). To translate engine size in cubic inches to liters, multiply cubic inches by .0164 (a 1.8 liter engine is about 112 cubic inches).

But what if you don't have an owner's manual or your dog chewed up that page? Then it's time to figure out the vehicle identification number (VIN).

You transcribed your car's VIN onto the Car Care card, right? Good. It's going to look something like this: 1G1AZ377XRD101234. Yes, all that gibberish means something, but don't try to pronounce it. It's a unique code that identifies your specific car. Depending on the manufacturer, it identifies the engine, transmission, chassis, date and location of manufacture, and your mother's maiden name (just kidding!).

To keep everyone honest, the VIN is also stamped on one or two places on your car. Such a precaution helps the police find stolen cars and parts, and it also identifies vehicles that have received engine transplants.

How can you figure out what this VIN really means? The car's owner's manual, if you have one, may help you read it. Otherwise, you need a service manual for the car to fully decipher the code. We'll talk about those documents in the next chapter. The point is that, now or later, you need to identify the engine your car uses to catapult you down the road.

In the VIN example (from a Chevrolet, repeated here: 1G1AZ377XRD101234), the tenth digit (R) means the car was built in 1994, and the eighth digit (7) indicates that the engine is a 350 cubic inch V-8 with electronic fuel injection (lucky you!). How the heck do I know this? I looked it up in the service manual!

After you've identified the engine in your car, you can begin gathering and using its specifications, or *specs*. The owner's manual or service manual (did I mention that they're covered in the next chapter?) give you the needed info. Here's the kind of stuff you'll need: engine size, number of cylinders, type of fuel-delivery system (carburetion or injection), how it's kept cool (air or water), what grade of and how much oil it needs, and facts about replacement filters. Stuff like that.

You can record this information, as you get it, on your Car Care card, in the "About Your Car" section. It should include the following:

➤ Engine displacement

➤ Number of cylinders in engine (4, 6, or 8)

➤ Cylinder firing order

➤ Engine oil type and capacity (with filter)

➤ Carburetion or fuel injection

➤ Fuel tank capacity and recommended octane

➤ Spark-plug type and gap

➤ Distributor parts numbers

➤ Air filter part number

➤ Fuel filter part number

➤ Oil filter part number

➤ Drivebelt part numbers

➤ Radiator capacity and recommended coolant level

➤ Manual transmission fluid type and capacity

➤ Automatic transmission fluid type and capacity

➤ Power steering fluid type

➤ Battery size and CCA (cold crank amps)

➤ Tire size and pressure

Why do you need all these numbers? Because it's the American Way. Actually, you use them to make sure that your car is operating as designed and to select parts and fluids if it doesn't. You don't want to have to look up this information each time you need it, so you'll refer to the Car Care card. Much easier.

Along the way, you may discover equivalent part numbers. Your oil filter might be a NAPA #1515, for example. Maybe you can buy an equivalent oil filter on sale: Motorcraft FL-1A, AC PF2, Fram PH8A, or Purolator PER1A. As you buy these equivalent parts, write down the numbers on your Car Care card (if there's room) or in the back of this book.

My Mechanic Says. . .

Just like people, car engines need to idle for at least a minute or two each day before moving forward. Imagine starting your day without coffee or tea. Running your car for one or two minutes warms up the engine, circulates the oil, and reduces wear. Yes, it also produces some extra emissions, but that's more ecologically correct than prematurely replacing an engine.

The Great Maintenance Tracker

Keeping your car trouble-free means not only performing regular maintenance (or having it done); it also means knowing what has been done and when.

Part 2 of this book, "Maintaining Your Car," guides you through each step of preparing for and performing maintenance on your car. It also offers an easy way to remember what service is needed. The "Car Maintenance Schedule" section of the Car Care card gives you a place to keep track of maintenance on your car. Together, Part 2 and the Car Care card can help you cut maintenance time and costs, and make your car more trouble-free.

Take a few moments now to look over the "Car Maintenance Schedule" section of the Car Care card.

The Least You Need to Know

➤ Your car is unique. Learning as much as you can about it helps you reduce maintenance time and costs.

➤ Cars have families that can be useful when you need help.

➤ Your car's title and registration offer important clues to maintenance and repair.

➤ Keeping track of maintenance is vital to owning a trouble-free car.

HEY HONEY, WHAT'S THAT?

OWNERS MANUAL

Chapter 3

Using Manuals: Doing It by the Book

> ## In This Chapter
>
> ➤ Learn how to find service information for your car
>
> ➤ Figure out how to read and use the owner's manual
>
> ➤ Learn to find and use a service manual for your car
>
> ➤ Learn where to get more help if you need it

If all else fails, read the manual.

That truism can help you keep your car trouble-free and your checkbook intact—or at least more so. Using your car's owner's manual and its service manual can save you hundreds of dollars in repairs, even if you never pick up a wrench. Information in these manuals can help you keep your car in top shape by telling you when and how to service it.

This is the third consecutive chapter in this book in which you're not going to get your hands dirty. Even so, it will show you more about how your car runs and how to keep it running—by the book.

Do It by the Book

You can maintain and repair your car using the book you have in your clean little hands right now. However, at least two other books offer more specific and technical information about your make and model of car. They are the owner's manual and the service manual. What's in them? How can you find and use them? Will there be a test at the end? Do you have to buy them? Good questions!

Owner's Manuals

An owner's manual is typically included with every new car sold. Most are about the size of a *Calvin and Hobbes* book and usually contain fewer than 100 pages. An owner's manual shows you how to use and maintain your car. Topics include how to read instruments and warning lights, how to find and replace fuses that regulate parts of the electrical system, how to operate the radio and climate controls, and related fun things.

Most owner's manuals also include maintenance information: how to check and replace oil, how to check tire pressure without kicking the tire, how to change a tire, how to safely jump the battery, and how to tow your car.

The owner's manual usually includes a *maintenance schedule*—a chart of recommended service tasks and when to do them. It might recommend that you change the oil and oil filter every 7,500 miles, for example, and that you change the spark plugs every 30,000 miles. It probably also recommends a time frequency for maintenance, such as 7,500 miles or 12 months, whichever comes first. So if you drive your car only 6,000 miles a year, you'll service it at the end of 12 months. If you drive it 12,000 miles in a year, you'll service it every 7,500 miles.

Most maintenance schedules are easy to read. If your maintenance schedule suggests some form of maintenance every 7,500 miles, for example, the chart shows you what service to perform at each 7,500-mile interval. If your car is still under warranty, the manual tells you what maintenance must be performed to keep the warranty in effect. The manual may include two maintenance schedules: one for normal driving conditions and one for severe conditions. Your manual describes normal and severe conditions. Evaluate your driving conditions and choose the appropriate schedule. If you are unsure which schedule to follow, ask your dealership's service manager for a recommendation. Following the severe condition maintenance schedule just might prolong the life of your car.

You don't have to have an owner's manual for your car (and, in fact, you might not have one if you bought a used car). Part 2 of this book, "Maintaining Your Car," clearly describes auto maintenance for all kinds of cars. However, you might want the owner's manual as a reference to determine what equipment and features your car has.

The owner's manual usually includes specifications that are useful as you maintain your car. There's stuff like the size of your car's engine; how large your fuel tank is; how much oil and other fluids it requires; and useful info about tires, brakes, lights, and more.

Where can you find an owner's manual for your car if you don't have one? You can sometimes purchase one through a new car dealership that sells your brand of car. If the car is older, you can find an owner's manual through a bookstore that sells used books, especially one that sells used automotive books. Or you can visit automotive swap meets in your area. Make sure you have the exact year, make, and model of your car (as verified in Chapter 2, "Learning About Your Car: What Does What").

Service Manuals

Service manuals, also called *technical* or *shop* manuals, are thicker books on how to maintain and repair your car. They get pretty specific. Part 3 of this book, "Repairing Your Car," guides you through common repairs for typical cars. However, if you really get into repairing your car, you might want to invest in a shop manual that's more specific to your car.

Shop or technical manuals are written by the car manufacturer (the car's family) to be read by automotive technicians. Who should know your car's needs better than those who gave it birth? However, their manuals are often difficult to decipher unless you've taken a year or two of college-level automotive classes. Shop manuals are available through new car dealers' parts departments or directly from the manufacturer. You may find an order form in the back pages of your owner's manual. Manufacturer's shop manuals usually cost from $30 to $75 each.

Aftermarket service manuals are published with the car owner in mind. They are simplified versions of the manufacturer's service manuals. Service manual publishers include Chilton, Haynes, Clymer, Motor, and others. Aftermarket service manuals typically are published for a model or group of models rather than a specific year. One service manual for my 1984 Honda Accord, for example, covers the Accord and Prelude for 1976 through 1985. Another aftermarket manual covers imports from 1980 through 1989. By featuring a wider group of cars, more copies of the manuals are sold and the price is reduced. Aftermarket manuals are sold for $15 to $30 each. They can be purchased at auto parts stores and at larger bookstores.

You might also be able to find aftermarket service manuals at your local or regional library. If you borrow a service manual, make photocopies of the pages you'll use in the garage or driveway so that the library book is not smudged, or you could end up buying it anyway.

The book you're holding is an aftermarket manual written to help you understand, maintain, and repair your car. You can use it alone or with another service manual to help you keep your car trouble-free.

Here are the features to look for in a usable service manual:

➤ **Contents page:** This page, near the front of a service or shop manual, tells you what's in the manual. Pretty obvious. Consumer-level service manuals usually start with general information about automotive tools and safety. They then show you how to troubleshoot common problems. General service is covered next, followed by specific maintenance and repairs for each system. Technical or shop manuals jump right into maintenance and repair for your system. Chapter 1, "How Cars Run: What Makes Them Go?" of this book briefly described automotive systems to prepare you for finding your way through the manual.

➤ **Index:** The back of the service manual usually includes an index. Unfortunately, not all indexes are created equal. Some are simply a listing of the chapters arranged alphabetically. Others are more useful, such as Maintenance, Routine Checks...33–34. A few don't even have indexes. A comprehensive index can save you time when you're trying to look up a specific problem.

➤ **Photos and drawings:** They are usually included in service manuals to help you visualize the task. Some illustrations help you pinpoint the location of a part or an adjustment. A cutaway diagram can show you how components work as a whole. An exploded view of a component shows how the parts are assembled (or disassembled). Some illustrations include *callouts*—words or arrows to show you what's where. A picture really can be worth 1,000 words, or even more. Good illustrations can help you understand the problem or the solution much more quickly.

➤ **Part identification:** Depending on the type of manual you use, parts are identified by name, number, or both. The numbers are long and usually not very useful unless you're ordering through the dealer's parts department. Besides, who wants to be known by a number? An easier way to understand the part's name is by looking at the illustration callout—Power Steering Reservoir Filter, for example.

➤ **Charts:** These, too, help you keep your car trouble-free. The maintenance schedule chart was mentioned earlier. Other service manual charts can help you identify your car's engine, troubleshoot your car, or select the right replacement parts. Good charts can answer some of your questions rapidly and direct you to solutions described elsewhere in the manual.

Doing It Manually

Owner's, service, shop, technical, and aftermarket manuals are useful tools in your quest for a trouble-free car. You've learned how to select a good one. Unfortunately, just owning the book isn't enough. Let's consider how to use your new manual.

You can quickly find the information you need when you need it, if you take time to acquaint yourself with how the manual is set up. Thumb through it at your leisure. Read the troubleshooting chart if it has one. Look at the illustrations to see if there's anything you recognize. If not, don't worry. You soon will be using it like a pro, and you'll be learning more about your car with every page.

As mentioned, this book on trouble-free car care includes a section on maintaining your car (Part 2) and a section on repairing your car (Part 3). Take some time now to flip through the pages of these parts and learn more about them.

Service and other instruction manuals are usually written as step-by-step procedures. The steps might be numbered or they may simply be chronological. Take a relatively simple procedure like changing the oil or changing a spark plug and read over the instructions a few times. You'll quickly catch on to how information is presented. It can also give you confidence for the day you actually follow the instructions.

This book offers a description of what's done and why, and then follows with steps for performing that procedure on the typical car. Feel free to make your own notes in this book or in your owner's or service manual. Underline, circle, cross-reference, check off, or otherwise mark your own book or a photocopy of someone else's book pages. Notes you make as you disassemble a part can be critical to getting it put back together in the same way.

Manuals written for more than one car model (such as this one) cannot be specific or even accurate to all makes and models. What can you do about it? You can photocopy diagrams from specific manuals found in the library. You can make your own notes and diagrams in this book or modify the diagrams presented. Or you can ask for help.

Hell-p! When the Book Isn't Enough

Books and manuals can guide you through trouble-free maintenance and repair. However, sometimes you might have a question or need an explanation that you just can't get from the book. What can you do?

Depending on your question, automotive parts suppliers might be able to help. If you're not sure how much oil your car should get during an oil change, for example, check the oil can for a toll-free number, or call the local dealership and ask the parts department how much oil you should buy for an oil change.

You can also take your manual in as you buy parts. The parts clerk might be able to give you some ideas on making the job easier if you can show the illustration and instructions you're using. Clerks working in auto parts stores and the auto section of some large retail stores are usually trained in automotive mechanics with additional training in parts identification and installation. If they're not too busy, most are glad to help. Clerks in most discount general merchandise stores work in the automotive section this week and the gardening section next week, so they might not know as much as you do about cars.

Automotive magazines can also help. There are dozens of magazines available at larger newsstands on every topic from how to buy a new car to how to keep your old car running. Many include how-to columns answering reader's questions. The articles will make more sense as you learn more about your own car. The leading general-interest auto magazines include *Car and Driver*, *Road & Track*, *Popular Mechanics*, and *Auto Week*.

The best resource you can have is a friendly auto mechanic. Once you've found a good one (which you learn about in Chapter 7, "Finding a Good Mechanic: Who Can You Trust with Your Car?"), you can call the mechanic when you have simple questions that need answering. Why should the mechanic help you? If you let the mechanic know that you want to do some, but not all, of your own car maintenance and repairs, he or she might see the advantages of earning your business for jobs you don't want to tackle. It also strengthens your relationship if you refer other car owners to your mechanic.

The Least You Need to Know

➤ Your car's owner's manual includes specific service information as well as descriptions of options and features you should know about.

➤ Shop manuals are typically too technical for the non-mechanic, but many aftermarket service manuals are written specifically for consumers who want to work on their cars but don't have degrees in auto mechanics.

➤ Service manuals can be easy to read and use, offering step-by-step instructions and clear illustrations to make the job easier.

➤ There are many other valuable resources you can call on if you get stuck with a question as you maintain or repair your car. People want to help.

Chapter 4

Cars on the Internet

The latest rage is the Internet. Advertisements for products on TV include their "Web address." Friends try to give you their "e-mail address." What does it all mean and, more important, who cares?

What does it mean? The Internet isn't magic. It's a tool. It's really no different from any other latest-and-greatest invention in that some people use it for good and others don't. The Internet is nothing to be fearful of. It is simply a tool that can help you understand, maintain, repair, and enjoy your car. And have some fun!

Who cares? Contrary to what many folks say, you can live quite well, thank you, without access to the Internet. However, it is a tool that can help you get the information you need faster and, sometimes, more easily than in traditional ways. The printed word never replaced conversation as the primary tool of communication. Nor will the Internet replace the printed word.

Driving on the Internet

So what *is* the Internet? It's an interactive network of computers connected through telephone lines. Think of it as a telephone system between computers. One computer calls another to find out what's new. It asks questions, answers questions, and spend a lot of time saying "uh-huh."

For example, once on the Internet, you can get repair information on your car, find out what a new one costs, chat with others who have the same model—and problems—and write to your congressperson about the sad state of auto manufacturing today.

Money Saver

If you don't have a computer with Internet access or a friend who can get you on the Net, try the local public library. Some have computers with Internet access available to the public. Larger libraries may offer classes or assistance.

What You Need to Cruise the Internet

What do you need to get onto the Internet? You need a computer, a thing called a modem, some communications software called a browser, and a few bucks. The few bucks are needed to subscribe to an Internet provider, or IP (also known as *ISP* for *Internet service provider*). An IP is a service that connects your computer with other computers on the Internet. The typical charge is less than your cable TV bill. Some charge by the hour and others have a flat monthly fee or nearly unlimited access, so check around for the best deal.

If you want to get onto the Internet, first find a local IP, and then ask what software and hardware you need. They want you to become a subscriber, so will typically help you get set up. Where can you find a local IP? Ask at local computer shops, check the classified ads in area newspapers, check the local phone book yellow pages under "Internet," and ask friends.

Reading Signs on the Internet

There are lots of pieces to the Internet, many of them far beyond the scope of this book. The most popular—and the most friendly—is what's called "the Web." It's also known as the "World Wide Web" or WWW. In fact, many businesses include their Web address in advertisements and even on products.

For example, the Web address for BMW is www.bmw.com. What does that mean?

> **www** means it's a World Wide Web address
>
> **bmw** is the domain name
>
> **com** means it is a commercial site (**org** means organization, **gov** means government, and **net** means network)

Dots and slashes are used as separators.

There's a bit more to the address, however. To reach this location on the Internet, you need to tell the computer that you're using Hypertext Transfer Protocol. What? Don't worry about it. Just prefix the address with this:

http://

So this is the uniform resource locator (URL) address to reach BMW:

http://www.bmw.com

Type that Web address into the Web browser and watch the magic start.

Many automotive resources already have Web addresses and more are being added every day. They include government services, commercial sites, and organizations. Here are some useful Internet Web addresses to help you keep your car on the road rather than in the road.

Did You Know?

The Internet was first set up so people at university research departments could share information with their counterparts around the world.

Auto Manufacturers Around the World

Alfa Romeo	http://www.alfaromeo.com
Audi	http://www.audi.com
BMW	http://www.bmw.com
Chrysler	http://www1.daimlerchrysler.com
Citroen	http://www.citroen.com
Daewoo Motor Company	http://www.dm.co.kr
Daihatsu Motor Corp.	http://www.ingway.co.jp/~daihatsu
Ferrari (as if...)	http://www.ferrari.com
Fiat	http://www.fiat.com
Ford Motor Co.	http://www2.ford.com
General Motors	http://www.gm.com

Honda Motor Co.	http://www.honda.com
Hummer	http://www.hummer.com
Hyundai Motor Co.	http://www.hyundai-motor.com
Isuzu	http://www.isuzu.com
Jaguar	http://www.jaguarcars.com
Kia Motors	http://www.kia.com
Land Rover	http://www.landrover.com
Lexus	http://www.lexus.com
Maserati	http://www.maserati.it
Mazda Motor Corp.	http://www.mazda.com
Mercedes-Benz	http://www.mercedes-benz.com
Mitsubishi	http://www.mitsucars.com
Porsche	http://www.porsche.com
Saab	http://www.saab.com
Saturn	http://www.saturn.com
Subaru	http://www.subaru.com
Toyota	http://www.toyota.com
Volkswagen	http://www.vw.com
Volvo	http://www.volvo.com

Fun Destinations on the Internet

There are literally thousands of other resources to help you buy, maintain, repair, and learn more about your car. To whet your appetite, here are a few of the more popular ones:

➤ Info about the latest car models as well as car care at http://www.caranddriver.com.

➤ Source of thousands of car reviews at http://www.autohelper.com/carreviews/cr_bottom.html.

➤ Consumer Reports Online offers reviews and reports on new and used cars (for a monthly fee) at http://www.ConsumerReports.org/Categories/CarsTrucks/index.html.

➤ Great site for tips on maintaining and repairing the family car at http://www.familycar.com.

➤ Search a huge database of car problems at http://www.cartalk.cars.com.

➤ Valuable tips on auto maintenance and repair at http://www.autodigest.com.

➤ Daily automotive news and reviews at http://www.auto.com.

➤ Automotive resources (auto parts, dealers, news) at http://www.eauto.com.

➤ *Popular Mechanics*'s site for news, reviews, and tips on cars and trucks at http://www.popularmechanics.com.

➤ Useful source of information about cars, manufacturers, parts, service, and more at http://www.autodirectory.com.

➤ Tips and advice on cars at http://www.carseverything.com.

➤ Retail and trade-in values (Kelly Blue Book) for new and used cars at http://www.kbb.com.

➤ Lots of tips on car maintenance and repair from Bob, the Auto Answer Man at http://www.stretcher.com.

➤ Mister Fixit's excellent source of tips on repairing cars at http://www.MisterFixit.com/autorepr.com

➤ Learn more about the Automotive Service Association and its members at http://www.asashop.org.

➤ Find out what the U.S. government has to offer car owners at http://www.pueblo.gsa.gov/cars.

➤ Consumer and technical information about your car at http://www.motorminute.com.

➤ Check out the Consumer Automotive Repair (CAR) Show online at http://www.thecarshow.com.

➤ Learn more about cars, how they work, and what to do when they don't at http://www.autoshop-online.com.

➤ Lots of preventive maintenance information and tips at http://www.carcarecounsel.org.

➤ Taylor Automotive Tech Line helps solve car problems at http://www.nashville.net/~teklin19/index.html.

➤ Helpful advice on car maintenance and repair at http://www.autoshop-online.com.

➤ Answers to common car maintenance questions at http://www.autosite.com.

➤ Car maintenance for the novice at http://www.hunter.com.

➤ Audio files of the popular Auto Answers radio program at http://www.autoanswers.com.

➤ Source for technical manuals and data at http://www.alldata.com.

➤ Volunteer experts answer auto repair questions at http://www.allexperts.com.

➤ Order repair manuals for your car from http://www.autdigest.com.

➤ Find auto parts and resources at http://www.autobody.com.

➤ Online source of automotive books at http://www.autoliterature.com.

➤ Interactive troubleshooting plus other auto information at http://www.AutoDen.com.

➤ Troubleshooting guide for your car at http://www.diadex.com.

If you own a classic car (as I do), you'll find these Internet resources helpful:

➤ Learn about restoring your classic car at http://www.autorestorer.com.

➤ Find lots of classic car parts at http://www.supercar.com.

➤ More parts for antique and classic cars and trucks at http://www.antiquecar.com.

➤ Stuff for the car buff at http://www.automuseum.com.

➤ Scads of information on classic car restoration and maintenance at http://www.classicar.com.

➤ Biggest and best published source of antique and classic cars and parts for sale (Hemmings) at http://www.hmn.com.

➤ Information, photos, and resources for classic car nuts at http://www.myclassiccar.com.

➤ Companion to a TV show about classic cars at http://www.roadclassic.com.

➤ Classifieds for antique, classic, customs, and hot rod cars at http://www.yesterdays-cars.com.

➤ The Web site for a car club dedicated to the 1956–57 Continental Mark II at http://Markii/markii/cma/top.shtml.

Creating Your Own Maps

Now that you're plugged into the Internet, there is much you can look for. Searching, or "surfing," the Internet is relatively easy, and many tools are available. Most Web browser programs offer you ways to search the Internet for key words.

The problem soon becomes not how to find things on the Internet, but how to *selectively* find things. For example, asking for a search of the Internet using the term "automobile" finds literally thousands of Web addresses where the term is used. With practice and by reading the "help" screens, you'll soon learn how to find what you're looking for. The Internet holds plenty of information on auto resources (your local mechanic might even have a Web site!). You can also search for other information on specific car problems, tools, specifications, and low-cost insurance.

To get you started on your search, here are the URLs for popular Internet search engines:

➤ AltaVista at http://www.altavista.com

➤ Excite at http://www.excite.com

➤ Hot Bot at http://www.hotbot.com

➤ Infoseek at http://www.infoseek.com

➤ Look Smart at http://www.looksmart.com

➤ Yahoo! at http://www.yahoo.com

Visiting Friends on the Net

Once on the Internet, you'll meet people and find a few new and old friends. How can you correspond with them? By using electronic mail, or e-mail. Web browser programs usually have some type of e-mail writing and delivery system on them. Your IP can tell you more. In fact, your IP can get you an e-mail address.

For example, if your commercial Internet provider is named Acme and your account name with them is Bubba, your e-mail address is bubba@acme.com.

Folks who want to send you a message would do so using your e-mail address, and you would use their e-mail address to send them a message. It's like your street address or telephone number, except it's an electronic address.

Using Other Online Services

The Internet is a big network that nobody really owns. You buy the telephone time to get on the Internet. There are, however, many commercial networks called *online services*.

The two most popular online services with consumers today are America Online and CompuServe. Not only do they offer their own electronic resources, but both also offer access to the Internet.

America Online

America Online is a computer system that subscribers call up through their modem. Computer software provided by America Online manages the connection and makes it simple for the operator to move from topic to topic.

America Online (800/827-6364) offers access to products, discussion forums, and other resources for automotive owners and others.

CompuServe

Another popular online service is CSI/CompuServe. In the same way, CSI/CompuServe lets callers

Money Saver

If you're ready to join the Internet generation, first call a local computer store or community college about signing up for a class. It can give you hands-on experience under a guiding hand.

access service through supplied software and the customer's computer and modem. Access telephone numbers are located in all major cities and many medium-sized ones. CompuServe is older than AOL and more international in scope.

The monthly subscription rate for CSI/CompuServe (800/848-8199) is about the same as that for America Online and other consumer online services, such as Prodigy (800/776-0845).

Using CD-ROM Resources

You love their music. Now use them on your PC! They are compact discs, or CDs.

Compact discs store digital information that can be read but typically not changed. This digital information is what makes CD music cleaner and crisper than tapes and records that used analog information. But the information stored on the disk doesn't care if it is music or numbers. It's all the same.

So your computer uses a CD-ROM (compact disc read-only memory) player to interpret these digital signals into information you can see on your computer screen.

There's so much information that can be stored on a CD that you can have some pretty fancy computer programs on one to help you understand and maintain your car. If your computer has a CD-ROM drive, check with your local computer store for CDs that will help with car maintenance and repair.

Bring on the Questions!

Still have questions about cars on the Internet? Here are answers to a few of the most frequently asked questions (FAQs):

Q: Can someone on the Internet access my computer?

A: Not without knowing your passwords. If security is a concern, make sure your communications software and modem offer password protection, and make sure you don't give out your password to others.

Additionally, you should be aware that if you exchange information on the Internet (send e-mail or interact with a Web site), others can pick up any information sent (including your e-mail address or credit card numbers) without your knowledge. That's why people get spam (the Internet equivalent of junk mail) and why most vendors over the Internet use secure sites.

Q: How can I get information off the Internet?

A: Most Web browser software has features that let you download files or print information directly from the screen. They use programs called File Transfer Protocol, or FTP.

Q: What are newsgroups?

A: Newsgroups are groups of people who exchange information and chat among themselves on a common topic. There are newsgroups for car owners, do-it-yourselfers, and thousands of other topics. To learn more about newsgroups, talk with your Internet provider or read the information that comes with your Web browser. Subscribing to a newsgroup is typically free and takes just a few minutes.

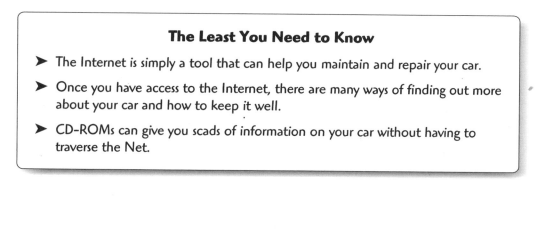

The Least You Need to Know

➤ The Internet is simply a tool that can help you maintain and repair your car.

➤ Once you have access to the Internet, there are many ways of finding out more about your car and how to keep it well.

➤ CD-ROMs can give you scads of information on your car without having to traverse the Net.

Chapter 5

250,000 MILES
SOLID GOLD!

Quarter-Million-Mile Car: Fact or Fiction?

> ### In This Chapter
>
> ➤ Why today's cars live longer
>
> ➤ How to keep track of your car's life
>
> ➤ How to set up a safe and efficient workshop

Cars have traveled far over the past 50 years.

The post-WWII automobile was big, obese, and not very efficient. It looked like a remodeled Army tank and offered about the same gas mileage. It had vacuum-powered windshield wipers, column manual transmission, and a bland interior.

To overcome these limitations, teens of the 1950s began putting bigger engines into lighter cars of the 1930s. Then they started rebuilding the engines and adding more carburetion to get even more power; the car bodies were nothing more than a shell. The hot rod was born. It didn't look anything like dad's Studebaker or Chrysler, and it was even less efficient than dad's car.

Then Detroit caught on to the new market and began putting sleeker styling and bigger engines in stock cars. The Boss Mustang, Plymouth Barracuda ('Cuda), and Chevy Corvette ('Vette)—the so-called muscle cars—were born.

Then the '70s came along and we found ourselves with gas-guzzlers and no gas. Foreign auto manufacturers, who had been making fuel-efficient cars for decades, stepped in and took over the American automotive marketplace. Making cars became a much more competitive field.

The average miles-per-gallon doubled. Smaller cars were now getting 30 mpg and medium-sized ones earned at least 20.

More important, competition bred an increase in quality. American auto manufacturers of the 1950s were so intent on styling that they made very few mechanical advances. The carburetor of the 1960s, for example, was similar in design to that of 1950. It was just bigger. But competition brought efficient carburetion and, later, fuel injection.

The application of the computer to cars also advanced their quality and longevity . They're not perfect, but computers have added to the life expectancy of today's cars.

Sure, I love my 1956 Continental Mark II. Its classic styling represents the best designs of its era. But cars of the 1950s weren't expected to live into the 21st century, and it takes lots of ongoing maintenance to keep it on the road. Cars of the 1950s hoped to keep the same engine for about 75,000 miles and the transmission about 100,000 miles with regular maintenance. Some didn't last that long. A few made it to 200,000— a very few.

Today's car has the birthright of living to a quarter-million miles or more with regular maintenance, and maintenance is easier on modern cars than on your father's car.

I was hesitant to buy our 1984 Honda a few years ago because it had nearly 100,000 miles on it. But I was confident enough to give it to our daughter at 160,000 miles a few years later because I knew it would roll 200,000 someday. It sold me on the improved quality of modern cars.

The styling of a Honda or other modern-day car will probably never be called classic, but these cars are great transportation. And that's really what cars are supposed to be about.

So how can you have a quarter-million-mile car? Again: with regular maintenance. And you've learned in this book that you don't have to do all the work yourself, but you should know how it is done and how to pick a good mechanic.

This chapter offers valuable tips to make sure you keep your car trouble-free longer.

Your Car Notebook

Life is complicated enough without having to remember the date of your car's last oil change. Did I get 40,000 miles on the last set of tires, or just 30,000? What's the part number of that oil filter I need? Which filter do I get if they don't have my brand in stock?

There are hundreds of facts about your car that you should remember to keep it in top running condition. And, if you're like me, you could easily forget them. One solution is to use the Car Maintenance Schedule tear-out in the front of this book to remember what to service when. A more complete solution is to start a Car Notebook.

When I first purchased my 1956 Continental Mark II, I also bought a 5×7 pocket notebook for a couple of bucks. It has been my best investment in keeping my car on the road. I began entering things like the date it was purchased, from whom, the mileage, and what the previous owner told me about the car's history and mechanics. I use the following pages as a log: "7/17/95: Ordered two power steering hoses from Jack Rosen. $44 + $12 ship. Arrived 7/20; installed."

Then I set aside pages in the middle of the notebook for "Needs & Wants." As I found something I needed or wanted to fix, I added it to the list and checked it off when done (or crossed it out if I later decided it wasn't needed): "Fix center brace on front seat."

Other pages were devoted to special projects, such as preparing the car for a show or jotting down tips from a magazine on touching up paint chips.

Finally, my Little Black Book includes "Parts and Equivalents": "Oil Filter: Napa 1515, Motorcraft FL-1A, AC PF2, Fram PH8A, Purolator PER1A." I prefer one brand, but if it isn't available, I consider the others.

The book also includes facts I should know: tire pressure, amount of oil needed for an oil change, spark plug gap, and other useful information.

Best of all, this notebook is typically kept in my car's glove compartment. If something breaks or I want to see how long it's been since my last oil change, the information is with my car.

All these parts numbers aren't as important for newer cars, but you should have a list of your preferred filters, oil brand and weight, and hose parts numbers. (Many problems can occur if the wrong hose is installed.)

And, if you do your own maintenance, your Car Notebook becomes a record of service that you can pass on to the next owner. Think of it as a buyer: wouldn't you love to get a book like this with a used car you purchased?

So the first step to keeping your car on the road for a quarter-million miles or more is keeping track of parts and service.

Money Saver

The smartest way to keep your car running for a quarter-million miles or more is to set aside just a few minutes each week for checking over your car. Plan to spend some quality time with it, checking tire pressure, fluid levels, and general condition.

Money Saver

Advertisements for automotive wonder products that sound too good to be true probably are. Buy quality fuel, oil, and replacement parts instead of cheap products and a bunch of expensive additives.

Your Workshop

Having an organized place to work on your car makes car care easier. You'll be reluctant to take care of maintenance chores if you always have to find a flat parking spot, dig out the tools from here and there, and use the ground as a workbench.

If you already have a garage that isn't preoccupied with storage, you can set up a small car maintenance center there. Even if it is full of stuff, you can clear out a small area near the door where you can keep tools, parts, and books for driveway repairs. Small is better than nothing.

If you have some room and a few bucks, consider building or buying a workbench. The bench should reflect your current and future abilities. You don't need a large bench if all you'll be doing is changing plugs and filters. But a larger surface is needed for disassembly of larger parts.

My current workbench is an old desk at the side of a garage. On it is my main tool chest with drawers of tools and a couple of Snickers bars. Under the desk is a floor jack and stands. Nearby is a rolling chest that includes gauges, testers, battery charger, and some more Snickers bars. I'm ready for any emergency!

The key to a good workbench is organizing tools so that they are readily available and easily returned. I use lined toolbox drawers to organize my tools. In other garages I've mounted tools on pegboard walls. I prefer toolboxes because I can then take the tools to the car instead of vice versa.

Did You Know?

Many colleges and adult education sources offer consumer-level classes on auto care. They not only give you hands-on experience under the supervision of a professional mechanic, they also give you a handy place to work on your car and all the tools you'll need.

To decide what setup you prefer, sneak a peek at how neighbors repair their cars, or drive through neighborhoods on a Saturday morning. Be careful, though, as not everyone will appreciate your interest in their garage. Others will be most happy to show off the shop.

Fortunately, you can rent a garage if you need it. Some cities are big enough to support do-it-yourself shops where car owners can rent a shop and maybe even some tools on a per-hour basis.

If you have a major repair job to do and nowhere to do it, consider renting a storage unit for a month. but make sure the managers will let you use it for repairs. Some won't let you access a storage unit daily. Others don't want the mess (and liability) of having you work on your car there.

If you live in a small town, consider renting a bay of a service station or asking to work alongside the mechanic. You might not be able to save much money this way, but you'll learn a lot about car maintenance.

So you don't really need your own garage to keep your car trouble-free.

Planning

This book groups maintenance tasks so you can plan ahead. You can do all the monthly tasks at one time or maybe just those under the hood on one day and those underneath and beside the car the following day.

Another reason for planning your maintenance tasks is to free you from worry. Not only will you know that your car is safe, but you can also enjoy today's football game because car maintenance isn't scheduled until *next* weekend.

Your car notebook should include a calendar or some type of scheduling to make sure that

➤ Scheduled maintenance *is* scheduled.

➤ Maintenance is planned before major trips.

➤ You know what parts and tools to gather in advance and when you need them.

Fortunately, a number of useful chapters about scheduling maintenance are on the horizon. Chapters 6 through 13 get pretty specific about my CAR Maintenance System.

And don't forget to use the tear-out in the front of this book to help you plan and schedule trouble-free car care. Yes, you can keep your car on the road for a quarter-million miles or more!

My Mechanic Says. . .

If you really want to know more about your car, or would like to encourage a young person who wants to be a mechanic, check an area college's bookstore for textbooks that the automotive courses use. They often include *Auto Service and Repair* by Stockel, Stockel, and Johanson (Goodheart-Willcox Co., 1996) and *Automotive Encyclopedia: Fundamental Principles, Operation, Construction, Service and Repair* by Toboldt, Johnson, and Gauthier (Goodheart-Willcox Co., 1995). For those who want to know the physics of cars (stuff like gear ratio formulas and brake circuit configurations), look for *Automotive Handbook* published by Robert Bosch, GmbH. They're not cheap books, but they offer lots of information per pound. My mechanic has a set on his bookshelf!

The Least You Need to Know

➤ Today's cars live longer because of better engineering and reduced maintenance needs.

➤ Keep track of your car's life in a Car Notebook that records what has been done, when, and even how.

➤ Set up a safe and efficient workshop that will make maintenance and repair easier.

➤ Plan for trouble-free car care.

Part 2
Maintaining Your Car

Cars are amazing things, aren't they? They can take you places your grandparents never saw—at speeds they never dreamed of. The world has changed dramatically over the past century, and much of the world's movement has been made by the car.

So it's really frustrating when the *%$#@! things don't work! Don't blame the car. Today's cars are designed to run 100,000, 200,000, even 500,000 miles or more— with proper maintenance.

That's where you come in. Whether you do the maintenance yourself or have it done, it's your job to make sure it happens. Actually, it's not that big of a job. You can handle it. You can spend just a few hours each year to check, adjust, and replace parts and fluids on your car—and you can save scads of money. The chapters in this section show you how.

Chapter 6

Do-It-Yourself Maintenance, or Getting Your Hands Dirty

In This Chapter

➤ How to keep car maintenance costs down

➤ Saving money with the right tools

➤ Using the CAR Maintenance System

I can't do that!

I can't work on my car!

Sure you can!

If you can eat and watch TV at the same time, you can do at least some of the maintenance on your own car—or at least know how to hire someone to do it for a fair price.

The purpose of this chapter is to convince you that you can safely do some or all of your own car's maintenance. The next chapter will help you find professional help for tasks you'd rather not do.

Pickpockets in Overalls

The fact is that the cost of most car repair jobs is about 50% parts and 50% labor, so that $80 tune-up required only about $40 in parts. In fact, the mechanic also made at least 20% more on the parts because he or she buys the parts at a low price and sells them to you at a profit. So you could have done the same tune-up for about $32 in parts and pocketed the rest—if you knew how.

Before you get started taking over the maintenance of your car and saving money left and right, here are some tips to make the job easier and maybe even more fun. Well, at least easier.

Tip #1: Buy tools only as needed. Later in this chapter, you'll learn what tools you need for maintenance and repairs. Some eager folks go right out and buy a $500 set of top-of-the-line tools before they open the hood of their car. Instead, start gathering a few tools needed for basic maintenance, and then build your set as you discover what jobs you want to do and which you'd prefer others do for you. In most cases, you'll be able to pay for needed tools with savings from the first job you do yourself. Then the tools are yours, free and clear to save you money on future jobs.

Tip #2: Buy parts at a discount. That's not the same as buying cheap parts. *Cheap parts* are those made to sell at the lowest possible prices. *Discount parts* are quality parts that you purchased at less than the suggested retail price—sometimes just a few pennies or bucks more than the cheapies. By learning the year, make, model, and engine of your car (see Chapter 2, "Learning About Your Car: What Does What"), it becomes easier to compare the prices of specific parts by number. You don't have to shop at Wally's Superduper Phantasmagoric Store to get a low price. In fact, you might find a local auto parts retailer who will give you a discount (as much as 35%) on purchases of quality parts that are more durable and reliable. You'll also get knowledgeable answers to your questions—something that Wally's clerks might not be able to offer.

Tip #3: Group maintenance tasks. One way to make your work easier is to do more than one job during a maintenance session. When you check the oil, check the coolant and other fluids at the same time. Use a maintenance plan that helps you use your time efficiently.

Tip #4: Make maintenance a habit. Keeping your car in good condition actually won't take much time at all. In fact, if you make maintenance a regular habit, you can do much of it using the time you'll save being frustrated by needless repairs. Later in this chapter I'll give you an easy-to-remember method of making car maintenance a habit you can live with.

In Your Driveway or in the Parking Lot

One big reason why more people don't do maintenance on their own cars is they just don't seem to have a good place to do it. They think that they need a garage and shop. Not so. Most car maintenance can be done nearly anywhere the law allows. Following are some ideas about where you can get the work done.

Depending on the task, you might be able to do much of your car's maintenance right where it's parked in the morning. You can open the hood, check and fill engine fluids, and visually inspect your car where it is.

If you're changing oil, you might be able to get permission to drain and replace the oil and filter in the parking lot where you buy the parts. Of course, you'll need an oil-collection can to eliminate spillage and allow recycling, but many auto parts stores can sell you the collection system and even help you recycle the old oil and filter. The same can be said for refilling other engine fluids.

You can also replace many worn car parts, *such as filters,* right there in the parking lot where you bought them—if you don't have a better place to do so. Some parts stores offer a specific area to do so. If not, ask permission. *Make sure you can do so safely and can clean up after yourself when done.*

What about maintenance in colder or wetter climates? Some cities have do-it-yourself maintenance shops where you can buy and install parts in a heated garage bay—for an hourly fee. Or you can borrow a friend's garage for a few hours. Or you can do your own maintenance when the weather's nice and have your mechanic do it when it's not so nice.

How To Get Your Hands Dirty

As you'll soon discover, most car maintenance can be done in a couple of minutes a week and a couple of hours every few months. It's really not going to take that long once you know what you're doing and how to do it.

The first step to trouble-free car care is planning what you'll do. The CAR Maintenance System described later in this chapter will help you with that task.

The second step is gathering the needed fluids and parts. Having a system also helps you make sure you have what you need for normal maintenance. Chapters 8 through 13 give you step-by-step instructions and suggest what fluids and parts you'll use.

The third step is gathering the tools you'll need for the maintenance procedure. What tools? This is a good time to look over the scads of tools found in an auto parts store and figure out which ones you'll need—and which ones you won't.

Let's do that right now.

It's Tool Time!

Tools are simply extensions of your hands. If you had eaten enough spinach when you were younger, you wouldn't have to use tools to loosen bolts. You could do it with your bare hands. You didn't, so now you must. (Fortunately for the toolmakers, few of us liked spinach.)

Cars stay together because of fasteners. Bolts, screws, clips, and other fasteners are used to attach car parts to each other, and so they work together. Most of the tools you need for maintaining your car simply tighten or loosen these fasteners. A few perform related functions. The key tools to have are listed here:

➤ Wrenches or sockets move bolts

➤ Screwdrivers move screws

➤ Pliers grab parts

➤ Lubrication or lube tools lubricate parts

For now, that's about all you'll need. So let's start selecting tools for your maintenance toolbox.

Wrenches

Wrenches come in two sizing systems: SAE and metric. What's the difference? As you learned in Chapter 1, "How Cars Run: What Makes It Go?" *SAE* is an acronym for *Society of Automotive Engineers*. These fine folks established a standard for parts and fluids for American-made cars. Tools that fit these parts are labeled *SAE*, *standard*, or *US* and are sized in fractional inches, such as $^3/_8$ inch. *Metric* is what the rest of the world uses, including European and Asian auto manufacturers. Metric parts and tools are measured in millimeters (mm).

Because there are two common sizing systems for cars sold in the U.S., many tool sets include wrenches for both systems. A $^1/_2$-inch bolt is just a bit larger than a 12-mm bolt, so the tools are not interchangeable. If you own and maintain only German, Korean, or other metric cars, you'll need only metric wrenches. If you have only older American cars, you may need only SAE wrenches. But if you own—or plan to own—cars that use the other system, you will eventually need a set of both. Keep them separate, though, so you don't mangle a bolt by using the wrong size wrench.

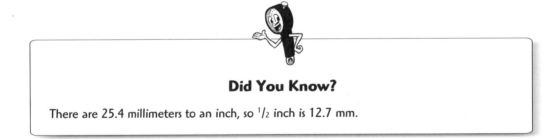

Did You Know?

There are 25.4 millimeters to an inch, so $^1/_2$ inch is 12.7 mm.

An *end wrench* is a flat-handled tool of hardened steel with an opening at each end. The opening is designed to grasp the outside edges of a bolthead so that it can be turned by rotating the wrench handle. Some wrench ends are open on one side so that the wrench can be slipped around them. These are called *open-end wrenches*. The ends of others, called—surprise!—*closed-end* or *box wrenches*, encircle the bolt's head to get a better grip.

An open-end wrench applies its force on two sides of the bolt. A closed-end wrench applies its force to the corners of a bolthead. The closed-end wrench gives you better grab to turn the bolthead. In addition, a closed-end wrench has 6 or 12 notches to make it twice as easy to find six corners of the bolthead to grasp.

Some end wrenches have an open end and a closed end, both of the same size. These are called *combination wrenches*. Other wrenches have both open ends or both closed ends, but of slightly different sizes, such as $^1/_2$ and $^9/_{16}$ inch.

A cousin of the open-end wrench is the *adjustable-end wrench*. It was made popular by the Crescent Tool Co., so the adjustable-end wrench often is called the *Crescent wrench*. Because the jaws of an adjustable wrench contact only two sides of the bolthead and because one of the jaws is movable, the adjustable-end wrench isn't as powerful as the closed-end wrench. Even so, every toolbox should have one or more Crescent wrenches.

Another relative of the end wrench is the *ratchet wrench*, a closed-end wrench in which the end can rotate. A locking device called a *ratchet* makes sure it rotates in only one direction. To make the ratchet wrench turn bolts in the other direction, simply turn it over.

Car Speak

Know your fasteners! A *bolt* is a fastener with a head larger than its body and grooves or threads on the body. A *nut* is a fastener that can be screwed or twisted onto the body of a bolt. A *screw* has a tapered body that doesn't require a nut to fasten. A *pin* is inserted into a hole to keep a part from moving.

Socket Wrenches

From the ratchet wrench, it's a simple progression to the *socket wrench*. A socket wrench is a socket and separate driver. The *socket* is a round cylinder that surrounds the bolthead. The socket is named for the size of the bolt it fits: $^3/_8$ inch, $^9/_{16}$ inch, $^3/_4$ inch, and so on. The *driver* is a ratchet handle with a square tip that fits in the end of the socket. The driver is named for the size of this square tip: $^1/_4$-inch, $^3/_8$-inch, or $^1/_2$-inch driver. A set of socket wrenches is also named for the size of the ratchet handle tip.

Which socket wrench set should you buy? Consider $^1/_4$-inch socket wrenches for fasteners on electrical equipment, $^3/_8$-inch for most other non-engine car care, and $^1/_2$-inch if you plan to take apart an engine or transmission. Folks usually buy a $^3/_8$-inch socket wrench set to handle most car maintenance tasks.

Spark plugs require a longer socket than most boltheads. You can buy a spark plug socket to fit a $^3/_8$- or $^1/_2$-inch driver. The most popular size of spark plug socket is $^{13}/_{16}$ inch (21 mm).

The big brother of the socket wrench is the *torque wrench*. Bolts and nuts that need to be tightened to a specific pressure (measured in foot-pounds) need this wrench with its special long-handled driver with a torque-measuring device. The device can have a gauge, a scale and pointer, or a dial. You won't need a torque wrench for many tasks, but if you get into the car-fixing hobby, tell Santa you want one. He probably delivers quite a few each year.

Screwdrivers That You Can't Drink

Screws are common fasteners for attaching or adjusting car parts. Some screws fasten body parts together. Other screwheads are used to adjust the amount of fuel that is dumped into a carburetor, for example.

Screwdrivers are alcoholic beverages mixed to make your head rotate. They are also tools for turning screwheads. The tip of the screwdriver is designed to fit snugly into the screwhead. The handle of the screwdriver is then turned to rotate the screw.

Screwdrivers are available in many tip designs and sizes that work with corresponding screwheads. Most popular are the *straight* or *standard tip* (a.k.a. *flathead*) and the *Phillips* or *cross tip*. *Hex-head* or *Allen wrenches* are used to turn hex-head screws—screws with a six-sided hole in the screwhead.

Pliers: They're Not Just for Pulling Teeth

Pliers grip things. Pliers shouldn't be used to turn boltheads (because it's hard to keep a firm grip and you could slip and "round" the bolthead), but they can be used to hold a nut while the bolthead is turned—or vice versa. Two wrenches are better. Pliers can grasp and remove a clip fastener or another part. Some pliers have blades that can cut wires. Others compress or crimp electrical connectors.

For all-around use, make sure you have one pair of slip-joint pliers and one pair of needle-nose pliers in your maintenance toolbox. *Slip-joint pliers* let you widen the jaws to grasp larger objects, as needed. *Needle-nose pliers* have long, pointed jaws that can grasp small parts and hold them in place.

Your toolbox should also have a pair of *locking-jaw pliers*. They sometimes are referred to as *Vise-Grips* for the name of the company that first made them popular.

Lubrication Tools

Car maintenance often means replacing fluids and lubricants. A *grease gun* holds cartridges of grease lubricant. You snap the tip of the grease gun around a *lubrication* or *zerk fitting* and then squeeze the handle to force grease into the fitting. And no, it isn't fair to reach for the grease gun when your spouse irritates you.

A *filter wrench* helps you grasp and turn an oil filter for removal.

Other lubrication tools help you pour oil into an engine. A *small oil can* helps you lubricate parts needing lightweight oil. A tube or spray can of *white grease lubricant* can be used to lubricate door, hood, and trunk hinges.

Other Maintenance Tools

You may eventually want several other handy tools for your trouble-free maintenance toolbox:

➤ A **jack** can lift your car so that jack stands can be placed under it to give you safe room to work under your car. *Make sure your car still has the original or a replacement jack.* Alternatively, use maintenance or wheel ramps onto which you drive your car to raise one end.

➤ A **tire pressure gauge** makes it easy to check the air pressure in tires without having to drive to the gas station.

➤ A **file** is useful for removing small amounts of metal as well as for breaking out of jail.

➤ A **hammer** is sometimes useful for venting frustration on inanimate and inexpensive objects. I believe that it has other uses as well.

➤ A **voltmeter** can help you check electrical wiring and components in your car.

➤ A **tachometer** can help you set your engine's idle speed.

Using Tools To Make a Dent

There's a logic to how cars work. There's a related logic to how tools work with car parts. Understand the logic and you're on your way to making maintenance easier.

First, most fasteners have grooves or threads on them so that they can be rotated into or out of other parts. So it's very important that the threads aren't damaged or, if they are, that the replacement fastener has the same thread pattern.

Auto parts stores usually have small bins where you find a variety of bolts. The labels on the front of the bins tell you about the bolts inside. The label that says $1/2 - 13 \times 1$ is telling you that these are $1/2$-inch-diameter bolts with 13 threads per inch and that the bolt shaft (not counting the head) is 1 inch long. The bolthead may have lines on it pointing to its corners. These lines tell you what grade or strength the bolt is. No memorization here. Just make sure a replacement bolt has at least as many lines on the head as the one it is replacing. Remember to take the original bolt with you when you're buying a replacement so that you can check the match.

For you metric fans, the label on the bolt bin might say $M12 - 1.75 \times 25$. It describes a metric bolt with a head width (tip to tip) of 12 mm, a distance of 1.75 mm between threads, and a shaft length of 25 mm. Be careful, folks, because this size is almost identical to the standard size described in the last paragraph. Bolt strength is indicated by numbers stamped on the bolt's head. Make sure a replacement bolt has the same or higher numbers as the old bolt.

Most clocks now are digital, displaying the time numerically. Although that makes reading the time easier, it makes it more difficult to define the term *clockwise*. Bolts, screws, and other threaded fasteners are installed by turning them clockwise. Looking down on the top of the fastener, turn the upper side toward the right. To loosen a fastener, turn the upper side counterclockwise or toward the left. This rule applies for all right-handed screws, bolts, and most other threaded fasteners. Less common left-hand threaded fasteners are installed by turning counterclockwise and are removed by turning clockwise.

Another way to remember which direction to turn the bolt is to think "righty-tighty, lefty loosey," meaning turn the head to the right to tighten and to the left to loosen.

Did You Know?

Put it back where you found it! Parents love to use that line. Unfortunately, it's good advice. As you finish using your tools, return them to where you got them and they usually will be there when you need them again—unless someone else didn't listen to his or her parents.

Finding Parts the Legal Way

Your car has more than 10,000 parts. Trouble-free car care means replacing a part once in a while. No, they don't fall off—they wear out. How can you make sure you have the correct replacement part? The first step is to identify the part. Chapter 2, "Learning About Your Car: What Does What," showed you how to identify your car. That's the starting point for finding replacement parts.

Parts you need to replace during routine maintenance include filters, ignition components, and a few other parts that are easy to identify and remove. To identify the specific part, look it over for a brand name and any numbers. An oil filter might say *Atlas F-14* on its casing, for example. A battery might be labeled *Interstate Group 24, 60A* on the top. A spark plug might say *Autolite BRF42*. (Okay, you caught me. A spark plug doesn't "say" anything. You have to "read" it. Feel better?)

What if the part you need to replace doesn't have a number or other identification on it (such as an air filter)? If possible, remove the part and take it to your auto parts retailer. With year, make, model, and engine specs, the retailer probably will be able to find the exact replacement part for you.

And what if you can't remove the part without losing your ride? Then identify it in other ways, such as description, size, and location. With other specifications on your car, an auto parts retailer usually can identify the part and furnish a replacement. If you can drive the car to the auto parts store, do so and ask a counterperson to look at the part.

And what if the auto parts store doesn't have the part you need? Ask whether they can order it for you or where else you might be able to get it. It's out there somewhere. I've found tune-up parts for my 40-year-old Lincoln on the shelf in small-town parts stores.

As you begin to do some repairs on your car, you might not be able to find all the parts you need in parts stores. This is especially true of damaged body parts (sounds gory, doesn't it?). Fortunately, there are auto recyclers or salvagers who dismantle damaged cars and sell the good parts. Some even inspect and guarantee their parts. An auto recycler can furnish a transmission or other major part at less than half the cost of buying a new one.

Depending on the age and popularity of your car, mail-order parts companies can furnish nearly any component. One of the oldest and largest is J.C. Whitney & Co. (312/431-6102). Others furnish replacement parts for Ford Mustangs, Chevys, imports, and others. Car magazines will have ads from these resources.

My Mechanic Says. . .

Oops! What if you accidentally damage the threads on a bolt hole? Hopefully, all you'll need to do is replace the bolt or nut with a new one of the same size and thread. If you've damaged the part, you can buy or rent a tap and die set to cut new threads in it. You can buy a tap and die set if you think you'll be doing this on a regular basis. However, you might be able to rent one from a tool rental shop or from larger auto parts stores.

Did You Know?

To check a maintenance-free battery's condition, look on its top for a charge indicator. A spot of light will tell you whether the battery is charged. No light means no charge. Most battery-condition indicators have a label on the battery that tells you how to interpret what you see.

The CAR Maintenance System

I've been promising you a system that can make maintenance easy to remember. It's time to deliver on my promise.

The easiest way to memorize something is to picture it. You can obviously picture a car. The second-best way to remember is to find an acronym or letters that stand for words. So here goes my system.

There are three types of maintenance on your car:

➤ Check your car.

➤ Adjust your car.

➤ Replace fluids and parts.

The first letters of these three maintenance procedures can be remembered as the acronym C-A-R.

Hang on, it gets easier.

Car maintenance should be performed on a regular basis:

➤ Fluids should be checked about every week.

➤ Adjustments should be made about every six months.

➤ Fluids and parts should be replaced every year or two.

These guidelines fit most modern cars. Cars older than about 25 years need more frequent adjustments and replacements, depending on age and how much they are driven. Some need monthly adjustments and yearly replacements.

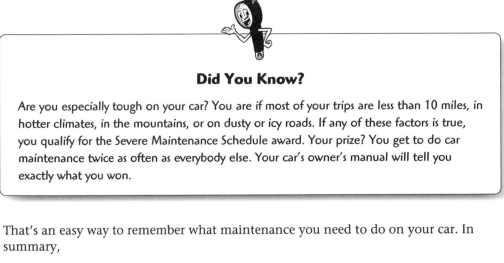

Did You Know?

Are you especially tough on your car? You are if most of your trips are less than 10 miles, in hotter climates, in the mountains, or on dusty or icy roads. If any of these factors is true, you qualify for the Severe Maintenance Schedule award. Your prize? You get to do car maintenance twice as often as everybody else. Your car's owner's manual will tell you exactly what you won.

That's an easy way to remember what maintenance you need to do on your car. In summary,

➤ Check your car every week and every three months.

➤ Adjust your car every six months.

➤ Replace fluids once a year and parts every other year.

Check what? Adjust what? Replace what? I knew you would ask. The next chapter in this book will help you find a good mechanic for the car-care jobs you don't want to do. Then, I'll devote an entire chapter to the specifics of each of these maintenance tasks. I'll include a description of each task with step-by-step instructions on how to do it.

These chapters (8 through 12) also group maintenance tasks by where they are done. Those marked with an (H) are done by opening the **hood**. The (U) means that the maintenance step requires you to climb **under** the car. A (B) means you will do the job **beside** the car. This system not only helps you work more efficiently, but it also identifies which jobs require you to get under the car—jobs you might prefer to have a mechanic do for you.

The HUB acronym is cute, but has no significance other than it's easier to remember than VQMLTZPVXS.

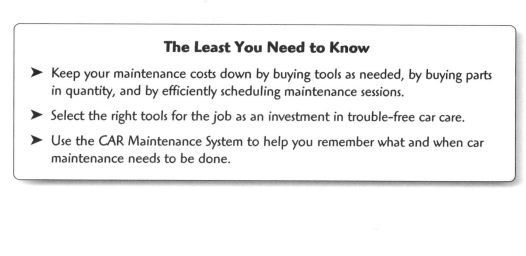

The Least You Need to Know

➤ Keep your maintenance costs down by buying tools as needed, by buying parts in quantity, and by efficiently scheduling maintenance sessions.

➤ Select the right tools for the job as an investment in trouble-free car care.

➤ Use the CAR Maintenance System to help you remember what and when car maintenance needs to be done.

Chapter 7

Finding a Good Mechanic: Who Can You Trust with Your Car?

In This Chapter

➤ Selecting a dealer service shop that takes your plastic, not your body parts

➤ Discovering a really good independent garage

➤ Finding a specialized shop without a criminal record

Trouble-free car care doesn't mean that you have to do it all yourself. It means doing as much as you feel comfortable with and finding a trustworthy mechanic (or mechanics) to do the rest. Understanding how your car runs and knowing what's involved in its maintenance and repair are important steps in finding a good mechanic and knowing when to hire him or her to do the work.

You might want to select more than one mechanic, depending on what work you would rather not do and the quality of the mechanic you've found to do those jobs. You might prefer to do your own tune-ups and oil changes, for example, but leave other parts replacement to a dealership's garage. Or you might use the local service station mechanic for some work and a local muffler shop for other work.

It's your choice, and your choice is based on understanding your car and your own preferences. This chapter gives you the information you need to choose and find qualified, reasonably priced mechanical help when you need it.

Did You Know?

Mechanics have a certification program managed by Automotive Service Excellence (ASE). There are more than 300,000 ASE Automotive Technicians. Some hold certifications in one or two types of auto repair. Those who are certified in all eight areas earn the designation of Master Automobile Technician. Only about 25% of the certified techs become master techs. Certified technicians must have at least two years' experience, have ongoing training, and be recertified every five years. So look for ASE certificates on the wall or ask to see them. Any mechanic that's earned them will be proud to show them off.

The Dealer's Service Shop: Returning to the Scene of the Crime

Remember our drive down Auto Row in Chapter 2, "Learning About Your Car: What Does What"? This is where all the new car dealers live and prey. Most have a service shop for maintaining and repairing cars they've sold or cars from the same family (Ford, GM, VW, and so on). For new cars, this should be your first stop for maintenance service. Dealer service shops know your car, know the maintenance requirements, and usually have exact replacement parts on hand. In fact, some new car warranties are void if anyone other than an authorized shop does any maintenance or repairs on the car. The purchase price of some cars includes basic maintenance work.

So if your car is "under warranty," read the car's warranty and find out what you can and cannot do to maintain your car. You typically can perform any scheduled maintenance without voiding the car's warranty if you follow instructions in the manufacturer's service manual and use approved parts. Keep receipts for parts so that you can prove you did the work, and that you didn't just write it down in a book.

Is your dealership's service department honest and fair? The best way to find out at the least cost is to have some regular maintenance done at the shop. Take it in for a lube and oil change, for example, and stay in a customer area where you can watch while it's being done. Just as important, you want to watch the entire service department at work and take note of issues like these:

➤ What is the attitude of the mechanics toward the cars?

➤ Does the service manager seem genuinely helpful or is he or she full of excuses?

➤ Is the shop organized well?

➤ Ask other customers waiting for cars about their experiences with this shop and with other shops.

➤ Ask the service manager what training programs are used to keep the mechanics up-to-date.

➤ Ask the service manager what the hourly shop rate is, and then use this figure as a comparison to the rates of independent shops.

➤ Check with your local Better Business Bureau or Chamber of Commerce to see if consumer complaints have been filed against the dealer or shop.

How can you make sure you get the best price from a dealer service shop? Keep these guidelines in mind:

➤ If you bought the car at the dealership, ask your salesperson or the sales manager for a discount on the standard shop rate—in writing. If you can't get a discount on labor, ask for one on parts. You might not get it, but it's worth a try.

➤ Ask for a written estimate before any work is done. Most shops do this anyway to protect themselves. However, by making sure the service manager knows you will watch the bill closely, the manager usually will, too.

➤ Let the service manager know you're not a complete idiot when it comes to cars. Ask the manager to explain what is being done and why. If the explanation isn't clear, ask for a clearer explanation. They're working for you.

Money Saver

What should you tell your mechanic? Describe what you see, hear, or smell: clanking in the right front corner, low grinding when driving up hills, a wet spot in the garage below the right wheel, a rotten-egg smell from under the hood after a short drive. Don't diagnose the problem. If you do, the mechanic might fix something without solving the problem.

What if you're not satisfied with the work done by a dealer service shop? Don't walk away without letting them know they have a dissatisfied customer. Dealers understand what that means to their future business and often will try to do something about it. If the service manager doesn't make it right, talk to the sales manager, the dealer, or the manufacturer. The manufacturer's customer service telephone numbers are typically found in the owner's manual. You have that right.

General Mechanics: One-Stop Shopping

Not all good automotive mechanics work for a dealership. Some prefer to operate an independent garage. An independent garage may work on all cars, on foreign cars only, on older cars, or on other specialized groups of cars. However, a general mechanic probably will work on any part of the car: engine, transmission, electronics, whatever. And the hourly shop rate for an independent garage is typically (but not always) about 10% to 20% less than that of a dealer's service shop.

Some general mechanics have their own garages, whereas others own or lease bays in service stations. A few work on a percentage of sales, keeping half and giving the garage owner the other half. It doesn't matter as much where they are located as how professional and honest they are.

Selecting a good general mechanic is similar to selecting a dealer shop. Some shops are operated by ex-dealer mechanics who wanted to be independent. Others are run by those who have no training and little experience. As a consumer, it's up to you to sort out one from the other. Need some tips?

➤ Look for ASE and other certification programs for automotive technicians.

➤ Ask for the hourly shop rate and compare it with that from dealer shops and other automotive service shops. A shop rate that is too low will tell you as much as one that is too high.

➤ As with dealer shops, take your car in for minor service and watch how it's done. Watching the mechanics work will tell you about their knowledge and attitude.

➤ Ask the service manager how much of the work is done by trainees or apprentice mechanics. Is the hourly shop rate for apprentices lower than that for experienced mechanics? It should be.

➤ Ask your friends and neighbors for recommendations about independent mechanics. You'll also get horror stories. From these, you can better decide which mechanics to consider and which to avoid.

Money Saver

Many larger libraries have an *automotive flat rate manual* that estimates the amount of time required by a trained mechanic to perform defined jobs on specific cars. Knowing this helps you estimate how much time it will take a non-trained mechanic to do the same job (about double) and helps you figure how much it will cost to have it done.

What can you do if you're not satisfied with the work done by a general mechanic? First, complain to the service manager or owner. If you don't get satisfaction, contact the local Chamber of Commerce to find out what options you have. Some chambers have a grievance committee. Others will refer you to a local or regional Better Business Bureau. Another option is to file a small-claims suit against the shop. By doing a little research in advance, you probably won't have to take it that far.

Specialized Shops: I Don't Do Electric Windows!!!

Some mechanics specialize in servicing and repairing one or more systems on cars. An engine shop, for example, rebuilds and installs engines on all brands of cars.

A transmission shop services and repairs all types of transmissions, or may specialize in manual or automatic transmissions. A muffler shop installs mufflers, pipes, and related components. A brake shop services brake systems, no matter what brand of car. Some muffler shops also work on brakes.

Why should you consider a specialized shop for servicing your car? For the same reasons you would see a specialist rather than a family physician. You already know what part isn't working well, and you want someone with lots of experience to fix it. A dealership mechanic might repair a couple of transmissions a week. In the same time period, a transmission shop's mechanic might work on two dozen of them. A muffler shop will have or can make tailpipes to fit any car rather than wait a week for one to be ordered.

Of course, to use a specialized shop, you need to have an idea of what your car needs. This book will help you define service needs and diagnose problems so that you can select the right specialty shop for service and repair.

Specialized shops have boomed with franchising. You now can go to any major city (and a few minor ones) and find names you know: AAMCO, Mr. Transmission, Midas, Meineke, and so on.

Tune-up Shops: Adjusting Your Car's Attitude

A tune-up shop specializes in automotive maintenance called the *tune-up*—the adjustment or replacement of parts needing frequent service. Operating parts such as spark plugs and fan belts are designed to be replaced every so often. However, even if you own a car with a carburetor, it probably won't need replacing. It can be adjusted. A tune-up shop might also use sophisticated electronic equipment to diagnose the car's operation and to make needed adjustments.

The hourly shop rate for many tune-up shops is lower than that for full-mechanic shops. Service can be done by mechanics who know lots about ignition and fuel systems, but aren't trained in automatic transmission repair, for example. They know more and more about less and less.

Lube Shops: Fast Food for Your Car

Lube shops have sprouted up across the country. Why? Because all cars need periodic lubrication and because it can be done efficiently by shops that specialize in it.

The typical lube shop has two or more bays or work areas. Your car is driven in from one side. A technician in a pit under the floor lubricates your car from underneath while another technician opens the hood and works from above. Standard servicing includes changing the oil and filter, checking and maybe changing the air filter, lubricating the steering components (if your car needs it), and checking fluid in the transmission and other parts. Your car then is driven out the other side of the bay to make way for another car. Pretty efficient.

Most lube shops take 15 minutes or less to perform a lube service. Depending on the car's needs and what's done, the service costs $20 to $40. About half of that goes for parts and the rest for labor costs. Many shops also print a service report that tells you what has been done, what's been checked, and any service needs your car may have. It also tells you when you should bring your car back for the next servicing. Depending on how many miles you drive each year, this will be about every six months.

Money Saver

Don't buy cheap! The difference between a good lube job and a cheap one is about five bucks—or 1,000 bucks. A lube shop that uses low-grade oil or filters or hires untrained people who forget to tighten the drain plug, can cost you 1,000 bucks for a new engine. Don't shop for the lowest price. Shop for the best value.

Money Saver

Service needed to certify your car may be covered under warranty or service bulletins at little or no cost to you. A service or recall bulletin is issued by the manufacturer defining a known problem and what the manufacturer will do about it. To learn whether your car is covered under a service bulletin, contact the dealer or the National Highway Traffic Safety Administration (202/366-2768).

Idea: Your car needs a lube every six months and you're supposed to visit the dentist every six months, so how about a franchise that offers both services at the same location? Call it Cavity City or Drill 'n Oil.

Lube shops have become popular because they are faster than taking a car to a dealership or even an independent garage. They usually are conveniently located next to a shopping mall or a restaurant where you can spend money while you wait. And because lube shops don't require certified mechanics to do the service, costs are usually lower. Lube shop service people typically are not trained mechanics, however; they can't help you spot, diagnose, or repair problems. You're on your own.

The same rules apply for finding a good lube shop as for finding any mechanic: ask your friends, take your car in once and watch how they work, and compare costs. Know what you're buying and what you should expect for your money.

Many lube shops are franchises. The advantage of any franchise is consistency. The technicians are trained, the products are comparably priced, and good service is important to repeat business. Make sure that the people who serve you and service your car have a professional attitude. There are too many competitors for a lube shop to be less than courteous and professional.

Don't Pollute! And Do It Safely!

Depending on where you live, your car may need periodic inspection for emissions or safety. Your state or county may require an annual or biannual inspection and certification by an authorized shop. This job can be done by your regular mechanic, if certified to make the needed inspections, or by a shop specializing in such inspections. Unfortunately, you can't do this one yourself.

As a consumer, your best bet is to already have a regular mechanic or dealership lined up that is certified. Why? Because the inspector has you in a difficult position that may require you to use that shop to do any required repairs. You want someone you can trust to do needed repairs as well as to tell you what repairs are really needed. Don't go to strangers.

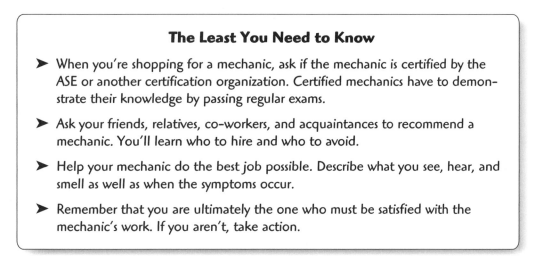

The Least You Need to Know

➤ When you're shopping for a mechanic, ask if the mechanic is certified by the ASE or another certification organization. Certified mechanics have to demonstrate their knowledge by passing regular exams.

➤ Ask your friends, relatives, co-workers, and acquaintances to recommend a mechanic. You'll learn who to hire and who to avoid.

➤ Help your mechanic do the best job possible. Describe what you see, hear, and smell as well as when the symptoms occur.

➤ Remember that you are ultimately the one who must be satisfied with the mechanic's work. If you aren't, take action.

Chapter 8

CAR Weekly Check Up

In This Chapter

➤ How to check the big three: oil, coolant, and windshield washer fluid

➤ Giving the power steering and brake systems a drink

➤ Keeping the pressure on: taking a look at tires and air

Pride of ownership really begins here. People who consider themselves car klutzes have miraculously been transformed into auto aficionados by the simple process of weekly car care.

It's a wonder what a little engine oil on the fingertips can do to bond man or woman and machine.

So let's get started.

The first step in the CAR Maintenance System outlined in Chapter 6, "Do-It-Yourself Maintenance, or Getting Your Hands Dirty," is performing simple checks of your car's systems once a week. These checks are easy to do and can save you thousands of dollars in unneeded repairs. They also offer you peace of mind and a chance to get your hands just a little bit dirty.

Every Seven Days or Once a Week—Whichever Comes First

Got a couple of minutes? That's all it takes once a week to make sure your car is in good shape. In fact, it takes less time to check your car every week than to worry about it.

Your car is a drinker; it uses several fluids. These fluids include oil, coolant, windshield washer fluid, brake fluid, and maybe power steering fluid. Your car also uses pressurized air to keep tires inflated. The fluids can evaporate, deteriorate, or leak out, and the air can leak out. In each case, the fluid or air must be checked and replaced as needed. That's something you can easily do on a regular basis to help keep your car trouble-free.

Your weekly checks can be done over the weekend or before you drive to work on Monday morning (or whenever your work week starts). If you don't drive your car very often—maybe it's your second car—you can check the fluids and pressure less frequently, but make a habit of it. Make your checks on the 1st and 15th of the month, or on even-numbered Wednesdays, for example. If you'd rather watch the odometer than the calendar, make these checks after every 250 miles of driving. Or you can make these checks every time you fill your gas tank. The important thing is to do them regularly.

You might not need tools for these checks. They are mostly visual checks. However, you might need a wrench or pliers to open a power steering or brake fluid reservoir. You will need an air pressure gauge to check pressure in your car's tires, but you can probably borrow one from a service station attendant. By keeping a rag in the trunk or under your car's seat, you can make sure you don't get your hands dirty as you make these checks.

You can perform these checks just about anywhere. Some people do them in their garage. Others do them in the driveway or in the parking lot after work. You should be able to efficiently complete these weekly checks in just a few minutes. To ensure that fluids are settled (and you don't get burned), make sure your engine hasn't been running within the past half hour.

Did You Know?

To keep you from putting water where the oil should go, most car manufacturers clearly label where to add liquids. Look for parts under the hood with the words **OIL FILLER, COOLANT, WINDSHIELD WASHER FLUID**, and so on. A few manufacturers use symbols deciphered by logic. If you're not sure, ask a gas station attendant, mechanic, or friend who does his or her own maintenance.

To make the process easier, the weekly checks described in the rest of this chapter appear in a logical order. First, check fluids under the hood; an *H* in a section title indicates that the section covers items under the hood. The figure in this chapter shows where to find various fluid reservoirs under the hood. Then check the car's tire pressure as described in the section with the title marked with *B* (for beside the car). Always check liquids when the car is sitting level.

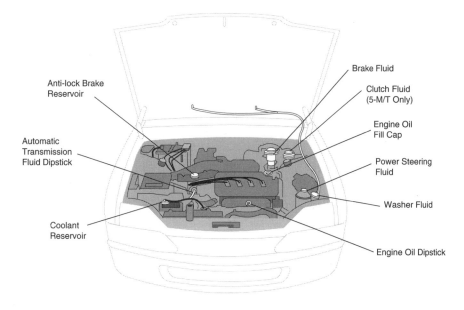

Check Oil Level (H)

Parts in your car's engine rotate at tremendous speeds. Oil circulates in the engine to lubricate these parts and keep them from wearing out. When the engine is off, this oil settles to the lowest spot in the engine—the oil pan. An oil pan stick or dipstick was installed on the engine by the manufacturer to allow you to check the level of the oil.

Warning: Don't attempt to check your oil in a white tuxedo.

To check the oil level in your car, follow these steps:

1. Have an old rag on hand to wipe the dipstick. Make sure your car is level and the engine is cool. Open the hood and look for the dipstick. It is a rod with a curved handle sticking up from one side or the other of your engine. Push the dipstick down in its tube, if needed, to make sure it accurately measures the oil level in the oil pan.

2. Pull the handle up to remove the dipstick rod from the engine. There should be a light or dark brown liquid coating the last couple of inches on the rod. Hold the rod away from your fine clothes to make sure oil doesn't drip on them. (If the liquid is reddish-brown, you have the automatic transmission dipstick. Replace it and keep looking for the engine oil dipstick.)

3. At the lowest end of the dipstick rod will be marks and maybe the word *FULL*. Lower on the rod will be another mark and maybe the word *ADD*. Some dipsticks have only a narrow area stamped with a criss-cross design or just two dots. If so, the highest point of the design indicates FULL and the lowest point means ADD. Visually check to identify the highest point on the stick covered by oil. This point should be somewhere between the FULL and ADD words or marks.

4. If the top edge of oil is above the ADD mark, the oil level is okay. If the top edge of oil is below the ADD mark, you must add oil without overfilling it. How much? For most cars, the distance between the ADD and FULL lines is about one quart of oil. So you can add one quart of oil. If the oil mark is well below the ADD mark, put one quart in, let it settle a few minutes, and then recheck the oil once.

5. To add oil, first find the oil cap on the engine. Some cars have a twist-off cap on the valve cover (a long and wide part on top of the engine that often has a design or lettering). Other cars have an oil-filler tube with a round cap that you should pull off. To make sure this is the right place to put oil, remove the cap and look for signs of dark brown oil buildup.

6. Remove the cap from the oil container (of course, you've made sure the oil is the same as that already in the car) and carefully pour oil into the engine. If this can't be done without spilling oil on the engine, use a funnel. (Oil won't hurt the outside of the engine, but it smells awful once the engine gets hot.)

7. Wait a few minutes until the oil settles into the oil pan, and then recheck the oil level to make sure it's between the ADD and FULL marks. Filling oil past the FULL mark can cause more harm to an engine than running it too low. Why? Because excess oil is worked up into a lather by moving parts, reducing the oil's lubrication qualities.

My Mechanic Says. . .

Oil is usually sold in one-quart plastic containers. To open, set it on a flat surface, grasp it near the neck, and twist the cap off. If you hold the container with one hand as you twist the cap with the other, hand pressure will force oil out the spout as soon as the cap is removed.

Did You Know?

The first oil well was invented by Edwin Drake in 1859, predecessor to J.R. Ewing.

Believe me, it takes longer to describe the process of checking the oil than to do it. Once you've done it for yourself, you can do it again once a week or every 250 miles in less than a minute.

Keeping Your Car's Cool (H)

Another important fluid in your car is the coolant. Coolant is a mixture of antifreeze fluid and water that circulates throughout your car's engine to remove excess heat. The coolant then circulates throughout the radiator where air flow cools the liquid before its journey back through the engine.

To check the radiator coolant level, follow these steps:

1. Make sure the engine and radiator are cool. If not, wait until they are before checking coolant level.

2. Open the hood and find the radiator. It's typically located at the front of the engine compartment just behind the bumper. On most cars, a coolant reserve tank located nearby holds the top layer of coolant from the radiator. If so, look at the side of the coolant reserve tank for two lines: one identifies MAX (maximum) levels, and one identifies MIN (minimum) levels. The highest level of coolant should be between these two marks.

3. If coolant is low, turn the radiator cap counterclockwise one-quarter turn to relieve any pressure remaining in the cooling system. Then push the cap down and turn it counterclockwise until it is off.

4. Check the coolant level in the radiator. If it is below the base of the filler neck, add coolant (remember: half-antifreeze and half-water), and then replace the radiator cap.

5. Open the cap on the coolant reserve tank and add coolant until the level is between the minimum and maximum marks. Replace the tank cap. Clean up any coolant that may have spilled on the floor or ground.

Safety First

Store coolant in a safe and secure place away from progeny and pets. Pets can die from lapping up antifreeze spilled on a garage floor.

Can You See Out of That Thing? (H)

Okay, let's do a real easy one. Most cars have apparatus that sprays a soapy liquid on the windshield when you push a button inside the car. This windshield washer fluid is stored in a reservoir or container under the hood of your car. Certainly it's not as critical as the oil, but running out of washer fluid can make it difficult to see through a dirty windshield.

To check the windshield washer fluid level in your car, follow these steps:

1. Find the windshield washer fluid reservoir. It is typically a clear or white plastic container holding a pint to a quart of colored liquid. The reservoir may look like a milk jug or a jar.

2. Visually check the fluid level. Some reservoirs have a mark on the side indicating the full level. If there's no mark, an inch or two below the top of the reservoir is the full level. Never fill the reservoir to the top because the liquid may expand with weather changes.

3. If the reservoir registers less than one-half full (or one-half empty, depending on your view of life), open the top of the reservoir, fill it with windshield washer fluid, and replace the top. Some reservoir tops snap on and off; others are screwed on and off.

What should you fill the reservoir with? You can buy replacement windshield washer fluid at nearly any large store for a dollar or two a gallon. You can also make your own using water and a windshield washer concentrate such as *20/20*, or you can use a drop or two of liquid dishwashing detergent. However, if you live in a colder climate, opt for the commercial stuff. It includes ingredients to keep the water from freezing during the winter.

Check Power Steering Fluid Level (H)

Not all cars have power steering. Steering systems have evolved over the years so that power steering is not necessary on many smaller cars. But if your car has it, you should check the power steering fluid level once a week or every 250 miles unless the owner's manual says otherwise.

My Mechanic Says. . .

Don't use automatic transmission fluid to fill a power steering fluid reservoir. The two fluids are similar in appearance and composition, but they aren't the same. Automatic transmission fluid has detergents that can break down the seals in a power steering unit, causing it to fail.

To check the power steering fluid level, follow these steps:

1. Find the power steering reservoir on your car. Power steering units pump or circulate hydraulic fluid to help you easily steer the car with reduced effort. This fluid is held in a reservoir attached to the power steering pump. On most cars, this pump is rotated by a fan belt at the front of the engine, so that's where to look first.

2. To check the power steering fluid level, remove the cap or top to the reservoir. The cap on some power steering reservoirs has a dipstick attached to the underside, indicating the full and add levels. Other reservoirs have a mark on the inside of the casing to show where the level should be filled to. *Note:* Power steering fluid expands when hot.

That means the level in the reservoir is higher if the engine has been running recently. Some power steering dipsticks are marked for FULL HOT as well as FULL COLD. Check the level when cold, if possible.

3. To add power steering fluid, check your car's owner's manual for the fluid brand recommended by the manufacturer. Then pour fluid into the reservoir as needed to bring it up to the full mark. Don't overfill. That's it. You should check your power steering fluid level weekly or every 250 miles, but you shouldn't have to top it off more than every couple of months. If you do, there's a leak somewhere and repair is in order.

Check Brake Fluid Levels (H)

Brakes are obviously important to your car. Without them, you would run right past where you wanted to stop. Brake systems use hydraulics to magnify the pressure of your foot on the pedal to stop the car. Hydraulic systems, in turn, use hydraulic fluid. In this case, the fluid is called *brake fluid*. Power brake systems also use a booster to enhance your power to stop the car.

To check brake fluid levels in your car, follow these steps:

1. Find the master brake cylinder. On many cars, look under the hood on the wall between the engine and the driver's area (called the *firewall*). The power brake booster, a large round unit, may be mounted on it. Some import and older cars have them under the floor below the driver, accessed by moving the carpet to expose a metal plate that is, in turn, moved to uncover the master brake cylinder.

2. Clean off the top of the reservoir before opening it so that crud doesn't fall into it. Then remove the cover from the master brake cylinder reservoir. The cover usually has a four- or six-sided head that can be unscrewed with a wrench.

3. Visually check the level of brake fluid in the reservoir. Make sure the fluid is up to just below the cover's threads or a FULL mark on the inside of the reservoir.

4. To add brake fluid, make sure you have a can of brake fluid (the owner's manual tells you which Department of Transportation, or DOT, grade to use) that you opened in the past year. At about two bucks a pint, you can afford to throw out older brake fluid and use only the fresh stuff. With the master cylinder cover removed, carefully pour brake fluid in until the level is about $1/4$ inch below the top. Replace and tighten the cap.

If the master brake cylinder is empty or nearly empty, you might have to bleed the brakes. For this, you'll need to call the American Red Cross...

My Mechanic Says. . .

Brake fluid is really tough on paint jobs. Never the twain should meet.

just kidding. *Bleeding* (removing air from) the brakes is covered in Chapter 24, "Brake System Repairs: Stop Ahead!"

One more related task: Some cars have a hydraulic clutch booster. This helps your foot move the car's clutch plate or disc. If your car has one, you can check your owner's manual to see where and what to do about it. In most cases, the clutch booster uses brake fluid, so checking the fluid level for that is the same as checking the fluid level for the hydraulic clutch booster.

Check Tires and Pressure (B)

Tires of a few decades ago, called *bias tires*, needed to be replaced once every year or two. Today's radial tires can, with regular maintenance, last five years (or one year of a teenage driver). Today's tires also are safer and make a car easier to steer when compared to the older, bias tires.

The key statement in the last paragraph is "with regular maintenance." That's where you come in. You can either check the air pressure in your tires or ask the gas station attendant to do it once a week. By doing so, you can make sure you get 50,000—not 25,000—miles from your 50,000-mile tires. It can also save fuel because underinflated tires reduce fuel economy.

To check tires and pressure on your car, follow these steps:

1. Read your car's owner's manual or the side of a tire to learn what air pressure you should have in your tires, measured in *pounds-per-square-inch* or *psi*. Most modern car tires have recommended pressure somewhere between 24 and 34 psi when the tires are cold. A typical recommended cold pressure is 28 psi. Add 2 to 4 psi when carrying a heavy load or pulling a trailer. The tire's maximum load pressure is embossed on the tire wall. Don't exceed it or the tire police will repossess your tread. Actually, excessive pressure makes tires wear unevenly and reduces their usable life.

2. Check tire pressure in your driveway or at a nearby gas station when the tires are not hot from driving. Find the valve stem on the front left (driver's side) tire. It protrudes from the wheel rim. If the valve stem has a cap, unscrew it and set it aside. Place the mouth of your tire pressure gauge (described in Chapter 6, "Do-It-Yourself Maintenance, or Getting Your Hands Dirty") against the end of the valve stem. Push it until you hear a rush of air, and then release it. The tire gauge has a dial or a sliding scale that indicates how much pressure is in the tire.

3. If air pressure is lower than it should be, add air using an air line at a gas station or tire shop, or a hand pump (and get the added benefit of exercise). If pressure is greater than it should be, use the nipple on the tire gauge to press the center of the tire valve stem and release air. Release a little, and then recheck the pressure. Remember to replace the valve stem cap if your tire has one.

4. While you're there, visually inspect the tire for wear. Some tires have a tread indicator that shows you when the tires are too worn to be safe. Inspect the tire for damage as well. A cut in the tire casing can become an auto accident just a few miles down the road. Wear across the tire tread should be even. If not, take your car into a tire shop—after reading Chapter 23, "Steering and Suspension System Repairs: No More Swerves or Bounces!."

5. Repeat this process for the left-rear, spare, right-rear, and right-front tires. This circling of the car makes it easier to remember which tires have been checked if you're interrupted. Don't forget the spare tire.

Why all this ruckus about tire pressure? Because the main reason why tires don't live as long as they're designed to is not high blood pressure; it's low tire pressure. Low tire pressure makes tires wear out at the edges. It also makes the car ride sloppy. Checking tire pressure once a week or every 250 miles is an easy way to increase the life and safety of your tires, and it takes just one to two minutes.

Did You Know?

Use a penny to check tire tread depth. Turn the head of a penny upside down so that President Lincoln is standing on his head. Place the penny between two center treads on a tire. If you can see the top of the President's head over the top of the tread, the tread is too thin—less than $1/32$ inch.

When the Bottom of the Tire Is Flat

Before driving anywhere, even a quick two-mile hop, make sure you have a good spare tire on board and the correct tools.

To change a flat tire, follow these steps:

1. If you're at the side of the road, turn on your emergency flashers and raise the trunk lid to signal to others that you are having a problem.

2. Use the flat edge of a tire tool or screwdriver from your trunk to pry the hubcap (if your tire has one) off the wheel rim. Use a tire tool to loosen, but not remove, the four or five lug nuts holding the wheel to the axle.

3. Place a block behind a wheel on the other axle. Then place the car jack under the car frame or on the bumper as described in the car's owner's manual. Stop

raising the jack when the wheel is high enough to rotate the tire without touching the ground.

4. Remove the lug nuts and place them in the hubcap so they don't get lost. Remove the tire and set it out of the way.

5. Install the spare tire on the car. Of course, you've been checking spare tire pressure during your weekly checks, so you know the tire is good! Screw the lug nuts on the car by hand, making sure the tapered side of each nut faces the wheel.

6. Lower the jack until the tire firmly touches the ground but isn't supporting the car. Use the tire tool to tighten the lug nuts in a criss-cross pattern.

7. When all lug nuts are tight, lower the jack until it can be removed. Replace the wheelcover by pressing it against the wheel rim. If the wheelcover won't easily go on, place it in the trunk and drive to a service station or tire shop so that they can install it for you.

8. Visit a tire shop immediately to have your flat repaired or replaced. You don't want to get stuck 15 miles from town without a spare tire!

That's about it. Invest a few minutes in your car once a week and you'll not only save hundreds of dollars in potential repair bills, but you'll also understand your car better. You might decide to hire everything else out—or not. In any case, you'll have a clearer understanding—and a sense of satisfaction—about your car.

Safety First

A space-saver spare tire should not be driven at highway speeds for more than 50 miles.

The Least You Need to Know

➤ Check your car's oil level on the engine dipstick and add oil as needed.

➤ Check your car's coolant level by removing the coolant cap and add coolant if the level is low.

➤ Check your car's windshield washer fluid level by removing the reservoir cap and add fluid as necessary.

➤ Check your car's power steering fluid level, if any, by removing the power steering reservoir cap and visually inspecting the dipstick, adding new fluid if needed.

➤ Check your car's brake (and clutch, if applicable) fluid level as recommended by the manufacturer.

➤ Check your car's tire pressure using a pressure gauge, adding air if it is lower than recommended by the manufacturer.

Chapter 9

CAR Quarterly Check Up

In This Chapter

➤ How to safely check your car's battery and charging system

➤ Checking hoses and cooling system

➤ Checking transmission and differential fluid levels

➤ How to check your car's suspension and steering system

➤ Checking the exhaust system quarterly

➤ Checking windshield wiper blades

By making the basic checks offered in Chapter 8, "CAR Weekly Check Up," you've moved ahead of most car owners and can now sit near the front of the classroom. I'm proud of you—as long as you keep up on your homework!

Once you've made these weekly checks a habit, maintenance not only becomes easier, it's more fun. You'll gain a better understanding of your car. We all need to be understood. And you'll be able to read your car's feelings more accurately.

The second step in the CAR Maintenance System is performing simple checks of your car's systems once every 3,000 miles and replacing parts as needed. Here's where you can really begin solving car problems before they happen.

A Quarter's Worth of Maintenance

Modern cars have a million—well, at least thousands of parts. Some of these parts can wear out or at least need periodic adjustments. You can minimize wear and cost by checking these components and replacing them on a regular basis.

The CAR Maintenance System presented in this book suggests that you check eight different components about every three months or 3,000 miles. (That's 4,800 km for you metric fans.) This chapter describes how to make those eight checks. Of course, the frequency with which you make these checks depends on the age of the car and how much you drive it. Older cars need more frequent checks, even once a month. For newer cars that aren't driven as much, you can get away with checking these components about every six months. However, running down the list takes less than an hour on most cars, so you might want to do it more often. Better safe than sorry, right?

This chapter first covers tasks you complete under the hood (designated by an *H* in the section title), moves on to tasks you handle under the car (indicated by a *U* in the section title), and finally describes tasks you perform from beside the car (designated by a *B* in the section title). Again, you don't have to do them yourself. Just make sure you tell the mechanic or lube service which checks you want done. You're the boss!

All Charged Up (H)

Batteries store electrical power for starting the car, running the radio, and other necessities. Modern cars use 12-volt batteries; your house uses about 120 volts. Even so, there's still enough power in a car battery to get your attention in a decidedly unpleasant way. The charging system (the alternator and voltage regulator) replaces the used-up electricity. If it doesn't get replaced, your car won't start.

Did You Know?

The first car radio was the Motorola, designed by William Lear and Elmer Waverling in 1929. Rock music was invented soon thereafter to test the components.

It's very important to work safely around your car's battery. First, the battery uses acid and lead to store electricity. Second, electric current from a battery (at 50 or more amps) can quickly destroy a car's computer system or smaller wires and components. Wear rubber gloves and safety goggles when working around the battery, and make sure you don't touch metal objects between the battery terminals and other metal.

The only tools you'll probably need are a battery terminal cleaner (a couple of bucks at any auto parts store) and a wrench for loosening bolts. You could use a standard wire brush, but, if you do, don't use it for other cleaning purposes because the battery acid can be transferred to other surfaces and cause damage.

Also, put out that cigarette first! A flame or spark near a battery—even a "sealed" battery—can cause an explosion.

To check the battery and charging system on your car, follow these steps:

1. Identify the terminals. One has a + (positive) symbol on or near it and one has a - (negative) symbol. The cable on one of these two terminals is attached to the engine block and the other goes to the starter. The one that goes to the engine is called the *ground terminal*; this is usually (but not always) the *negative terminal*.

2. Remove the plastic terminal caps, if there are any, from the terminals and carefully brush away any white powder (corrosion). If the battery cables attach to the battery with a nut, remove the nut and clean the terminal and cable end with a wire brush, and then skip to step 6. If the battery uses terminal posts, follow steps 3 through 5.

Safety First

Rubber gloves should be worn any time you are working with caustic cleaners or solvents or any potentially harmful fluids from your car, such as battery acid.

3. Use a wrench to loosen the bolts at the end of the battery cable where it wraps around the ground terminal. Carefully wiggle the cable end up and down until it comes off the terminal. (If the end doesn't come off the terminal easily, buy and use a battery terminal puller from the parts store.) Then loosen and remove the cable on the other terminal. Warning: Striking a terminal or cable end with a hammer to loosen it can loosen the terminal inside, ruining the battery (I know from experience).

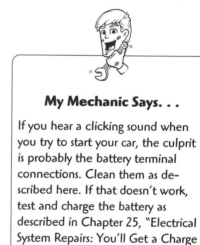

My Mechanic Says. . .

If you hear a clicking sound when you try to start your car, the culprit is probably the battery terminal connections. Clean them as described here. If that doesn't work, test and charge the battery as described in Chapter 25, "Electrical System Repairs: You'll Get a Charge Out of This!"

4. Place the end of the terminal-cleaning tool over each terminal and rotate it a few times. The wire brush inside the tool will clean the terminal post.

5. Twist and open the terminal-cleaning tool to expose the round wire brush inside. Insert this brush into the cable ends and rotate the tool to clean the inside of the ends. If the cable ends are broken or the wire is frayed, replace the cable with one of the same length.

6. Use an old paint brush or a Christmas tie to dust away dirt on the top and sides of the battery. Make sure the debris doesn't fall on other components or on the car's paint. If the battery is very dirty, remove it from the car and carefully clean it with a solution of a pint of water and a teaspoon of baking soda (season to taste). Make sure the solution doesn't get inside the battery.

7. If you have one, use a voltmeter ($10 at Radio Shack) to check the battery's voltage. A fully charged battery should read 12.5 to 13.5 volts of power. If it is less, take the battery to a gas station for charging or do it yourself with a battery charger (about $25 to $50). A mechanic's battery charger (a few hundred dollars) also can tell you the condition of the battery and whether it will hold a charge. If it won't, replace it now before you get stranded in a land where batteries cost twice as much.

8. When reinstalling your car's battery, attach the grounded terminal last. Install treated felt washers (from your parts store) under the cable ends to reduce corrosion. Place the cable end over the terminal and then tighten the bolt until the end fits snugly. Don't overtighten the bolt because cable ends are made of soft metal that can break easily.

Hosing Around (H)

The most intimidating components on your car are also pretty easy to check and maintain: hoses. Open the hood of your car and you'll see all shapes and sizes of hoses from $1/2$ inch to 4 inches in diameter. These hoses deliver fuel, circulate engine coolant, move refrigerant, and much more. Check them once every three months and replace them if they seem soft or have cuts in the surface. If you wait until they actually break, you may have to call for an expensive tow truck to get you off the highway and then a taxi to get you to Aunt Minnie's wedding on time. Here's how to inspect and, if necessary, replace worn hoses.

To check hoses on your car, follow these steps:

Safety First

Be very careful when working around an engine that's running. Engine surfaces quickly become hot to the touch and can burn you. Fan blades and belts are moving quickly and can bite. Mechanics take a moment to look for such dangers before working on a running engine. You should, too.

1. With the engine running, open the hood and begin looking for patterns to your car's hoses. To help define the maze, check the underside of the hood for stickers that serve as a map. You may see stickers labeled *Vacuum House Routing, Emission Hose Routing,* or *For Pizza Delivery, call 1-800-555-1234.* Other hose systems are self-explanatory, going to and from the radiator (cooling system), to the carburetor (fuel system), or to the car's heater (heating system). If hoses are not color-coded, you can often identify families of hoses by their relative size. Vacuum lines, for example, are all about the same diameter. You can often identify hoses by the end connection as well (see step 3).

2. Inspect each hose, squeezing it to see whether there are any cuts, leaks, or wear. Listen for soft hissing that identifies a loose vacuum line. Look for liquids that

identify a leaking hose or fitting. A shower when you squeeze means a definite problem.

3. Check the ends of each hose to make sure they are securely attached. If they are not secure, tighten them. Vacuum lines usually slip on. Cooling system hoses use screw clamps on the ends that you can tighten with a screwdriver. Fuel lines often use spring clamps with tips you squeeze to loosen pressure on the hose.

4. Turn off the engine before replacing any hoses, or you will have fluid everywhere. If you cannot easily remove a hose from the car to find a replacement part, take measurements. Remove one end of the hose, if you can, and measure the inside and outside diameters. Then measure the length. Write down any identifying numbers, such as *TA1-05*, that appear on the hose. If you have a service manual for your car, look up the part to determine what it's called.

My Mechanic Says. . .

Don't mess with air conditioner hoses. They are pressurized and contain a refrigerant gas. If your air-conditioning system hoses are in poor condition, take your car to a licensed air conditioner service shop with the tools and training to do the work for you.

Cool It! (H)

As you learned in Chapter 1, "How Cars Run: What Makes Them Go?" the cooling system is a critical part of your car. If your engine gets too hot, it can quickly damage itself, so checking your car's cooling system is an important step in keeping it trouble-free.

To check the cooling system on your car, follow these steps:

1. With the engine cold, open the radiator cap. Some caps require you to lift a lever on the cap that releases pressure. Others are twisted one-quarter turn to relieve pressure. Newer systems might have a cap on a separate coolant reservoir near the radiator instead of on the radiator itself.

My Mechanic Says. . .

Don't mess with hoses on fuel-injection systems. They are pressurized and contain gasoline. If your fuel-injection system hoses are in poor condition, take your car to a mechanic with experience in repairing such systems.

2. Visually inspect the cap and clean off any rust deposits. If the cap leaks or is more than a couple of years old, replace it. The cost of a new cap is typically less than $10—a fraction of the cost of a new engine damaged by overheating.

3. Visually inspect the coolant in the system. The top of the coolant should be near the top of the radiator or near the FULL mark on the coolant reservoir. Fill as

needed with a mixture of half coolant and half water. Chapter 11, "CAR Yearly Replacements," will show you how to flush your cooling system.

4. Inspect the cooling system hoses if you haven't already done so. There are usually two: one between the top and one between the bottom of the radiator and the engine. Radiator hoses should feel firm, not mushy. Check and tighten the screw clamps on the end of the hoses.

5. Inspect the front and back side of the radiator for debris and damage. Bugs, leaves, papers, and other debris can block the airflow and reduce the radiator's efficiency. Use a soft brush or compressed air to remove debris. Make sure you don't bend any of the honeycomb fins on the radiator. They allow the passing air into the radiator to keep your engine cool.

6. Inspect the top and bottom of the radiator for small leaks or rusty spots that may soon become leaks. If you find any, take your car to a radiator shop where it can be repaired before the problem becomes big enough to mean replacing the radiator rather than repairing it. More important, preventive maintenance can mean getting to the big game on time and avoiding a costly towing bill.

Safety First

If your car overheats, cautiously lift the lever on top of the cap to release pressure. After a minute or longer, place a folded cloth over the cap and twist the cap counterclockwise one-quarter turn to relieve more pressure. Remember, you're working with boiling water. Wait a moment or more, then place the cloth over the cap again and remove the cap. Allow the engine to cool 20 minutes before refilling.

My Mechanic Says. . .

The fluids used by automatic and manual transmissions are very different. An automatic transmission uses a hydraulic fluid, which is reddish-brown and usually of a thin consistency. A manual transmission uses a heavy lubricant, which is light brown and at least as thick as the oil in your car's engine. These transmission fluids are not interchangeable.

Shifting Fluidly (H/U)

Your car has either an automatic (shifts automatically) or manual (you shift gears) transmission. Each uses a fluid or lubricant to keep it healthy. At least four times a year, you should check the fluid level in your transmission to make sure it is full. You'll need a clean rag to check the automatic transmission fluid from under the hood. You'll need to get under most cars to check the lubricant level in a manual transmission.

To check the automatic transmission fluid level in your car, follow these steps:

1. Make sure the car is level. Set the car's parking brake and start the engine. When the engine is warm and at idle speed, move the transmission selector through each gear range a couple of times, ending at neutral.

2. With the engine still running, lift the car's hood and look for the automatic transmission dipstick. It looks like the engine oil dipstick but is located behind a rear-wheel-drive engine or above the transmission on a front-wheel-drive car. The dipstick often is painted a different color to distinguish it from the engine's oil dipstick.

3. Got it? Pull the transmission dipstick out from the tube and visually check that the fluid appears reddish-brown, identifying it as automatic transmission fluid. Carefully touch the liquid on the end of the dipstick to make sure it is warm. It should not be hot. Then, using a clean rag, wipe the dipstick clean and replace it in the tube until the dipstick cap seats.

4. Pull out the transmission dipstick again and read the level. Some automatic transmission dipsticks are stamped with words like *MAX. LEVEL HOT IDLING IN NEUTRAL*—or not. The safe operating range is marked.

5. If the automatic transmission fluid is low, add fluid through the dipstick tube. You'll need a special funnel (from your handy-dandy auto parts supplier) to get the fluid into the small tube, but it can be done. Use the type of automatic transmission fluid recommended by the manufacturer. It's probably identified in the owner's manual. If not, ask the auto parts clerk what type is recommended for your car. Add just a little at a time until it is near the top of the operating range shown on the dipstick.

My Mechanic Says. . .

Don't check automatic transmission fluid immediately after pulling a trailer or when the engine is cold or overheated because the dipstick will give a false reading. Automatic transmission fluid should be checked with the engine running at normal operating temperatures.

To check the manual transmission lubricant level in your car, follow these steps:

1. Look under your car to find the transmission. On a rear-wheel-drive car, the manual transmission is below the floor-mounted gear shifter. On a front-wheel-drive car, the transmission or transaxle unit is under the hood and beside the engine (usually on the passenger side of the car). You might need to safely jack up the car and place stands underneath it to find room to work. Because the transmission fluid must be as level as possible when checked, don't raise the car any more than necessary to get to it.

My Mechanic Says. . .

An automatic transmission that hesitates before it changes gears may simply need fluid. Check and replace. If that doesn't solve the problem, the transmission might need adjustment (see Chapter 22, "Transmission Repairs: Those Troublesome Trannys," or your mechanic).

2. To check the level of fluid in the transmission or transaxle, first find the level plug. It's typically a bolthead on the side of the transmission casing. Use a wrench to turn it counterclockwise and remove it.

3. It's pinky-finger time. The transmission lubricant should be filled up to the bottom of the level plug hole. Insert your smallest finger inside the level plug hole to see if it is. If not, add the manufacturer's recommended lubricant through the level plug hole until the top of the liquid is at the bottom of the hole.

For manual transmission fluid, some car manufacturers recommend a heavy lubricant such as SAE 80-90 weight, and others use the same oil as in the engine. Check your car's owner's manual or service manual for recommendations.

Check the Differential Lubricant Level (U)

A car's *differential* includes the gears that distribute the single drive shaft's rotation to two or four wheels. Rear-wheel-drive cars have a differential on the rear axle. Front-wheel-drive cars include the differential in the transmission, so there isn't a separate differential unit. Four-wheel drive cars use a transfer case to distribute power to all four wheels.

Most car manufacturers recommend that the differential be filled with an SAE 80-90 weight lubricant. Transfer cases for four-wheel drive vehicles typically use a lubricant similar to (but not the same as) automatic transmission fluid. You might need to order this special concoction from the car's authorized dealer. It's refined from pure gold found only in the Andes. Check your car's owner's manual or service manual for requirements.

To check the differential lubricant level in your car, follow these steps:

1. Look under your car to find the differential. On a rear-wheel-drive car, the differential is a round metal case between the two rear wheels. The transfer case for a four-wheel drive car is on either the front or rear axle. If necessary, safely jack the car up and place stands underneath it.

2. To check the level of fluid in the differential or transfer case, first find the level plug. On many cars, it's a bolthead on the side of the casing; use a wrench to turn it counterclockwise and remove it. On some cars, it's a rubber plug on the side of the casing; pry it off with a small screwdriver.

3. Use your finger to check the lubricant level. It should be filled up to the bottom of the level plug hole. If it isn't, add the manufacturer's recommended lubricant until the top of the liquid is at the bottom of the level plug hole.

You're Suspended! or Steering the Right Course (U)

Problems with your car's steering and suspension come on gradually and might not even be noticed until the system fails. That's a situation you devoutly wish to avoid, so it's very important that you check these systems every 3,000 miles. Fortunately, it's an easy process that you can do while you're making your other quarterly checks.

To check the suspension and steering on your car, follow these steps:

1. With the car sitting in a level spot, push down on the top of the front left fender and quickly release it. Do the same on the front right fender. You're trying to make the corner of the car bounce as though it just hit a bump in the road. If the car bounces more than once or twice, the shock absorbers may need replacing. Chapter 23, "Steering and Suspension System Repairs: No More Swerves or Bounces!" shows you how.

2. With the front end of the car raised and safely blocked, inspect the steering mechanism underneath the car. Especially look at the shock absorbers for possible fluid leaks. Then ask someone to repeatedly turn the steering wheel left and right as you watch how the mechanism works. Most of it is common sense. Trace the movement from the steering gear box through the rods to the back side of the wheels. Movement should be smooth with no clunks or metallic sounds.

3. From beside a front wheel, grab the tire and move it from side to side. Movement should be smooth, not jerky or noisy. Then grab the tire at the top and bottom, moving it toward and away from you a few times to see whether it seems loose.

4. Now spin the tire and listen for noises. A grinding sound can mean that the wheel bearings need lubrication (see Chapter 11, "CAR Yearly Replacements") or the brakes are dragging (see Chapter 24, "Brake System Repairs: Stop Ahead!"). When you are done, remove the stands and lower the car.

Repairs to your car's suspension and steering systems can be done either by you (see Chapter 23) or by your favorite mechanic (see Chapter 7, "Finding a Good Mechanic: Who Can You Trust with Your Car?"). Don't let these repairs go. Avoidable tragedies result from neglected suspension and steering systems.

When Your Car Is Exhausted (U)

Send your car on a vacation after it has been overworked. Not unless you get to go along, you say?

You might think your car's exhaust system always tells you when it's not working well by making noise. That's not completely true. A leaking exhaust can also quietly send dangerous fumes into the passenger compartment, making folks sick or worse. Instead of waiting for problems to happen, make sure to check your car's exhaust system quarterly. It's actually quite easy.

To check the exhaust system on your car, follow these steps:

1. Make sure the engine of your car has been off for at least a couple of hours to allow the exhaust pipes and parts to cool down. The catalytic converter can hold heat for many hours.

2. If necessary, raise and safely block both ends of your car to gain access to its belly.

3. Visually trace and inspect the exhaust pipes from where they exit the engine (called the *exhaust manifold*) to the rear of the car. If you have one, use a rubber mallet to softly strike the exhaust pipe, catalytic converter, resonator, and muffler. A small piece of wood can be used instead. You're checking for holes caused by rust.

4. Inspect the exhaust system hangers. They consists of strips of metal and strapping that hang the exhaust system from the bottom of the car. Make sure they are doing their job.

5. Inspect the underside of the car for holes that can allow noxious exhaust fumes to enter the passenger compartment. They must be sealed for your passengers' safety. Depending on the size and type of holes, they can be sealed as you would repair body damage (see Chapter 27 "Body and Paint Repairs: Giving Your Car a Makeover").

If exhaust system repairs are needed, refer to Chapter 26, "Exhaust System Repairs: Fixing an Exhausted System," or visit your friendly mechanic or muffler shop. They're always happy to see you!

Wiping Away the Raindrops (B)

Unless you live on Mt. Waialeale on the Hawaiian island of Kauai (where 480 inches of rain fall a year!), your windshield wiper blades probably won't wear out very often. Instead, they will deteriorate from sun exposure, or they will build up with automotive lubricants thrown up by cars passing in the rain.

Don't wait until a rainy day to check and service your car's windshield wiper blades. You don't want to stand outside in a downpour in your shirtsleeves trying to make your wipers do their job. Check them as you make your other quarterly checks. Then, when you need them, your windshield wipers will be ready to serve you. "Would you like catsup with your fries?"

To check the windshield wiper blades on your car, follow these steps:

1. Visually inspect the windshield wiper mechanism for damage or loose parts. Also clear the area around the wiper arms of debris that can slow down their movement.

2. Inspect the windshield wiper blades for tears and other damage. Replace damaged or deteriorated blades with identical blades. Remove them in the auto parts store's parking lot and take them in for a match. Blades and their frame are removed by lifting the arm and unhooking the end of the arm from the center of the blade's frame. Some blades require you to push a button in the center of the frame to release the blade. Helpful auto parts clerks can find the exact replacement for you, and often even install them on your car in the parking lot.

3. If the blades are simply dirty, clean them with a mild detergent. Also clean your car's windshield to ensure that elongated but colorful bug carcasses don't obstruct wiper travel.

Did You Know?

Besides the sun, car washes are your windshield wiper blade's worst enemy. Car washes often deposit a waxy spray on windshields and wipers. Wax buildup on the blades actually increases friction between the surfaces. In addition, rain can mix with wax on the windows to blur lights and make driving more difficult. What a relief to know that it's not your eyesight that's blurred. If you do have hot wax added at your car wash, ask the attendant to wash your windshield with a mild detergent or do it yourself.

The Least You Need to Know

➤ Check your car's battery and charging system every three months, cleaning and tightening terminals.

➤ Check cooling system and vacuum system hoses quarterly, tightening and replacing as needed. Also check the radiator for leaks.

➤ Check transmission and differential fluids, replacing as needed every three months.

➤ Once a quarter, check steering and suspension components for wear. While you're lounging around under the car, check the exhaust system for rust and damage.

➤ Inspect windshield wipers every three months and replace as needed.

Chapter 10

CAR Semiannual Adjustments

In This Chapter

➤ How to replace the oil and filter on your car

➤ Adjusting the carburetor and throttle linkage on older cars

➤ Adjusting brakes for a smooth and safe stop

➤ How to increase tire mileage by rotating them every six months

Many car owners check and replace fluids, but draw the line at making adjustments to their cars. Others see adjustments as another area where they can save some money and, just maybe, increase their pride of ownership.

This chapter describes the steps you can take every six months or 6,000 miles to keep your car well adjusted. As with other tasks in this book, you can do them yourself, or you can hire others to do them for you. In either case, this chapter will help you understand what needs to be done, why, and how.

Semiannual Specials

There are thousands of parts in your car. Some just sit there like car potatoes, enjoying the ride. Others are hard workers with a mission. Depending on how much they are called upon to work (and how well they were made), these hard-working parts will need to be adjusted every once in a while. On average, once in a while means about every six months or 6,000 miles of driving. Your mileage may vary.

Your car's carburetor (if not fuel-injected) mixes hundreds of gallons of fuel with the appropriate amount of air before it needs to be adjusted, for example. Your car's tires will roll many thousands of miles before their position on the car needs to be rotated to even out the wear. Other adjustments your car will need include throttle linkage and brakes.

You'll need to break out the toolbox (Chapter 6, "Do-It-Yourself Maintenance, or Getting Your Hands Dirty") for most adjustments: screwdrivers, wrenches, and a few special tools. I'll point them out as you need them.

The remaining sections in this chapter describe the adjustments you might need to make and how to make them. Remember: *H* means under the hood, *U* designates adjustments done under the car, and *B* notes adjustments made beside the car.

Dirty Oil and Filter Adjustments (H, U)

Okay, okay. You're technically not adjusting your oil and filter; you're replacing them. But it should be done every 6,000 miles, so I used my unexpired poetic license to keep this important step in the chapter with other adjustments. Sue me!

An oil filter is simply a can with a paper-like filter in it. Think of it as a can of coffee filters (bet what it filters doesn't taste like coffee, though). The oil is forced through the filter, depositing carbon, bits of metal, and other contaminants on the filter's surface. Instead of periodically cleaning the oil filter, you replace it with a new one—hopefully before the contaminants block the flow of oil through the engine.

What oil should you buy for your car? Flip back to Chapter 1, "How Cars Run: What Makes Them Go?" for some basic info and flip through your car's owner's manual for their specific recommendations.

Some cars are designed to be run 7,500 miles between oil changes. Others require an oil change every 3,000 to 6,000 miles. How you drive is as important to oil-change frequency as miles. Cars driven only short distances, pulling trailers, or in the mountains require more frequent oil changes than those driven regularly at highway speeds.

My Mechanic Says. . .

Learn as much as you can about your car's maintenance needs. By carefully reading the owner's manual, you might learn that your car has a sealed carburetor, doesn't require frequent ignition timing, has self-adjusting brakes, has self-adjusting drivebelts, and can do quite well, thank you, without much maintenance. Now if it would just make its own payments to the bank...

Some folks say it isn't necessary to replace the oil filter with every oil change. They say you can replace the oil filter with every other oil change. Let's think about this for a moment. When you change oil in a car you replace all the oil except that in the oil filter, so about 20% to 25% of all the oil in the car will still be dirty. Not only that, but the oil filter contains the contaminants filtered from the oil. It's the yucky stuff. Three quarts of clean oil plus one quart of dirty oil equals four quarts of dirty oil! Makes more sense to me to start with it all clean each time.

Okay, let's weigh this against the cost of a new oil filter: less than five bucks (less than three bucks for many cars). So here's the new rule I ask you to follow: Always change the oil filter when you change the oil. On behalf of your car, thanks!

In addition to getting an oil filter for the oil change, you need oil! How much oil? Look in the owner's manual. It may say something like *oil capacity:* or *crankcase capacity: 3.5 L (3.7 qt.) including filter.* Oil containers usually have marks on the side to indicate milliliters (ml) or ounces (oz).

To replace the oil and filter on your car, follow these steps:

1. As usual, make sure your car is parked in a level spot. Start your car and let the engine run for about 15 minutes to warm up the oil. Warm oil drains more thoroughly and brings with it more built-up sludge. Use this time to gather the tools you'll need: a wrench (to remove the oil pan plug), an oil-draining pan, and an oil filter wrench. Rubber gloves will keep warm oil off your skin. Shut off the engine when you are ready to start. Wait about five minutes for the warm oil to drain to the lowest spot in the engine, the oil pan.

2. Place the drain pan under the oil pan plug. The plug has a bolthead and is located at the lowest point underneath the engine. If necessary, jack up the car and install safety stands. Using a wrench, turn the plug counterclockwise to loosen it. Set the plug and washer aside for later. Alternatively, you can use a hand-operated oil siphon to draw oil from the oil pan through the dipstick tube without having to crawl under the car.

3. After all oil is drained into the pan, reinstall the old plug and a new washer on the oil pan. Tighten the plug with a wrench. Don't forget this step or your car's engine could be ruined by operating as oil drips out the bottom. It would slowly bleed to death—not a pretty sight.

4. Move the pan to below the oil filter. On some engines, the oil filter can be reached from under the hood. Others require that you remove it from underneath the car. If necessary, jack up the car and install safety stands. Be careful when working around the underside of your car because the exhaust pipe and other components are hot.

5. Using an oil filter wrench, twist the filter counterclockwise two or three turns. Oil should begin dripping from the filter to the pan. Use your hand to rotate the oil filter until it comes off the shaft. Then tilt the filter so that oil in it can drain into the drip pan.

6. Make sure the new oil filter is the same size as the old one. Open a can of new oil, get some oil on the end of a rag or your finger, and spread it around the circular rubber seal on the end of the new oil filter. Place the new oil filter on the screw-on filter shaft and turn it clockwise. Tighten the new filter by hand only, about two-thirds of a turn after the gasket makes contact with the filter holder. Don't tighten the filter with the oil wrench.

7. Replace the oil by following the instructions in Chapter 8, "CAR Weekly Check Up," on checking oil level: find the oil filler location and use a funnel to pour in

the appropriate amount of oil, and then recheck the oil to make sure it's between the ADD and FULL marks.

8. Replace the oil filler cap securely. Wipe off all tools with a clean rag and put them away for later use. Make sure you take the used oil to a recycling center or an auto parts store to have it properly disposed of. If you DON'T recycle oil properly, a large fellow who grunts with an accent will recycle you!

Check your oil level after your next short drive. Make sure the oil level is within range: above ADD and below FULL on the dipstick. Add oil as needed. Also look under the car to see whether there are any new oil drips, indicating that the oil plug or oil filter is not tight.

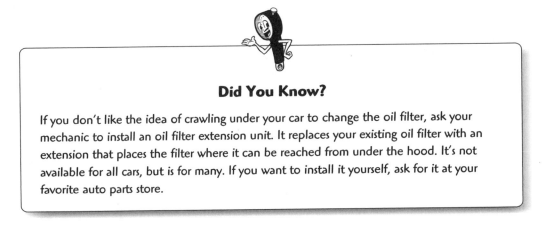

Did You Know?

If you don't like the idea of crawling under your car to change the oil filter, ask your mechanic to install an oil filter extension unit. It replaces your existing oil filter with an extension that places the filter where it can be reached from under the hood. It's not available for all cars, but is for many. If you want to install it yourself, ask for it at your favorite auto parts store.

How Much Gas Do You Want? Adjust Throttle Linkage (H)

The *throttle linkage* is simply the part of your car that uses your foot pressure on the accelerator pedal to control the amount of fuel going to the carburetor or fuel injectors. It's a mechanical system of linkage, cable, and connections. Some cars seem to need throttle adjustment many times a year, but others require it only every few years.

The best way to adjust the throttle linkage on your car is to refer to the car's service manual. Every car has a slightly different linkage. Even so, they all work on the same principles. If you don't have a service manual or you just want an overview of how the throttle works, keep reading.

This job requires an assortment of wrenches and maybe a screwdriver or two (no, still not the liquid kind). You might also need some lubricant, depending on the linkage and its condition.

To adjust the throttle linkage on your car, follow these steps:

1. Open the hood of your car and look for the throttle linkage system. It consists of one or more rods, cables, springs, and metal plates between the car's firewall and carburetor. You may have to remove the air filter from the top of the carburetor to see all of it.

2. Starting at the firewall, wiggle the parts to make sure they are fastened securely to their mountings and to each other. Tighten any loose mounting bolts. Don't move the throttle linkage forward and back too often because it will put fuel in the carburetor, "flooding" it and making starting the car more difficult.

3. Carefully spray the linkage joints with WD-40 or similar cleaning lubricant so they move freely. Wipe away excess lubricant.

4. If possible, disconnect the end of the linkage from the side of the carburetor. Some connections snap off, others might require removing a pin or clip. Then move the throttle linkage forward and back a few times to make sure it works smoothly. Tighten and lubricate as needed. Reconnect the linkage when done.

Give Him Some Air: Adjust the Carburetor (H)

If your car has a fuel-injection system instead of a carburetor (refer to your owner's manual), there's not much you can or have to adjust. Fuel is regulated by an electronic signal from your car's computer. Fuel injection systems are covered in Chapter 18, "Starting and Ignition System Repairs for the Clueless."

The carburetor is an important part of many cars over a decade old. It mixes the right amount of fuel and air to make a combustible vapor that your engine's spark plugs can ignite. The adjustments you can make are the ratio of fuel to air (rich or lean) and the amount of fuel fed to make the engine operate when the car isn't moving (at idle).

Most newer carburetors are sealed at the factory and don't allow owner adjustments. So you can spend the time required to adjust the carburetor doing something else.

But if you have an older car and need to adjust the carburetor, here's how to do it:

1. Attach a tachometer to your car's engine following the manufacturer's directions—unless your car already has a tach in the instrument cluster. *Tachs* measure the engine's operating speed in revolutions per minute (rpms).

2. Start the engine and let it run for about 15 minutes to warm it up. Look it over. You're looking for screwheads that can be turned to adjust the idle speed and the idle mixture. Hints: The idle speed screw is at the end of the throttle linkage and at the side of the carburetor; the idle mixture screw (or screws) is on the carburetor itself.

3. To adjust the idle speed, you use the tachometer to set the engine's speed at idle. Your car's owner's manual tells you what that speed should be, or there may be a sticker on the inside of your car's hood that indicates the idle speed. For many cars, idle speed is 500 to 750 rpm. Using a screwdriver, turn the idle speed adjustment screw clockwise to increase rpms or counterclockwise to decrease rpms. If your carburetor has an idle solenoid adjustment, you need to make a second adjustment for a high idling speed. There are many carburetor designs out there. Follow instructions in your car's service manual for this adjustment.

4. To adjust the idle mixture, make sure the tachometer is connected to the engine to tell you its operating speed. Find the idle mixture adjustment screws on the carburetor (underneath the air cleaner). A single-barrel carburetor (on smaller or older cars) has one idle mixture screw, whereas a two- or four-barrel carburetor has two screws. Turn the screw(s) in, or clockwise, until the engine is at its lowest speed. Then turn them out, or counterclockwise, until further turning doesn't increase speed. That's the best mixture for the idling speed. Do this a couple of times to get the best mixture, especially if your car has two idle mixture adjustments.

Did You Know?

Don't get busted by the carb cops. If your car's carburetor has plastic limiter plugs covering the idle mixture adjustment screws, stop. Don't adjust them—under penalty of federal law. Your idle adjustment could make you idle for many years. But seriously folks, don't attempt to adjust a carburetor that has limiter plugs.

Stopping on Time: Adjusting Brakes (U)

When ya gotta stop, ya gotta stop—and you won't if your brakes aren't in good shape and properly adjusted.

The brakes on your car should be checked and, if necessary, adjusted about every six months, depending on mileage. City drivers probably use brakes (and horns) more frequently than rural drivers. However, cars driven on dusty rural roads can collect dirt on brake components.

Foot pressure on the brake pedal is transferred hydraulically to the four brakes, one at each wheel. Two types of brake systems are in use today. The wheels may have either drum or disc brakes, or both—drums in the rear and discs on the front. *Drum brakes* slow down the car by pressing two half-circle brake shoes against the inside of a round brake drum. *Disc brakes* perform the same function by squeezing brake pads against both sides of a round brake disc.

Adjusting brakes simply means making sure the brake shoes or brake pads are close to the friction surface but not so close as to drag and wear out. Smart folks that they are, brake manufacturers include provisions for adjustments of their systems. In fact, many drum and all disc brake systems are self-adjusting and really don't need your help to keep themselves well-adjusted.

Besides basic tools, you may need a brake spoon, a tool that looks like a bent flat screwdriver. In fact, if you don't have a brake spoon, use a screwdriver for the adjustment.

To adjust drum brakes on your car, follow these steps:

1. Safely jack up the car and place stands under it. You will be working from the back side of the wheels, so give yourself enough room to work.

2. Find the brake adjustment access hole on the back side of the wheel. Many are near the bottom edge of the hub and covered with a rubber plug. Uncover the hole using a screwdriver to pry off the plug. Inside is a star wheel adjusting nut with lobes or bumps on it. Moving the lobes up or down rotates the star wheel and moves the two brake shoes into or out from the drum.

3. Insert a straight screwdriver or a brake spoon into the adjustment hole until it contacts the star wheel adjusting nut. Grab the tire and spin it. At the same time, rotate the star wheel up by moving your end of the screwdriver or spoon down until the brakes stop the wheel from moving. The brake shoes are now in contact with the inside of the brake drum.

4. To back the brake shoes off the brake drum, rotate the star wheel down by moving your end of the screwdriver or spoon up. Remove, reinsert, and repeat the movement three more times to back the brake shoes off the drums. Spin the wheel by hand and listen for the drag of brake shoes on the drum. As needed, repeat the process of moving the star wheel, one lobe at a time, until the brake shoes don't drag against the drum.

5. Reinstall the brake adjustment access hole cover.

6. Repeat the process on the other drum brakes.

My Mechanic Says. . .

Some brakes adjust themselves as they are applied while the car moves in reverse. Apply brakes while backing up in an empty parking lot. Or insert a stiff wire with a hook on the end through the access hole to hook around the self-adjusting lever. Pull the spring-loaded lever away from the star wheel, and then use a brake spoon to adjust as described.

As you adjust your car's brakes, or even if they are self-adjusting, spend a few moments visually inspecting the system. The brake system uses hydraulic pressure that presses brake parts together to slow the wheels. Brakes use hydraulic fluid inside heavy-duty hoses, so look for these hoses running to the back side of your car's wheels. Inspect the hoses for wet spots where fluid may be leaking. Also look at the back side of the wheel where the brake hose attaches. If you find a leak, don't try to patch it. Instead, refer to Chapter 24, "Brake System Repairs: Stop Ahead!" for information on how to replace a brake line.

The Wheels on the Bus Go 'Round and 'Round: Adjust Tire Rotation (B)

Car tires are, literally, where the rubber meets the road. As they roll their way to your destination, they also wear out. Old bias tires wore out in 10,000 to 20,000 miles. New radials last four times as long—unless they don't wear evenly. It's easy to reduce uneven tire wear by making sure tires are inflated properly (see Chapter 8, "CAR Weekly Check Up") and rotated or moved to different positions on the car to equalize wear (forthcoming).

Need to change a flat tire? Read the tips on doing so in Chapter 8.

Not all car and tire manufacturers recommend rotation. Some suggest that tires should be replaced when they are worn, without first trying to rotate them. Tests have shown that rotation doesn't prolong tire life; it only makes wear more even among the four tires. They suggest that front tires frequently wear faster than rear tires (which is why they are rotated) so they should be replaced as a set. The rear tires also should be replaced as a set when worn. Check your car's owner's manual for the tire rotation pattern, if any, suggested for your car.

The only tools you'll need for the job are those that came with your car: a jack and a lug wrench, also known as a tire iron.

To rotate the tires on your car, follow these steps:

1. Safely jack up and place stands under all four wheels of your car. If you cannot lift all four wheels, jack up and place stands under one side of your car or the other.
2. Remove wheels as needed, reinstalling them on the car for the most even and efficient wear, as recommended by the car's owner's manual.

For front-wheel-drive cars and front-engine, rear-wheel-drive cars with radial tires, move the front left tire to the left rear and vice versa. Then move the front right tire to the right rear and vice versa.

For front-engine, rear-wheel-drive cars with bias-ply tires, move the front left tire to the rear right, the rear right to the front right, the front right to the rear left, and the rear left to the front left wheel. Got that?

If your car's spare tire is a standard tire (rather than one of those weird spare-only tires that look like a large chocolate cruller), you might want to rotate it among the others. If so, rotate as recommended by the manufacturer.

Did You Know?

Can you speak tire? Tires are marked with their size, rating, and other useful information right on the side. They're easy to interpret. A tire marked with *P195/75/R14*, for example, indicates that it is a passenger car tire (P), 195 millimeters in width at the widest point, with an aspect ratio of 75 (the lower the number, the quicker the steering). The R means that it's a radial tire, and 14 is the wheel's diameter in inches. The tire also has a temperature rating (A is better than B, B is better than C) and a tread wear rating (300 lasts longer than 200).

Tires should wear evenly, with approximately the same amount of tread at the center as near the edges. If the edges wear faster, the tire probably is underinflated. If the center wears faster, the tire may be overinflated. The solution: Check tire pressure weekly, as described in Chapter 8. If one edge of a tire wears faster than the other, the wheel alignment (Chapter 23, "Steering and Suspension System Repairs: No More Swerves or Bounces!") is probably incorrect and should be checked by a wheel-alignment shop.

The Least You Need to Know

➤ You've picked up a lot of useful information in this chapter about adjusting your car's throttle, carburetor, brakes, and tire placement.

➤ Adjustments are made every six months or 6,000 miles, depending on the type and age of the car as well as the type of driving you do.

➤ Many cars have self-adjusting components that would just as soon avoid owner intervention.

➤ You can perform any or all of these adjustments yourself.

Chapter 11

CAR Yearly Replacements

In This Chapter

➤ How to adjust ignition timing on older cars

➤ Replacing drivebelts that keep your car running smoothly

➤ Lubricating your car's chassis—or having it done for you

Everybody still with me?

Back in Chapter 8, "CAR Weekly Check Up," you learned to check your car's fluids on a weekly basis. Well, 52 of those weekly checks have come and gone, and it's time to replace some of those fluids. And some parts, too.

Why replace them? Automotive fluids are your car's blood, sweat, and tears. They are the fluids that circulate and lubricate within your car. Every once in a while, they need to be transfused with new fluids. At the same time, there are automotive parts that need replacement about every 12 months.

This chapter offers instructions on how to replace automotive parts and fluids that need attention annually. Of course, there are so many car designs and needs that there can't be a hard-and-fast rule for much of anything having to do with cars. So read your car's owner's manual, apply your common sense, ask your mechanic, and determine when your car needs parts and fluids replaced.

You'll need your handy-dandy toolbox (see Chapter 6, "Do-It-Yourself Maintenance, or Getting Your Hands Dirty") to replace parts. I'll point them out as you need them.

Don't forget: *H* means under the hood, *U* designates adjustments done under the car, and *B* denotes adjustments made beside the car. There will be a surprise quiz on this later.

Keep Firing, or Readjusting the Ignition Timing (H)

An engine is poetry. Maybe it's not Carl Sandburg, but at least it's pentameter. At the exact moment that fuel is compressed in the combustion chamber, a spark comes along to ignite it. So the timing of the ignition is critical. Without correct ignition timing, power is lost.

Correct ignition timing ensures that each spark plug fires at exactly the right microsecond. How does this happen? Fortunately, there's an indicator on your car's engine that tells you exactly when a specific cylinder (usually #1) is ready for the spark. This indicator is mounted on the front of your car's engine. It's the crankshaft pulley that rotates as the engine does. When a mark on the rotating pulley aligns with a mark on the stationary engine block, the ignition is in time.

You might ask now, "How do I know when those two marks are aligned?" The engine is running so fast. Here's how: Attach a tool called a *timing light* to the spark plug wire on the #1, or reference, cylinder. The light will go on each time electrical current is sent to that cylinder's spark plug. Point the timing light at the engine's timing mark, and it will light up to show you the relationship between the mark and the reference point. Pretty snazzy, eh?

Did You Know?

Modern engine compartments are pretty crowded. What if you can't reach the spark plug wire for cylinder #1? Use the companion cylinder spark plug wire. How? Find the firing order of your engine, which is printed on top of the engine on a sticker under the hood or in the car's service manual. (A V-8, for example, may have a firing order of 1-5-4-8-6-3-7-2.) The companion cylinder is the third cylinder in the firing order on a four-cylinder engine, the fourth cylinder on a six-cylinder engine, and the fifth cylinder on an eight-cylinder engine (#6 in the V-8 example). Put another way, the companion cylinder is the one that starts out the second half of the firing order. You can attach the timing light to the companion cylinder's spark plug wire and time the engine as though it were attached to #1. Impress your friends with this trick at parties.

The other question you probably have is "What do I do if the timing is off?" Answer: You adjust it by rotating the distributor slightly. A bolthead below the distributor, where it attaches to the engine block, can be loosened to allow the distributor to be turned and then tightened when the timing is correct.

To adjust the ignition timing on your car, follow these steps:

1. Before starting the engine, use chalk or touch-up paint to identify the timing marks on the crankshaft pulley and the stationary pointer. Mark the scale as indicated by specifications. The manual or a plate or sticker on the car tells you where the mark should be. *TDC* means *top dead center*. *BTDC* means *before top dead center*. *5° BTDC* means *five degrees before top dead center*.

2. Connect the timing light to the engine following the manufacturer's instructions. For most models, this means attaching the black lead wire to the negative terminal on the battery, attaching the red lead to the positive terminal, and attaching the third lead on or around the reference spark plug wire.

3. Loosen the adjustment nut or bolthead on the distributor base so that the distributor can be rotated to adjust the timing. Be careful not to move the distributor yet.

4. If your car's manual says so, disconnect and plug the vacuum advance on the distributor. The vacuum advance (on older cars) uses increasing vacuum pressure to advance the timing at higher engine speeds. You don't want this to happen because it will throw off your ignition timing test, so disconnect the vacuum line and plug the hole with tape or a golf tee for now.

5. Make sure all the timing light wires and other tools are clear of the fan blades before starting the engine. Start the engine and let it warm up for about 15 minutes. If the engine is running at a high idle speed, press the accelerator a couple of times to bring the engine down to normal idling speed.

6. Point the timing light at the ignition timing mark on the crankshaft pulley. If the marks line up, tighten the adjustment bolt on the base of the distributor. If they do not line up, slowly rotate the distributor with your hand until the timing marks on the pulley are lined up and then tighten the adjustment bolt. If no amount of adjustment aligns the marks, or if aligning them makes the engine run very rough, you might not be using the correct spark plug wire. Stop, check everything for accuracy, and then start over.

7. After the distributor adjustment nut or bolthead is tightened, recheck the timing to make sure nothing was moved in the process. If everything is okay, reinstall the vacuum advance (if any), and then remove the timing light connections.

8. Take your car for a test drive, this time stopping off for a milkshake or other frozen artificial dairy product.

Safety First

Never allow test driving your car to distract you from watching traffic and practicing good driving habits. Remember to watch traffic signals and consider other drivers.

Belts Do More Than Keep Your Pants Up, or Replacing Engine Drivebelts (H)

The rotation of your car's engine not only rotates tires; it also powers the radiator cooling fan, the alternator, the air-conditioning compressor, the power steering (if any), and the washing machine. That's efficient! The power is transferred from the engine to these components through *drivebelts*. The belts wrap around the crankshaft pulley (introduced in the last adjustment) and pulley wheels for these other parts. Rubberized belts are used rather than chains because they are more pliable—and less expensive.

If the belts are too tight around the pulleys, the belts are stretched, and they break. If they are too loose, the belts don't efficiently transfer power to the driven pulley. So your job, should you decide to accept it, is to make sure the drivebelts are adjusted properly. Which drivebelts? Your car's service manual is more specific. Don't lose any sleep. Check them every six months or so and you'll be fine.

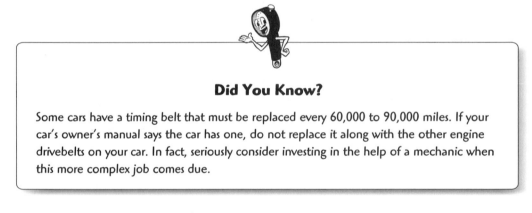

Did You Know?

Some cars have a timing belt that must be replaced every 60,000 to 90,000 miles. If your car's owner's manual says the car has one, do not replace it along with the other engine drivebelts on your car. In fact, seriously consider investing in the help of a mechanic when this more complex job comes due.

To check and replace the engine drivebelts in your car, follow these steps:

1. With the engine off, open the hood of your car and find the radiator and cooling fan. Behind the fan will be one or more drivebelts wrapped around one or more grooved wheels called *pulleys*.

2. Visually inspect each drivebelt for tears, small cracks, grease, and other signs of wear or damage. Especially inspect the inside of the drivebelts—the part that fits into the pulley grooves—because this side gets the most wear. ReplZ/e worn drivebelts with ones of the exact same size, shape, and function. Some drivebelts have the manufacturer's name and part number stamped on the outside edge of the belt. If not, a parts dealer can help you identify the exact replacement part.

3. To install a drivebelt, first find the adjustment bolt. Loosen the adjustment bolt to allow movement of the driven pulley. Some drivebelts have an automatic

tensioner that also must be loosened. Remove the old drivebelt and replace it with the new one. Use a prybar to move the driven pulley back to near where it was with the old belt and then tighten the adjustment bolt. Adjust the drivebelt tension (unless done so by the automatic tensioner).

4. To adjust the drivebelt tension, press against the outside of the belt about half-way between two pulleys. The movement of the drivebelt is called the *deflection*. Typical deflection is about $1/4$ inch for drivebelt spans (between pulleys) of less than 12 inches and about $1/2$ inch for spans of 12 to 18 inches. Loosen the adjustment bolt, use a prybar to move the driven pulley until the belt has the correct deflection, and then tighten the adjustment bolt.

Did You Know?

There may be two, three, or even four drivebelts on your car's engine. Because they all work about the same amount—and because it's easier to do so—replace all drivebelts at the same time instead of just one or two. The exception (as previously preached) is a timing belt.

What can you do with the old drivebelts you replace? If any are still in good condition, place them in your car's trunk for use in an emergency. Otherwise, you could try using them as slingshots.

It's Transfusion Time, or Replacing Chassis Lubricant (U)

Is there a doctor in the house? This patient needs a transfusion.

There are many moving parts on your car. The engine, transmission/transaxle, and differential all have their own lubrication systems. Everything else that needs lubrication gets it under the category of *chassis lubrication*. The chassis includes the frame and secondary systems of your car: suspension, steering, and braking. Lubrication minimizes wear.

Does your car's chassis need lubrication? Probably. Depending on the design of your car, some or all of the lubrication may be done for you by the manufacturer. Many newer cars are designed with sealed lubrication points. Others need lubrication on only a couple of parts every 12,000, 24,000, or more miles. Older cars require chassis lubrication as frequently as every 3,000 miles and at as many as 25 places on the car. Your car's owner's manual or service manual includes specific recommendations on chassis lubrication.

To replace the chassis lubricant in your car, follow these steps:

1. Gather the tools you'll need: wrenches, lubricating spray, and a grease gun. A grease gun, available at auto parts stores for about $10, forces thick lubricating grease into a fitting on your car when you squeeze the gun's handle.

2. Find the lubrication fittings on your car. A lube chart or service manual for your car shows you where they are. Most of them are on or around the steering linkage and the suspension system between the front wheels.

Car Speak

Cars have moving joints just like you do. Instead of elbows and knees, they're called *universal* or *constant velocity (CV) joints*. Cars with straight drive-lines (rear-wheel drives) use universal joints. Cars with angled drivelines (front-wheel drives) use CV joints. Both types need chassis lubrication.

3. Lubricate the steering and suspension parts as needed. Some parts have a nipple, called a *zerk fitting*, on which you press the end of the grease gun. Other lubrication points have a small plug that must be screwed off to reveal the lubrication point.

4. Make sure you lubricate all the miscellaneous chassis components as needed. They include the emergency or parking brake linkage, the transmission shift linkage, and universal or CV joints. These are lubricated either with a grease gun or by smearing grease on friction points with your finger. Many cars also require a drop of light oil on some parts. Make sure you hit the right part because oil is a conductor that can short out electrical components that are errantly doused.

The Least You Need to Know

➤ Automotive parts and fluids are necessary for the life of your car and should be changed on a regular basis. You can do it.

➤ Older cars require that the ignition timing be adjusted annually. Newer cars have preset timing or need it less frequently.

➤ Engine drivebelts should be regularly inspected and adjusted or replaced.

➤ You can lubricate your car's chassis for longer life using basic tools and procedures.

Chapter 12

CAR: Biannual Replacements

In This Chapter

➤ How to safely and easily replace radiator coolant, cap, and hoses

➤ Replacing fuel and air filters in just a few minutes every couple of years

➤ How to replace spark plugs, plug wires, and other ignition parts using basic tools

➤ Replacing your car's lubricants without getting too dirty in the process (oh, go ahead and get your fingers dirty if you want)

Cars are getting smarter and smarter. Mine can now beat me at chess. Just a couple of decades ago, cars required more frequent servicing to keep them in good running condition. Ignition systems were tuned up every six months to a year. Fuel and air filters were replaced as often. On the other side of the issue, emission-control devices were simple. Today's cars are more complex but need less frequent service. It's a trade-off.

Whether your car is 2 or 25 years old, some parts and fluids need replacement. You can do the replacement yourself, as you'll learn in this chapter. These parts include some filters, spark plugs, ignition wiring and parts, and emission-control components. Fluids include transmission, differential, and wheel-bearing lubricants. Even if you don't replace them yourself, you can learn more about what they are and how to make sure you get your money's worth from someone who does replace them.

It's pop (or mom, if you like) quiz time! What does the acronym H-U-B stand for in this book? Give up? Hints: *H* means under the hood, *U* designates adjustments done under the car, and *B* notes adjustments made beside the car. Did you pass the quiz?

So grab your car care toolbox (see Chapter 6, "Do-It-Yourself Maintenance, or Getting Your Hands Dirty") and let's get torquing. I'll let you know what tools are needed as we go along.

Keeping Cool, or Replacing Radiator Coolant, Cap, and Hoses (H)

Your car's radiator uses more than just water to keep your engine from overheating. It uses a mixture of water and antifreeze fluid, also known as *coolant*. An antirust ingredient in the antifreeze attempts to minimize the rust that's a byproduct of contact between water, air, and some metals. It's not totally successful, however, so every year or two, you should transfuse the rust-laden coolant in your car's radiator.

At the same time, consider replacing the radiator cap and hoses on your car. These components also break down with use and can fail when you most need them—like when you're crossing Death Valley, or when you're already late for a job interview.

My Mechanic Says. . .

Rust inhibitors should not be added to antifreeze or coolant used in aluminum engines. Your car's owner's manual recommends the appropriate antifreeze for your engine.

To replace the radiator coolant, cap, and hoses in your car, follow these steps:

1. Remove the radiator cap and drain coolant from the cooling system. On most cars, this means placing a 2- to 5-gallon open container under the radiator and opening the drain fitting or removing the lower hose on the radiator. Some engines also have one or two coolant drain plugs on the engine block that must be removed to drain coolant from the block. Drain the coolant reservoir if possible. Your car's heater might also have a drain plug. In each case, make sure you have a container to capture the draining coolant.

2. Flush the radiator system using fresh water and a radiator cleaner. You can purchase a radiator flush system at most auto parts retailers. It includes a cleaner as well as a plastic T-fitting that you install in a system hose. You then attach a garden hose to circulate fresh water through the system under pressure. Follow manufacturer's instructions rather than mine.

3. Check the condition of the radiator hoses by squeezing them. Replace them if they are soft, have cuts in them, or give you an unexpected shower. In fact, it's relatively cheap insurance to replace the hoses as you replace the coolant. Hoses usually cost less when replacing them isn't an emergency. Inspect and, if necessary, replace the hose clamps at the same time.

4. Replace the coolant. Recommended coolant is half water and half antifreeze fluid available from auto parts retailers. Make sure all drain plugs are tightened or replaced. Before adding the coolant to the radiator or reservoir, first open the car's heater temperature control to the maximum heat position so that the coolant also fills the heater core.

5. When you think the radiator or reservoir is full of coolant, start the car and let it warm up with the radiator cap off. The water pump inside the engine circulates the coolant, forcing air out of the system. When the upper radiator hose is warm to the touch, turn off the engine and let it cool. Then add more coolant as needed to fill the radiator or reservoir.

6. Replace the radiator pressure cap with a new one. Otherwise, it will fail 75 miles from town and you will have to purchase a new one at Joe's Hi-Way Robbery and Expensive Fuel and Auto Parts Station.

7. Start the engine again and let it warm up. As it does, inspect the radiator, reservoir, hoses, engine block drain plugs, and heater core for leaks. If you find leaks, refer to Chapter 21, "Cooling and Lubrication System Repairs: Fixing a Hot Car," or take your car to a radiator shop for repairs.

8. Properly dispose of the old coolant (*down a storm drain is a big no-no!*). Seal it in a plastic container and take it to your local recycling center for disposal. Coolant is both sweet and poisonous to pets, so clean up any spills thoroughly.

Keep It Clean: Replacing the Fuel Filter (H)

It's science lesson time. Gasoline is processed petroleum. During the processing, contaminants are removed. However, gas is then stored in imperfect tanks with rust and bits of metal or plastic. The worst culprit is your own car's gas tank, where contaminants can build up on the bottom. If the engine is operated when the tank is almost empty, these contaminants can be pumped to your engine along with the gas. They then can enter the carburetor or fuel injectors and block operation.

Fortunately, today's cars have filters in the fuel line to stop the big chunks from entering the carburetor or fuel injectors. Even older cars (like my 40-year-old Lincoln) have been retrofitted with fuel filters to minimize big chunks in the carburetors. Replacing the fuel filter on most cars is a piece of cake. So get out the cake server and....

To replace the fuel filter on your car, follow these steps:

1. Find the fuel filter. First, check your car's owner's manual or service manual for the location of the fuel filter. On some cars, it's under the hood—a small aluminum barrel in the fuel line between the fuel pump and the carburetor. On other cars, it's a plastic-cased filter installed on the carburetor, near the fuel-injection unit, or on the fuel pump. Some are installed near the fuel tank. A few cars have two fuel filters—one near the tank and one near the carburetor.

My Mechanic Says. . .

Fuel-injection systems pressurize fuel to deliver it to the engine. To replace the fuel filter on a fuel-injection system, you first must relieve system pressure. Refer to the car's service manual for specific information on how to do so safely.

2. Remove the fuel filter. In-line fuel filters can be removed by hand by carefully loosening clamps at each end of the filter unit and then pulling the fuel lines off the filter. Fuel filters installed on the carburetor or fuel pump require that you use a wrench to first loosen the fuel line and then remove the filter.

3. Replace the fuel filter. You can find a replacement fuel filter at your favorite auto parts store or many hardware stores. There probably will be a brand name and a parts number on the filter. If not, an auto parts counterperson or a reference book can tell you which filter you need. Also make sure the clamps or fittings on the filter are in good shape, and replace them as needed.

Cleaning Up the Air, or Replacing the Air Filter (H)

Air isn't what it used to be. A car's air filter can tell you this. Look at a used air filter and you can see a broad collection of stuff your car otherwise would have breathed. The history of air filters also illustrates the growth of pollution and a car's need for clean air. Early cars had no air filter. Later cars had an oil-bath filter system that caught bugs and bits before they were sucked up by the carburetor. Today's cars have large and fairly efficient filters to keep most objects out of the carburetor or fuel-injection system.

Wouldn't it be great if we all had replaceable air filters in us?

Fuel-injection systems are especially sensitive to clogged air filters. Although a clogged filter won't damage your car, it can dramatically reduce power. And a new air filter will probably cost you less than $10. Replacing your car's air filter is one of the easier tasks you can do for your car's health.

To replace the air filter in your car, follow these steps:

1. Find the air filter. For carbureted cars, the air filter is usually located above the carburetor in a large round object euphemistically called the *air cleaner*. For fuel-injected cars, the filter is located somewhere between the car's front grill and the engine.

2. Remove the air filter. For carbureted cars, remove the wingnut on top of the air cleaner and lift off the top to expose the round air filter. For fuel-injected cars, remove the clips or twistnuts on the filter cover and lift the air filter from the unit, noting which way it came out so that you can put the new one back in the same way. Use an old rag to wipe out the air cleaner, discarding any waylaid bugs or other foreign objects. (I found a live salamander in one of my car's air cleaners! Honest!)

3. Replace the air filter. Place the new air filter against the old one to make sure it's the same size. This also tells you something about the amount of contaminants your air filter stopped since it was last replaced. Install the new air filter in the same way the old one was installed. Some paper filters are wrapped with a foam

blanket that initially filters bugs that have committed suicide and other large projectiles. Filters for fuel-injection systems usually go in only one way, but those for carbureted systems can go in correctly with either side up. Make sure the filter sits well and isn't lopsided.

4. Replace other parts you took off to get to the filter.

Many cars have an air cleaner that controls the source of air going through the filter and to the carburetor or injection system. It pulls warmer air from the exhaust manifold when the engine is cold and from the outside air when the engine warms up. As you work around the air cleaner, make sure the air duct from the engine sits securely in place. Visually inspect the air cleaner housing and regulator for disconnections and damage.

Some older cars also have a rubber hose that feeds into the side of the air cleaner. This hose starts at a nearby tube where you pour oil for the engine crankcase, called the *crankcase inlet.* It recirculates fumes from the engine's oil system through the fuel system. If your car has one of these hoses, make sure it's snugly in place (between the crankcase inlet and the air cleaner).

Keep the Spark Alive: Replacing Spark Plugs (H)

Spark plugs are an important part of your car's engine. They supply the fire that ignites the controlled explosions within each cylinder.

Today's cars are sufficiently efficient that the spark plugs need replacement only every couple of years or about 25,000 miles. Unfortunately, car manufacturers have used this fact to make spark plugs less accessible than they were on earlier engines. In fact, on some engines, it's a chore just finding all the spark plugs, let alone trying to replace them. After you find them, you might decide to replace them yourself or to hire a dexterous mechanic for the job.

Did You Know?

Some high-performance cars use platinum spark plugs. The good news is that they run twice as long between replacements. The bad news is that platinum plugs cost at least as much as two body parts. Most auto parts stores offer a layaway plan.

To find the spark plugs, first find the car's distributor or ignition computer. It will have four to eight wires running from it. Follow each of these wires and you will, hopefully, find the spark plugs. Optionally, check your car's owner's manual or service manual for a drawing of the engine that may indicate where the spark plugs are hidden.

Don't bother cleaning and resetting the gap on used spark plugs. They're sufficiently used up and sufficiently cheap to replace every couple of years.

To replace the spark plugs in your car, follow these steps:

1. Purchase your spark plugs. Auto parts retailers can supply replacement spark plugs. However, a previous owner or mechanic might have installed spark plugs that operate at hotter or colder temperatures, so you might want to remove and check the brand and number on the plug before buying a set. Be careful of what you install because a spark plug that is too long can damage the engine's internal parts. Your best bet is to use the spark plug recommended by the manufacturer. How many? One for each cylinder: four for a four-cylinder engine, six for a six-cylinder engine, and eight spark plugs for an eight-cylinder engine. Enough math.

2. Set the gap for all the spark plugs. Spark plugs supply electrical spark to the cylinder by making it jump a small gap at the end of the plug. The gap between the center electrode and ground electrode must be exactly as recommended by the manufacturer. Use a gap gauge (a couple of dollars at the auto parts store) to set the gap between the electrodes. If the gap needs adjustment, you can carefully bend the ground or wire electrode until it is.

3. Remove the old plug. First, make sure your engine hasn't been run within an hour or more so that you don't burn yourself on hot engine parts. After you find the spark plug, grasp the spark plug wire where it attaches to the spark plug end or terminal and carefully pull it off. Depending on how easy the spark plugs are to reach, you may need to use a spark plug wire puller (less than $10 at you-know-where). Then use an old paint brush to sweep away any dirt and debris from around the spark plugs. You don't want that stuff falling into the cylinder hole when the spark plug is removed. Use a spark plug wrench to grasp and turn the spark plug counterclockwise to remove it. This may require some force.

4. Install the new (gapped) plug. Apply some anti-seize lubricant to the threads of the plug to make removal easier the next time. If you can easily reach it by hand, place the end of the spark plug in the cylinder hole and screw it in. If you can't quite reach it, push a 6- to 12-inch length of $3/8$-inch hose on the terminal to extend your reach. Don't force the spark plug into the hole or you will ruin the threads on the side of the plug. Tighten the spark plug into the hole using a torque wrench or a standard spark plug wrench. Overtightening can break the plug and add time and frustration to the job.

5. Reinstall the spark plug wire.

6. Repeat the process for the other spark plugs.

Your spark plugs may be trying to tell you something. You can learn much about the operation of your car's engine by inspecting the old spark plugs. A service manual or an auto parts store has a chart showing what spark plugs might look like and what caused the problem: overheating, carbon, oil, poor fuel, preignition, and so on. If you don't speak spark plug, don't be afraid to ask a knowledgeable clerk to help you interpret what the plugs are telling you.

Replacing Spark Plug Wires (H)

Spark plug wires used to be copper wires wrapped with a rubber insulator. Today's wires use a carbon or silicon conductor that is more efficient, but also more sensitive to mishandling and to age. I know that feeling! Many car manufacturers now recommend that the spark plug wires be replaced when the spark plugs are replaced.

To replace the spark plug wires in your car, follow these steps:

1. Purchase a replacement set of spark plug wires for your car as recommended by the manufacturer. A replacement set has wires cut to the correct lengths and includes contacts and boots (cowboy or hiking?) for each end. Some sets also have numbers on the wires to help you identify which cylinder they go to.

2. Find the spark plug wires on your car. To do so, find the car's distributor or ignition computer. Wires lead from it to the spark plugs. The wires may feed through one or more brackets, called *looms*, that isolate the wires from the maze of other wires and hoses under the hood. You might need to replace the looms, too, depending on how easy the wires are to remove from the looms. Some spark plug wire sets come with new looms or replacement bridges.

3. Replace the wires, one at a time. Select one spark plug wire and trace it from the computer or distributor to the spark plug. Then select the replacement spark plug wire of the same length. Follow the instructions that came with the wire set on how to install it on your car. Some spark plug wire conductors are more sensitive to handling than others. If it feeds through a hole in a loom, you may need to remove a boot from one end to do so.

4. Repeat the process for each spark plug wire until all are installed. Recheck both ends of each wire to ensure that they fit snugly.

Igniting the Fire, or Replacing Other Ignition Parts (H)

Depending on what type of ignition system your car uses, other parts can need replacement. Older cars have *breaker-point ignitions*. Newer ones have *breakerless ignitions*. The newest cars have *computerized ignitions*. You can replace some of these parts, but you may not want to, or be able to, replace ignition parts on newer cars.

To replace other ignition parts in your car, follow these steps:

1. Identify what type of ignition system your car has and what it needs. The car's service manual tells you and also identifies the parts to be replaced. Breaker-point distributors need new contact points, a condenser, a rotor, and a cap. Breakerless ignition systems need a new rotor and cap, and sometimes one or two other components. A computerized ignition might not need anything. To find out what your car needs, identify your car to an auto parts counterperson (see Chapter 2, "Learning About Your Car: What Does What").

Car Speak

A *breaker-point* ignition system distributes electrical current to spark plugs by interrupting current using two moving contact points. A *breakerless* ignition uses an electronic switch to do the same job. A *computerized* ignition uses all solid-state instead of mechanical parts. Chapter 18, "Starting and Ignition System Repairs for the Clueless," tells more about how ignition systems work.

My Mechanic Says. . .

If you don't have a service manual to verify the location of spark plug wires, ask someone to try starting the car while the distributor cap is off. Watch to see which way the rotor moves. Some distributor caps are marked for the first cylinder in the firing order. Follow the firing order around the distributor.

2. Disassemble the ignition and replace parts as described in the car's service manual. For many cars, this means first removing the distributor cap. The *distributor cap* is the round plastic part that gathers the ends of all the spark plug wires.

   To replace the cap, first align the old and new caps side-by-side with the notch underneath both caps at the same relative position. Then remove one spark plug wire from the old cap and place it at the same position on the new cap. One-by-one, repeat this process for all spark plug wires as well as the coil wire that fits in the center of the cap.

3. To replace the distributor rotor, first remove the distributor cap. Then lift the old rotor from the center of the distributor. Visually check to make sure the new rotor is the same size and shape as the old one. The hole on the underside of the new rotor has a notch that shows how it fits on the distributor shaft key. Install it by matching the notch and the key.

4. To replace contact points and the condenser on a breaker-point distributor, follow the car manufacturer's recommendations in the service manual. In most cases, the engine is rotated until the corners of the distributor shaft push the contact points open to a specific gap. Replace the old contact points with a new set and adjust the gap. Replace the *condenser* (this stores electricity between sparks).

5. To replace parts in a breakerless distributor or a computerized ignition, follow the manufacturer's recommendations. There are just too many variations to cover in this book.

Replacing PCV, EEC, and EGR Parts (H, U)

It's acronym time! In an attempt to reduce emissions from our cars, engineers and bureaucrats have worked overtime developing long names for simple devices. Here are a few:

➤ **EEC:** Evaporative emissions canister

➤ **EGR:** Exhaust gas recirculation

➤ **PCV:** Positive crankcase ventilation

➤ **RGDFMYCUC:** Rube Goldberg device for making your car unnecessarily complicated

Fortunately, replacing parts for these systems is not always as complicated. In fact, many cars have a road map to their emissions-control systems affixed to the inside of the car's hood.

To replace emissions-control system parts on your car, follow these steps:

1. Find the diagram of your car's emissions-control system. It will be under the hood, on the engine compartment firewall, or in the car's service manual. From this map, identify which parts need periodic replacement and when. They are usually marked.

2. Purchase the replacement part from your auto parts supplier (dealer or retailer). Ask the parts counterperson for directions or suggestions on installing the part. If the response is "Huh?" find another parts source.

Did You Know?

Emission-control systems reduce noxious gases released by internal combustion engines. Which ones? Hydrocarbons, carbon monoxide, and oxides of nitrogen—the ones you'd never invite to a party. To find out whether your car's emission-control system is working efficiently, a mechanic shoves a probe up your car's tailpipe. Ouch! An infrared gas analyzer then tests for these elements and measures them in parts per million, or *ppms*. Some states require that all cars take this test regularly. Cars that fail must be repaired or retired. Although you can't test and certify your own car, you can replace many of the emissions-control parts before the test.

3. Replace the part. In most cases, installation is straightforward: Remove the clips holding the part in place, remove the old part, install the new part, and replace

the clips. Fortunately, parts that are intended to be replaced on a regular basis are often designed to be replaced easily. Unfortunately, some automotive engineers clearly have a warped sense of humor. For example, EGR units are mounted on the intake or exhaust manifold. PCV valves are usually mounted on the engine's valve cover. EECs are often located near the front of the engine compartment, identified by two or more hoses.

Keeping It Automatic: Replacing Automatic Transmission Filter and Fluid (U)

Automatic transmissions are made to be trouble-free for 100,000 miles or more. However, they don't last that long if they don't get maintenance every year or two. What maintenance? Replacing the fluid and filter.

To replace the automatic transmission filter and fluid in your car, follow these steps:

1. Purchase the correct filter and fluid designed for your car's automatic transmission (refer back to Chapter 8, "CAR Weekly Check Up"). Depending on the transmission, you might also need a gasket. Don't buy cheap. Just a couple of dollars more could mean much improved quality. Also, find an open container, such as an oil change drip pan, for collecting the old automatic transmission fluid. Place the pan under the automatic transmission.

2. Safely jack up your car and place stands under it so that you have room to work. Gather your tools: screwdrivers or wrenches for removing the transmission plug or pan.

3. Remove the transmission plug or pan. Some automatic transmissions have a drain plug just like the one on the engine's oil pan. Other transmissions don't have such a plug so the pan must be carefully removed to drain the fluid. Here's how: Loosen the bolts attaching the pan to the front of the transmission three or four turns, but don't remove them. Then carefully loosen and remove the bolts attaching the rest of the pan to the transmission. Be careful because, once tipped, the fluid in the pan will begin draining over the edge. The fluid might be hot.

4. After the fluid drains completely, carefully remove the pan to expose the transmission fluid filter. Remove the filter and replace it with a new one following the manufacturer's instructions.

5. Clean the transmission pan with a rag, replace the gasket if needed, and reinstall the pan. Reinstall the drain plug if there is one. Remove the car from the safety stands.

Money Saver

If your car fails an emissions test, find out whether the needed repair is covered under your car's warranty before paying for it yourself.

6. Refill the transmission with the recommended automatic transmission fluid, using a funnel to pour it into the transmission dipstick tube. How much? Check your car's owner's manual or service manual for specifics. Three to six quarts is typical.

7. Start the engine and let it warm up. Make sure the brake is set. Slowly move the transmission through the gear selector a few times to circulate the fluid through the automatic transmission. Then stop the engine and recheck the fluid level using the automatic transmission dipstick. Add as needed.

8. Take your car for a test ride. Espresso stop is optional.

Trans Who? Or Replacing Manual Transmission/ Transaxle Lubricant (U)

This one isn't required, but it's smart motoring. Your car's manual may not suggest replacing the manual transmission lubricant. It makes sense to do so, however, just as you would replace any other lubricant that comes in contact with moving parts.

To replace the manual transmission/transaxle lubricant in your car, follow these steps:

1. Safely jack up your car and place stands underneath to give yourself a safe and spacious work area. You'll only need a wrench and a drain pan for this job.

2. Find the drain plug at the lowest point on one side of the manual transmission. Place the drain pan under it to catch the two to four quarts of lubricant that will drain from it. Use a wrench to turn the drain plug counterclockwise and remove the plug. After gravity has done its job, replace the drain plug.

3. Find the fill/level plug located above the drain plug on the side of the manual transmission. Remove the fill/level plug as you did the drain plug. Following the manufacturer's recommendations, fill the manual transmission with lubricant until it begins to flow out of the fill hole. Verify that the level is at the bottom of the hole with your pinky finger. Depending on available space and the size of the lubricant's container, you might need to use a suction tool to get the lubricant into the hole. There's not much room to move an oil can into position on some cars. Insert the tip of the suction tool's hose into the lubricant's container and pull on the plunger, drawing lubricant up into the tool's storage chamber. Then place the tool's hose tip into the fill hole and press on the plunger, forcing the lubricant into the *tranny* (the familiar version of *transmission*). It's actually kind of fun, *albeit* sloppy.

4. Replace the fill/level plug, making sure it's tight.

117

What's the Difference? Or Replacing Differential Lubricant (U)

Not all cars have a separate differential, as you learned in a previous chapter. The cars that do have them need a periodic change of lubricant to keep them in good running shape. Chapters 9, "CAR Quarterly Check Up," and 22, "Transmission Repairs: Those Troublesome Trannys," tell more about your car's differential.

Replacing differential lubricant is similar to doing the same for a manual transmission. To replace the differential lubricant in your car, follow these steps:

1. Safely jack up your car and place stands underneath the axle with the differential. You will need a wrench, a drain pan, and maybe a suction tool for this job. Turn the radio on loud to mask any cursing.

2. Find the drain plug at the lowest point on one side of the differential. If it doesn't have a drain plug, you need to remove the cover from the differential to drain the lubricant. Place a drain pan under the differential. Use a wrench to remove the drain plug or the cover. Once the lubricant has fully drained from the differential, replace the drain plug or the cover. If the cover was removed, inspect the gasket (a cork sheet around the cover's outer edge) for tears and replace as necessary.

3. Find the fill/level plug located in the center of the differential cover. Remove the fill/level plug and fill the differential with the recommended type and amount of lubricant, typically until it flows from the fill hole. Use your finger to verify that the level is at the bottom of the hole. If there isn't enough room under the floor pan for the lubricant's container, you might need to use a suction tool to get the lubricant into the hole. Insert the suction tool's hose tip into the lubricant's container and pull on the plunger, drawing lubricant up into the tool's storage chamber. Insert the tool's hose tip into the fill hole and press on the plunger, forcing the lubricant into the differential case.

4. Replace and tighten the fill/level plug.

Replacing Wheel Bearing Lubricant

Your car's wheels each rotate 600 to 900 times per mile, depending on the size of your tires. No wonder they wear out eventually! This rotation causes friction. To minimize wear between the housing or wheel hub and the axle, bearings are built into the center of a wheel and then packed with heavy lubricant. The bearings don't wear out very often—as long as the lubricant is replaced every year or two.

Wheel bearings are installed on unpowered axles. That is, front-wheel-drive cars have bearings on the rear wheels; rear-wheel-drive cars use bearings on the front wheels. Some newer cars have sealed bearings that don't require service. Lucky owners!

This job is especially popular recreation for those who enjoyed playing in the mud as children.

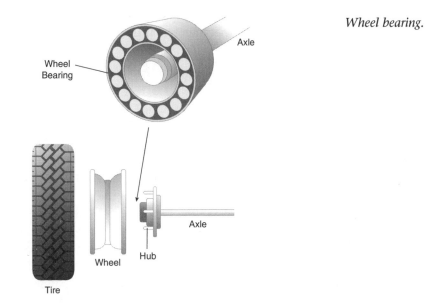

Wheel bearing.

To replace the wheel bearing lubricant in your car, follow these steps:

1. Safely jack up the unpowered axle until the tires clear the ground, and then install safety stands under the axle. Gather parts and tools. You'll need a small can of wheel-bearing grease, a wheel-bearing seal and cotter pins (from the parts store), a chisel or straight screwdriver, a standard wrench, a torque wrench, and a pair of pliers from your car care toolbox (see Chapter 6, "Do-It-Yourself Maintenance, or Getting Your Hands Dirty"). You'll also need some auto parts solvent for cleaning the old wheel bearing. If you like to clean up for dinner, hand cleaner will eventually be useful.

2. Remove a wheel from the car (see Chapter 8). Pry off the metal cap at the center of the wheel hub using the tip of a chisel or a flat screwdriver. You will see a nut with a wire cotter pin through it. Straighten the bent end of the cotter pin and pull the round end until the pin comes out of the nut. Discard the cotter pin.

3. Remove the wheel-bearing nut. The wheel hub now is loose. Remove the wheel hub by pulling it toward you and remove it from the wheel spindle (the wheel's center shaft). As parts come off, lay them out in the same order to make reassembly easier. This avoids the jigsaw puzzle syndrome of reassembly.

4. Remove the wheel bearings from the center of the wheel hub. The wheel bearing is a donut-shaped metal part with roller bearings around the perimeter. Turn the hub over and pry the seal out of the center of the hub using the tip of a chisel or a straight screwdriver.

119

5. Clean the wheel bearings, the wheel hub's center, and the end of the spindle with auto parts solvent and a small paint brush. Let the parts dry before reinstalling them.

6. Inspect the wheel bearings for wear or damage. If the bearings are damaged or worn, replace them with new ones.

7. Repack the wheel bearing with grease. Now comes the playing in the mud part. Here's how: Place a glob of grease in the palm of your less frequently used hand, and then use your more frequently used hand to press the wheel bearings into the grease. Roll the bearings back and forth in your palm. You're trying to pack the grease all around the bearings so that they remain lubricated for a long time and you don't have to do this messy job again for a while.

My Mechanic Says. . .

To efficiently repack wheel bearings, disassemble them from both wheels, clean both, repack both, and then reassemble both. It's faster and less messy than removing and repacking one wheel's bearings and then the other.

8. Install the rear (larger) wheel bearing. Then press the new grease seal on the back of the wheel hub. Reinstall the hub and use your fingers to push some grease into the area where the wheel bearing will go. Then install the outer wheel bearing unit and press more grease around it. Finally, install the washer, nut, new cotter pin, and grease cap. The nut should be tightened with a torque wrench to the manufacturer's recommended specifications. The cotter pin goes through a hole in the nut and spindle that first must be aligned. Bend the end of the cotter pin so that it stays in place.

9. Repeat the process for the other wheel.

The Least You Need to Know

➤ You can replace parts and fluids every couple of years to save money and learn more about your car.

➤ These parts and fluids include radiator coolant, cap, hoses, fuel and air filters, spark plugs and wires, ignition parts, and lubricants.

➤ Whether you do these jobs yourself or hire someone to do them, knowing how they are done will add to your enjoyment of your car.

Chapter 13

Body and Interior Maintenance: Keeping Your Car All Spruced Up

In This Chapter

➤ Washing and waxing with tips from the detailing pros

➤ Interior cleaning in only a few minutes to make your car look better

➤ Exterior touchup to save hundreds of dollars over a new paint job

When you bought your new car, you probably thought it was beautiful. Time and use might have since scribbled on your car, moving it more to the category of a utility vehicle. The paint may be chipped and faded. The interior has a couple of holes. There's that big stain from last summer's vacation mishap. You're beginning to see rust where paint used to be. Like many dream boats, yours is beginning to look more like a barge.

No sweat. With an investment of just a few hours and bucks, you can make your friends ask, "Did you get a new car?" Even if you're a technical klutz, you can participate in your car's maintenance by giving it a makeover, as described in this chapter.

Remember Ramsey's rule: A clean car runs better than a dirty one!

Before you start maintaining your car's finish and interior, read the owner's manual. It probably includes specific information on the type of finish on the car as well as how to care for it. If it doesn't, take your car to an auto parts store that carries a wide line of finishing products and ask for a counterperson or clerk with out-of-body...oops...auto body experience. You might have to try more than one retailer to find someone who knows car finishes and is willing to take a few minutes to look at your car. If you do find such an expert and the resulting advice is useful, buy your products there instead of at a discount store. The advice and service are worth the few extra pennies.

Splish, Splash, Give It a Bath

Your car is getting beat up by the environment every day. It's baked by the sun, pelted by elements, splashed on, and bumped into—to say nothing of what birds do to your car's finish.

Fortunately, there is a universal solvent that can remove such items from most surfaces. No, it's not a papaya-derivative sold on late-night TV commercials. It's plain old water. Water, without any help from other man-made products, can clean most foreign and domestic elements from your car's surface.

Unfortunately, car surfaces need some help. They need protection to minimize damage from the elements that gang up on them. They need a protective coating that keeps the elements from damaging the car's surface and makes cleaning the surface easier. After your car is clean, you need to protect your car's finish.

Wash Behind Your Mirrors and Under Your Fenders

Cars come clean with plain water. Most contaminants can be removed from the exterior surfaces of your car by simply washing them away. Unfortunately, a few contaminants require soap to remove them.

Depending on local conditions and your pride of ownership, you should wash your car once a week or once a month.

Here's how to wash your car:

1. Find a shady spot for washing your car—either in your driveway or at a do-it-yourself car wash. The sun heats up the surface of your car, evaporating the water before it can wash away contaminants. Make sure all windows are closed and your doors are firmly shut. If a door or window seal leaks water into the car, seal it temporarily by stuffing it with a clean rag.

2. Start with a rinse using plain water. Run water over the surfaces of your car, beginning at the roof and working down. Don't spray the surfaces with a hard blast of water. Instead, direct the flow of water over the surfaces by moving the end of the hose. If you're using a car wash pressure wand, hold it away from the surface so that the pressure doesn't scratch the paint with pressurized dirt particles.

3. Wash your car. If you're using soap, put it in the bottom of a small bucket and add one or two gallons of water. Don't use a dishwashing detergent unless you want to completely remove the old wax. If necessary, use a soap designed specifically for washing cars. Some manufacturers recommend separate products for the washing and cleaning steps. Major brands include Maguiars, Blue Coral, and Simonize. Use a sponge or soft cloth to apply and move the suds.

4. Rinse your car. Just as you did before, run water over the surfaces of your car. Flush away the contaminants, suds, and any residues.

5. Dry your car. Depending on the humidity of the air, you might need to first remove standing water from the car's surfaces. Use a soft sponge (that hasn't been used for cleaning anything else) to push excess water off the surfaces, starting at the roof and working down. You can then remove the remaining water with a chamois (pronounced *SHAM-ee*) or clean towel (pronounced *TOU-el*).

Your Car Needs Sunscreen, Too

Car *polishes* dress up your car's appearance, making it glossier. Car *waxes* protect your car's finish from damage by the elements. Some car-care systems combine polish and wax into one product, and others have separate products and procedures for each.

To protect your car's finish, apply a polish and wax in one or two steps, depending on the quality of results you want and the time you prefer to invest. This process takes one to two hours every three to six months.

Here's how to protect your car's finish:

1. Rinse, wash, and rinse your car as described in the preceding section. Make sure the car is fully dry before applying some finish products because water can mix and make the finish cloudy. Other products require a dampened application cloth.

2. Apply the polish/wax to flat surfaces first, spreading it and letting it dry as directed by the manufacturer. Some products suggest that you apply and dry a section at a time. Others tell you to apply the product to all surfaces before removal. Most products suggest that you apply with a circular motion. Sadly, none recommend that you drink a beer between applications.

3. Remove the polish/wax as directed by the manufacturer or a well-meaning neighbor in the adjoining driveway. Use soft cloths to polish the car, turning them frequently to minimize buildup.

Be Careful Not to Hurt the Soft Spot

Convertible car tops are fabric tops that fold down. They need special care. You can clean your convertible top with a special cleaner made just for convertibles or a mild solution of soap or detergent. Use as little water as possible and make sure it doesn't leak into the car's interior.

Convertible top windows typically are made of plastic that can easily be scratched by the wrong cleaner. Your auto parts retailer or a detail shop can

Money Saver

Small tears in a vinyl roof can be repaired using a kit made for just such repairs. Look for it at larger auto parts retailers. Make sure you buy one in approximately the same color as your vinyl roof.

sell you a cleaner made especially for convertible top windows. Follow the manufacturer's instructions—unless it's your brother's car.

Vinyl was a popular car roof covering for many years because it made the car look like a convertible. It also added an accent color. Although not as popular today, vinyl roofs can still be found on many new and used cars.

If your car has a vinyl roof, here's how to maintain it. First, clean it with a soft brush and mild detergent to remove dirt and contaminants that build up in the embossed pattern. Make sure the roof is rinsed and dried well, and then apply a vinyl roof dressing available from auto parts retailers. Products like Armor All also work well on vinyl roofs. If necessary, follow with a car wax to protect the surface.

Bathing Your Car's Engine

Engines get dirty. Although there are currently no engine laundromats, you safely can wash and dry your car's engine yourself. Not only is a clean engine compartment more aesthetically pleasing, it's also safer. Accumulations of oil and grease can be the starting point for a dangerous engine fire.

You can do this job in your driveway, but it will make a mess. Consider taking your car to a do-it-yourself car wash, where there's a pressure washer and adequate drainage for the job.

Here's how to safely clean your car's engine:

1. Start and run the engine for 15 minutes or until it reaches normal operating temperature.

2. Turn off the engine and open the hood. Remove the engine's air cleaner housing. Use plastic trash bags and tape to cover the carburetor, fuel-injector unit, and electronic components that can be damaged by water (distributor, alternator, coil, and so on).

3. Spray other components with a can of engine degreaser to loosen grease and oils. Let the degreaser stand for the time recommended by the manufacturer. On a warm engine, the standing time ranges from 15 minutes to an hour. The degreaser is breaking up petroleum buildups so that they can be rinsed away.

4. Carefully spray the engine compartment with pressurized water to rinse away the loosened grease.

5. Remove the trash bags from the covered components. Reinstall any other components you removed, such as the air cleaner.

6. Start the engine. If it doesn't start, water has probably entered the distributor; carefully open and dry the distributor with a clean cloth.

A Facial for the Finish

If your car needs more attention to renew the color and finish, use one of the polishes that include a *rubbing compound*. These compounds remove oxidation from the paint, renewing the color and even buffing out light scratches. They shouldn't be used on cars with a clear-coat finish because they will damage it; instead, use a polish that says it's safe for clear coat. Rubbing compounds also should not be used on finishes that are nearly worn off because they will take it down to the metal. It's time for a paint job. Follow the manufacturer's recommendations, printed on the container, for using rubbing compounds or polishes with a rubbing compound in it.

What can you do between wash jobs to maintain your car's appearance? You can use a soft, wet rag to carefully wipe away bugs, dirt, and bird messages. There are also spray-on products, such as Maguiar's Quik Detailer, that clean the surface and replace the protective coating. I use it and recommend it.

Chrome Is Chrome Is Really Plastic and How to Clean It

Car chrome isn't what it used to be. It isn't metal! *Chrome* used to be an electroplating of nickel and chromium on metal parts. Today's chrome is a silvery finish on plastic parts. Even so, both types are cleaned in much the same way. The only difference is that plastic chrome doesn't stand up to abrasive cleaners very well.

If your car's exterior metal chrome is pitted with some rust, clean it with an abrasive chrome cleaner to remove loose flakes and the rust. Then apply chrome paint to the exposed metal to color and protect it. Finally, apply a protective coating of wax to seal the surface and minimize future damage. If the chrome is gone, check the telephone book for a chrome plating service that can rechrome car parts.

If the exterior chrome is actually painted plastic, use a household surface cleaner to clean it. Touch up any chips with chrome paint made for the job (available from auto parts retailers). When the chrome is dry, apply wax to seal the surface.

Clean Wheels Go Faster

Well, okay, they don't go faster, but they do look better.

Soap and water do wonders toward cleaning and maintaining your car's wheels and tires. Use a soft brush to apply the same solution you use to wash your car. Then rinse it well with plain water. Perrier is too expensive for this job. White walls and red striping can be cleaned with a mild bleach solution or with spray cleaners made for the task.

The black surface of tires can be treated with Armor All or similar products to seal and shine them. A black tire paint is sold at auto parts stores for really gussying up the tires for a special date.

Can You See Through That Windshield?

Clean your car's windows using the same product you would use to clean household windows or with a special car window cleaner available at your nearby parts outlet. If you don't do windows, ask someone who does. Make sure you don't overspray the window cleaner because the chemicals in it can damage the car's wax finish.

Inside Tips

You can enhance the perceived value of your car by simply keeping the interior clean. Whether you're trying to sell your car or just want to feel better about owning it, cleaning the interior can help.

Money Saver

Sunscreens can help protect your skin from the sun's rays. It can do the same for your car. Install protective seat covers, use vinyl conditioners on interior plastics, and use a cardboard windshield screen to minimize the sun's power over your car. Just don't try driving with the windshield screen in place!

Start with a vacuuming. Heavy-duty vacuuming should be done at a car wash or with a shop vacuum. Maintenance vacuuming can be done with a household canister vacuum or a portable vacuum. First, remove, shake out, and vacuum floor mats. Next, starting on one side of the car, vacuum off the dashboard, seat, and floors. Then pass the vacuum hose across the front seat of the car, and walk around to the opposite side to repeat the process. Finally, vacuum the trunk.

Next, use an appropriate household cleaning solution or specialty car care solution to wipe off interior surfaces: the ceiling (called the *headliner*), door panels, the dashboard, instruments, the steering wheel, seats, etc. An exception is leather upholstery, which should be cleaned and conditioned with a product made for the job. If cloth-seat surfaces or carpeting is dirty, use a car upholstery cleaner to remove dirt and renew color.

Finally, apply a vinyl protector to vinyl surfaces.

Permanent Makeup for Your Car

Your car is a projectile in a world of projectiles. As you drive, road rocks strike the front of your car. As you park, posts reach out and bite your car. The world is tough on car paint.

You can fix the slings and arrows of outrageous fortune with handy-dandy touchup paint. Browsing through your favorite auto parts retailer's store, you will probably come across a rack of spray cans or mascara-type bottles identified as touchup paint. These little products can work wonders on your car. They come in assorted colors such as "Ford Motor Co., White, 1995–1986." They may also be cross-coded to the car manufacturer's paint code (in this case, "9M, YY") to make selection easier. You can also check with your dealership's parts department for exact match touchup paint.

Select touchup vials (with a brush in the cap) for fixing scratches and chips. Use spray cans for touching up larger areas, up to about one foot square.

Here's how to use touchup paint:

1. In the auto parts store, look for the touchup paints and especially for a chart that shows which paint color to use for your car. If possible, take a painted part of your car, such as a gas cap, into the store for comparison. If your car has been repainted since it was manufactured, you may have to guess. If you can't find a single color that matches your car's paint, select two that you can blend. I'll tell you how.

2. Purchase one or two cans or vials of touchup paint, one of scratch filler/primer, and a small package of very fine steel wool. If your car has a clear-coat finish, also purchase clear-coat touchup.

My Mechanic Says. . .

Paint shows its truest colors in soft sunlight. If possible, apply touchup paint in early morning or evening light. Alternatively, do it using artificial lights angled at the paint surface to show the greatest amount of color.

3. Find a chip or scratch on your car in the least obvious location so that you can practice your touchup skills. Smooth the surface around the boo-boo by carefully rubbing it with the steel wool. Make sure you remove any rust. Clean the surface.

4. Carefully apply the filler/primer to the scratch or chip area as directed by the manufacturer. If the paint is sprayed on, protect adjacent areas with masking tape. Let the paint dry the suggested amount of time. You might need a magnifying glass to read the instructions on the paint container.

5. Test the touchup paint. Shake the container to mix the paint inside. Apply the touchup paint to a small piece of glass or a mirror. Then hold the glass in front of the car or the mirror beside the car body to compare the touchup paint with the car's current paint. If the color isn't acceptable, mix a secondary touchup paint color with the first one until you get the color you want.

6. Apply the touchup paint. Shake the container vigorously, and then carefully brush or spray it on as directed. Let it dry. If your car has a clear-coat finish, apply clear-coat touchup paint.

The Least You Need to Know

➤ Washing and waxing your car on a regular basis can increase your pride of ownership and help retain your car's value and function.

➤ You can also protect the inside of your car using a variety of useful products available at most auto parts stores.

➤ The slings and arrows of outrageous driving can be covered by touch-up paints.

Part 3
Repairing Your Car

I'm impressed! You've stayed awake through 13 chapters of gobbledygook that would make most folks prefer the dentist's chair. As your reward, I'm going to make you the life of the party—even if it's the Republican Party—by feeding you a flood of facts on repairing your car. I bet you can't wait to tell your friends how to replace a strut or how to bleed brakes. No more than they can wait to hear it!

What you do with this new-found knowledge is up to you. Most folks tuck it away in their brain, filed under "M" for "Maybe someday." Or you might decide to grab a wrench and head for the garage. In any case, you'll be ready for the poker-faced mechanic who says, "I think it's your car's frazzinaggle—so you'll need a co-signer!" In the coming pages, you'll learn how to diagnose and implement or manage a wide variety of common automotive repairs on your car. The next dozen chapters help you decide which jobs to do and which to delegate.

Before you get down and dirty, you'll also need a service manual on your specific car. In the parlance of land navigation, my book gets you to the city and a service manual gets you around in the city. So let's get started on our trip!

Chapter 14

Why Cars Don't Run: The Little Car That Couldn't

In This Chapter

➤ Car components that wear out or fail—typically on an onramp

➤ Repairing your own car and living to tell about it

➤ Problems covered by warranties and repairs that are already paid for

Everything you've learned about cars so far in this book has involved how they run and how to keep them running. Unfortunately, we live in an imperfect world. Things break. The car's previous owner deferred some maintenance, the car's designer tried to save a few too many bucks, the car was assembled on a day ending with *y*, or some other lame excuse. The point is that your car isn't running when or as it should.

What can you do about it?

You are now a knowledgeable car owner. You've learned how your car runs and how to keep it running. You're now going to learn how to diagnose and troubleshoot car problems. Then you'll learn how to make or oversee any needed repairs.

First, let's put this book into reverse gear for a few minutes and back up to the first chapter. Those who were awake for it learned a few things about how cars run. You learned that

➤ Cars create and control power.

➤ Cars create power in the engine.

➤ Cars control power with everything else.

➤ I lied! Cars don't create power, they change chemical power into mechanical power with controlled explosions.

➤ These controlled explosions require fuel, air, and a spark in order to ignite.

➤ The controlled explosions turn a crankshaft.

➤ The crankshaft's turning is (eventually) transferred to the wheels.

➤ Other systems help you control your car: fuel, ignition, cooling, steering, brakes, et cetera, et cetera.

➤ Front-wheel-drive and rear-wheel-drive cars, old cars and new, foreign and domestic cars all do about the same thing in the same way. They just look different.

➤ And the wheels on the car should go round and round.

A front-wheel-drive car.

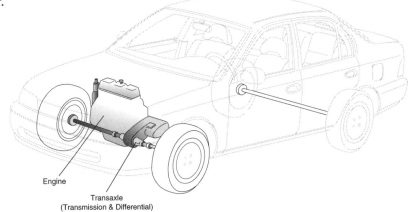

Engine

Transaxle
(Transmission & Differential)

A rear-wheel-drive car.

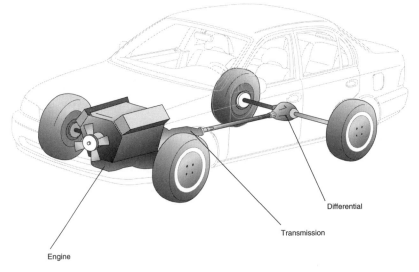

Differential

Transmission

Engine

Understanding these truths can help you figure out why your car doesn't run and help you decide what to do about it. Why? Because cars are designed logically based on the laws of physics, which Congress has never been able to modify, try as it might.

Making Sense of Your Car

The engine is the power factory in your car. All other systems in your car control something. Some systems control the engine (fuel and ignition). Others serve the engine by controlling heat, friction, or waste (cooling, lubrication, and emissions). Some systems apply the power to move the car forward (transmission, differential, and suspension). Others control the direction in which your car travels (steering) or stop forward travel (brakes). Some systems control the lights and creature comforts (electrical, heater, and air conditioner).

So why does the gosh-darn car choose not to run sometimes?

Cars sometimes don't run because the source of the power—the engine—loses one or more parts of the power equation:

Fuel + Air + Spark = Controlled Explosion = Power

So an engine that doesn't get enough fuel, or air, or spark doesn't run. That makes sense.

Cars also choose not to run because related systems (lubrication or cooling, for example) stop the engine from running or because the engine's power doesn't get to the wheels (transmission and other junk). That makes sense, too.

So what kinds of problems stop cars from running or reduce their efficiency?

Lots of them, as described in the rest of this chapter!

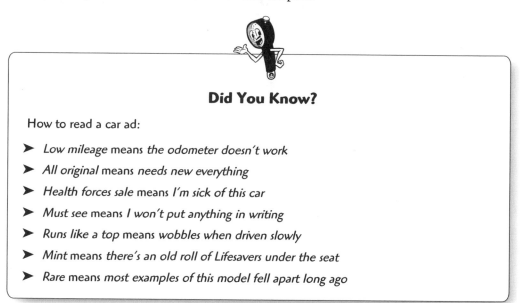

Did You Know?

How to read a car ad:

➤ *Low mileage* means *the odometer doesn't work*

➤ *All original* means *needs new everything*

➤ *Health forces sale* means *I'm sick of this car*

➤ *Must see* means *I won't put anything in writing*

➤ *Runs like a top* means *wobbles when driven slowly*

➤ *Mint* means *there's an old roll of Lifesavers under the seat*

➤ *Rare* means *most examples of this model fell apart long ago*

Driving with Murphy

Murphy's law says that if something can go wrong, it will—at the worst possible time. Murphy evidently owned a car. He or she (Murphy's gender is not a matter of public record) learned what can go wrong through first-hand experience. You don't have to. You can vicariously learn about common automotive problems from the experiences of others (with expletives deleted). The rest of this book will show you how.

Knowing what you already know about cars, the following short descriptions of common automotive problems can help you figure out why your car isn't running. They also make impressive party factoids.

Engine Problems: Did You Hear That?

Besides problems with supporting systems, the engine itself can have its own diseases in search of a cure. Like what?

➤ Worn valves that need replacement.

➤ Warped engine heads that need to be repaired.

➤ Combustion chambers or cylinders that need worn parts replaced or rebuilt.

➤ Worn crankshaft or camshaft that needs repair.

Solving engine problems will be covered in Chapter 19, "Performing Engine Surgery."

Fuel Problems: What To Do When Your Car Is Starved

What can go wrong with your car's fuel system? Many things. And when one does go wrong, your car may be as grumpy as a hungry child. In fact, a fuel system problem can stop your car.

➤ The fuel tank can become contaminated with junk (just like your arteries can become clogged by eating junk food) that blocks the fuel lines, carburetor or fuel injectors, or the engine itself.

➤ The fuel lines can spring a hole and leak fuel.

➤ The fuel pump can become clogged with debris or can wear out and not deliver enough fuel to the engine.

➤ The carburetor linkage can become bent or stuck, making it difficult to control fuel going to the engine.

➤ The carburetor can get too much (rich) or too little (lean) fuel for the engine's needs.

➤ The fuel injectors can become obstructed with debris, blocking the flow of fuel to the engine.

➤ The fuel-injection system's controller can become damaged or wear out and not work efficiently.

➤ The air filtration and delivery system isn't delivering.

➤ Your car is on a hunger strike because it wants the new flavor of gas at McQuickFuel.

Repairing your car's fuel system is covered in Chapter 20, "Fuel System Repairs: Fill 'Er Up!"—like it or not.

Ignition Problems: Rekindling the Spark

Your car's ignition system supplies the spark to the fuel/air mixture at the exact moment it's needed—in theory. When it doesn't, your car runs like a three-legged dog with a sore foot. Some of the more popular ignition system problems follow (vote for your favorite):

➤ One or more spark plugs misfire.

➤ One or more spark plug wires don't deliver a strong spark.

➤ The engine timing belt or chain is inaccurate or broken.

➤ The ignition switch isn't working as it should.

➤ The distributor isn't distributing spark very well.

➤ Your car's girlfriend had moved away.

Stick around for the exciting section on solving ignition problems, known to its friends as Chapter 18, "Starting and Ignition System Repairs for the Clueless."

Does It Compute?

Don't be intimidated by computers. They're actually pretty dumb. They know only two conditions: on and off. However, they do it so dang fast that they can control thousands of things in a fraction of a second. Here's how automotive computers can cause problems:

➤ Sensors are overriding common sense and stopping your car from functioning as designed.

➤ Wiring from your computer to components is damaged and doesn't deliver the signal.

➤ A large charge of electricity has damaged a computer chip or another component manufactured in a newly emerging country.

We'll cover the repair of automotive computers in Chapter 16, "Non-Nerd's Guide to Understanding Your Car's Computer." Computers in your car will also be discussed in Chapter 18 (ignition system) and Chapter 20 (fuel system).

Exhaust Problems: Cough, Cough

What can go wrong with your car's exhaust system? It can make lots of noise. It can stink like no other earthly odor. It can fail to pass an emissions test. Why?

➤ The exhaust manifold can leak and make excessive noise because of a damaged sealing gasket.

➤ The exhaust pipe can rust through, letting exhaust fumes escape into the already polluted atmosphere or into the passenger compartment.

➤ The muffler or resonator can be damaged or rusted through, releasing fumes and noise.

➤ The catalytic converter can quit converting all those little catalysts.

➤ The emissions-control systems can fail to control emissions.

Want to know more about exhaust system repairs? Sure you do. Check out Chapter 26, "Exhaust System Repairs: Fixing an Exhausted System."

Electrical Problems: Short Circuits and More

Electricity is vital to the continued operation of your car as well as to your stereo system. What can go wrong with your car's electrical system?

➤ The starter solenoid and motor can fail to rotate and start your car's engine.

➤ The alternator can fail to replenish electricity in your car's battery.

➤ The battery can fail to store electricity delivered to it by the alternator.

➤ The battery cables or other wiring can become damaged and leak electricity like water from a torn hose.

➤ The regulator can fail to regulate the electricity going from the alternator to the battery.

➤ Lights, gauges, clocks, and other electrical components can burn out or become disconnected.

➤ You can forget to pay your car's electric bill.

Solving automotive electrical problems will be covered in Chapters 18, "Starting and Ignition System Repairs for the Clueless," and 25, "Electrical System Repairs: You'll Get a Charge Out of This!."

Cooling Problems: Changing Hot to Cool

Your car's engine gets pretty hot as it converts chemical energy into mechanical energy. The car's cooling system helps keep the engine from getting too hot. Depending on the car, the coolant temperature must stay under 190° Fahrenheit. If it doesn't, your car's got cooling problems. Here are some of the causes of this problem:

➤ The radiator could be damaged.

➤ The radiator may be clogged with rust or other debris.

➤ The thermostat isn't controlling the coolant temperature as it should.

➤ The water pump isn't efficiently circulating coolant throughout the engine.

➤ The heater system is damaged or clogged.

➤ Your car's temper is flaring because it knows you've got your eye on a cute little sports car.

Chapter 21, "Cooling and Lubrication System Repairs: Fixing a Hot Car," will help you keep your car keep its cool.

Lubrication Problems: Keep Friction Out of Your Relationship

Parts inside your car's engine are rotating thousands of times per minute. That's pretty fast. To keep the parts from quickly wearing out, the lubrication system circulates oil under pressure. What can go wrong?

➤ The oil pump can become clogged with sludge or can fail.

➤ The oil passages in the engine block can become clogged with sludge and limit the flow of oil.

➤ Low oil level can starve some parts for lubrication.

We'll solve some common lubrication problems in Chapter 21, "Cooling and Lubrication System Repairs: Fixing a Hot Car."

Brake Problems: Stopping in Time

Today's car brakes are more trouble-free than their ancestors. They can adjust themselves nicely. However, when they fail, they can become hazardous. What are common brake problems?

➤ Drum and disc brakes wear out and need replacement.

➤ Hydraulic brake cylinders wear out and need repair or replacement.

➤ Power brake units wear out and need repair or replacement.

➤ Parking or emergency brake systems need repair.

Come to a halt in Chapter 24, "Brake System Repairs: Stop Ahead!," for more on brake problems.

Suspension Problems: A Shocking Story

Your car's suspension system helps smooth the ride, reducing wear on tires, components, and people. What can go wrong with your car's suspension system?

➤ Shock absorbers can wear out, making the car ride rough.

➤ Struts can need replacement, making steering more difficult.

➤ Steering components can wear out and need replacement.

➤ Power steering units need repair or replacement.

➤ Wheels can be damaged and need replacement.

➤ Your car has been to too many rodeos and wants to buck you off like an angry bull.

Chapter 23, "Steering and Suspension System Repairs: No More Swerves or Bounces!" will help solve many automotive suspension problems.

Transmission Problems: When Your Transmission Doesn't Transmit

Transmissions simply transmit the engine's power directly or indirectly to the driving wheels. Along the way, problems can happen that reduce the car's forward travel to little or nothing. What are these potential transmission problems?

➤ The automatic or manual transmission gears can wear out and need replacement.

➤ The automatic transmission's torque converter can lose its torque-converting capabilities.

➤ The manual transmission's clutch can lose its grip on the engine's flywheel.

➤ The car's universal or constant-velocity joints can wear out and need replacement.

➤ The car's gear shifting linkage can need adjustment, repair, or replacement.

➤ The transmission can run low on lubrication and tear itself apart.

Learn all about transmissions and how to solve their problems in Chapter 22, "Transmission Repairs: Those Troublesome Trannys."

Body and Interior Problems: Ouchies and Crunchies

Your car's body keeps everything moving in the same direction. The interior makes it a more-or-less comfortable ride. Common car body and interior problems follow:

➤ Window glass is damaged by flying rocks or vandals.

➤ Doors don't close well because of age or bent hinges.

➤ Paint needs to be repaired or replaced after being bitten by a fence post.

➤ Body dents need to be undented after meeting the same fence post as the paint.

➤ Interior surfaces need repair or replacement because of wear or woeful critters, including children.

Need to know more? Hang around for Chapter 27, "Body and Paint Repairs: Giving Your Car a Makeover."

Free Repairs!

Fortunately, you might not have to perform or even pay for some repairs. Your car may be "under warranty" and thus eligible for repair at the manufacturer's expense.

Three Years or How Many Miles?

A warranty is not a guarantee; it's an assurance. A warranty doesn't guarantee things won't go wrong with your car. It's a contractual assurance that if specific things go wrong within certain limits, the manufacturer will repair the problems or replace the parts.

A typical new car warranty assures the purchaser that failure of the engine, transmission, and other "drivetrain" components are fully covered for the first three years or 36,000 miles. All costs—parts and labor—are covered by the manufacturer. Some items on the car are covered under the car manufacturer's warranty, and others, such as tires and battery, are covered by a warranty from the component manufacturer. Don't be shy about asking the dealer or mechanic whether a repair to your car is covered under warranty.

Money Saver

Have your car inspected by an independent mechanic a couple of months before the warranty expires. For around $100, the mechanic can do a thorough check to discover whether there are any components that need repair. If so, get them repaired by the dealership while they are still under warranty. You don't really think your dealer's service shop would point these things out, do you?

Is Your Car Under Warranty?

Okay, you bought your car from Big Joe's Big Deal Used Cars and Yogurt Bar. The warranty on the car when new was for five years or 50,000 miles—whichever came first. The car is just two years old with 30,000 miles on the odometer. Is your car still under warranty?

Yes! Luckily, the manufacturer's warranty follows the car rather than the owner. It could have been a leased car or you could be the twelfth owner—it doesn't matter. As long as the mileage or time limit hasn't expired, the car remains covered by the manufacturer's warranty. You can find a copy of your car's warranty in the owner's manual or by contacting a dealer for that brand of car. Some states require used car dealers to put a sticker on each car indicating whether it's still under warranty.

Extended warranties often are available at a moderate cost, and you don't have to buy it when you buy a new car. You can usually purchase an extended warranty at any time in the first year (or first 12,000 miles). Ask the dealer for more information—and if the answer isn't totally clear, ask again.

Oops! When Your Car Gets a Recall

A *recall* is a notification of a repair that should be made to your car to ensure its safety or mechanical integrity. The repair is done by an authorized service center at the manufacturer's expense. Your car does not have to be under warranty to be subject to a recall.

How can you find out if there is a recall for your car? Contact the manufacturer, authorized dealer, or the National Highway Traffic Safety Administration (800/424-9393). Have information ready, such as the car's make, model, and vehicle identification number.

Be careful, however, because some dealer shops "find" other things to repair at the same time—things you'll have to pay for yourself.

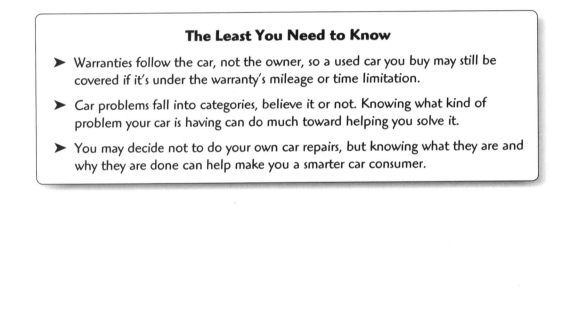

The Least You Need to Know

➤ Warranties follow the car, not the owner, so a used car you buy may still be covered if it's under the warranty's mileage or time limitation.

➤ Car problems fall into categories, believe it or not. Knowing what kind of problem your car is having can do much toward helping you solve it.

➤ You may decide not to do your own car repairs, but knowing what they are and why they are done can help make you a smarter car consumer.

Chapter 15

Don't Shoot! Troubleshoot

In This Chapter

➤ Using common sense to troubleshoot your car problems and save some bucks

➤ Performing an easy diagnostics test that the mechanic would charge you for

➤ Reading signs that tell you more about your car's condition

➤ Listening to telltale noises

No, troubleshooting doesn't mean shooting your car if it gives you trouble!

Troubleshooting means finding and fixing the source of car trouble. You don't necessarily have to fix the problem yourself—you can hire someone to do it—but you do need to know what the problem is. Why? So that you can demand, "Try that again?!" when the mechanic snickers, "A million dollars for a new muffler bearing."

This chapter offers a number of proven tips for troubleshooting your car and getting it repaired at a reasonable cost. The remainder of this book describes how specific repairs are done on unspecific cars.

I Can Answer That Question in Three Minutes

How do professional mechanics diagnose a car in just a few minutes? They use their common sense: They look for signs, listen for noises, and feel for problems. Knowing what a car should look and sound like, they easily recognize what shouldn't be. You can do the same thing; as you drive or perform routine maintenance, look, listen, and feel.

That's what your doctor probably does—uses common sense to find symptoms—before he or she tries to diagnose a problem. How are you feeling today? Where does it hurt? Does it hurt when I do this? Visa or MasterCard?

Learn and use these diagnostic techniques even if you have no desire to lift a wrench in repair. Why? Because you'll be better able to describe the symptoms to your mechanic. Mechanics are people, too. If you tell a mechanic that the valves need to be adjusted, that's what will be done—even if the problem is simply a loose wire. So don't tell your mechanic what's wrong; tell the mechanic the car's specific symptoms.

How can you clearly describe the symptoms?

➤ Describe what the problem looks, sounds, or feels like:

The muffler looks like it's red hot.

The engine sounds like marbles are rolling around inside.

The air from the heater feels moist.

➤ Describe where in the car the problem occurs:

The glow looks like it's emanating from behind the glove compartment.

The noise sounds like it's coming from the area around the right-rear wheel.

The wobble feels like it's in the rear half of the car.

There's a scream from the back seat every time I go over a speed bump at 50 miles an hour.

➤ Describe when the problem happens:

The front-left tire is low after it's parked overnight.

The car feels like it pulls to the right when I step hard on the brakes.

The engine sounds rough when I drive it at over 120 mph.

How to Listen When Your Car Talks

So what kinds of noises might you hear as you merrily roll along?

➤ Clicking

➤ Squealing

➤ Growling

➤ Whistling

➤ Thumping

➤ Humming

➤ Chirping

➤ Rattling

➤ Knocking

Knowing the type, location, and time of the sound often can help you pinpoint the problem. A growling sound from below the middle of the back seat when the car is moving is probably caused by a problem in the differential (on a rear-wheel-drive car), for example. If you hear a sound from the engine when accelerating that sounds like a bunch of marbles banging around, the problem is probably pre-ignition caused by low octane fuel or incorrect engine timing. A siren from behind accompanied by flashing lights might mean you were driving too fast.

Knowing what you now know about cars, you might be able to identify the source of the problem. If not, you can save money by accurately describing the sound, its source, and when you hear it to your mechanic.

How about smells? What kinds of unusual odors emanate from a vehicle that operates on gas?

➤ Burning oil

➤ Burning plastic

➤ Burning fabric

➤ Burning putridity

The smell of burning oil can be something as simple as oil spilled on the engine's exhaust manifold or as serious as engine piston rings failing. The smell of burning plastic can mean a problem with the electrical wiring or interior parts. Smells like burning day at the city dump are either that or the catalytic converter failing. A smell like a dirty diaper probably means the baby in the back seat needs a rest stop.

To troubleshoot smells, first stop the car as soon as safely possible, and then turn off the ignition. Get out and walk around the car, sniffing to identify the location of the odor. After you identify the odor, you can decide whether it's safe to go on or whether you should call for a tow truck.

Your sense of touch can also play a part in trouble-shooting. Descriptive terms follow:

➤ As hot as a radiator cap

➤ Colder than it usually is

➤ Mushy, not firm like normal

➤ Very smooth or very rough

➤ As hard as the proverbial rock

Hot or cold, soft or hard—you've determined that its touch is not normal. That's a start toward troubleshooting.

Money Saver

Do you still like to play doctor? You can listen to your car using a homemade stethoscope. Attach a piece of rubber vacuum hose to the end of a metal rod. Holding the rubber end to your ear, carefully place the metal tip against the running engine until you've identified the noise's source. Don't touch electrical wires, hot parts, or fan blades. Your car's service manual can also help you identify the culprit.

If Your Car Is in a Coma

So how can you troubleshoot a car that isn't running? There's nothing abnormal to see, smell, or touch. About all you can do is review what happened just before it stopped. An older car may show no symptoms of problems, but then stop running a week after a tune-up, for example. Knowing this, troubleshooting could lead to the distributor, where you discover that the wire on the new condenser had vibrated loose. No spark = no go.

Most car parts that fail don't just give up the ghost at a young age. They fail due to abuse or neglect. Reviewing the last few days or weeks of driving may offer a number of ideas on why your car quit. You might ignore a clunking sound in the engine, for example, until one day, both the engine and the car quit. A leaking battery may not be immediately discovered and cleaned up, and acid can eat through some wiring. A transmission that refuses to go into gear could have been acting up for a month.

Handwriting on the wall—but you're learning to interpret that handwriting and understand what to do about it.

Do Idiot Lights Have an IQ?

A *gauge* measures and numerically reports the status of something. Coolant temperature is 175°. Oil pressure is 40 psi. The speedometer is broken, officer.

A warning light gives you a yes or no answer. Coolant temperature okay? Off is yes and on is no. Oil pressure okay? Off is yes and on is no. Driving under the speed limit? Flashing light off is yes and on is no.

How can you be sure your car's gauges are telling you the truth? Experience. Yes, you can test them, but driving your car gives you the experience to know which readings are normal and which aren't. Gauges report trends.

How can you be sure your car's warning lights are equally honest? Warning lights report status. You can make sure your warning lights work by watching the dashboard as you turn on the ignition. Most modern cars light all warning devices then to let you know that the bulbs work. Your car's owner's manual will tell you what the lights mean and whether they are tested as the ignition switch is moved.

Hold on. There is a point to this. The point is this: Whether you are dealing with gauges or lights, learn to read them. Make a habit of scanning your car's dashboard on a regular basis. When starting your car, turn the ignition switch to the on position and watch the gauges and/or lights. With gauges, know what's normal. If necessary, apply a piece of tape on gauges to clearly identify normal operating ranges (some gauges are as useless as warning lights).

Troubleshooting by the Book

The lone figure in this chapter provides a useful troubleshooting guide to help you find later chapters in this book to help you solve common automotive problems (or at least to help diagnose what's going on). Begin in the upper left-hand corner of the flowchart and answer the questions down the left-hand side. When you get to a question you answer "no" to, look to the right to learn which chapter in this book offers more information about your car's problems. If your car doesn't start okay, read Chapter 18, "Starting and Ignition System Repairs for the Clueless," for troubleshooting tips and repair techniques. If your car starts okay, runs okay, but doesn't shift okay, look to Chapter 22, "Transmission Repairs: Those Troublesome Trannys," for help.

For precise help, most service manuals include a troubleshooting guide that covers a specific make and model of car. Not only are such guides more accurate to your car's symptoms, but they typically cross-reference the solution.

Troubleshooting Guide

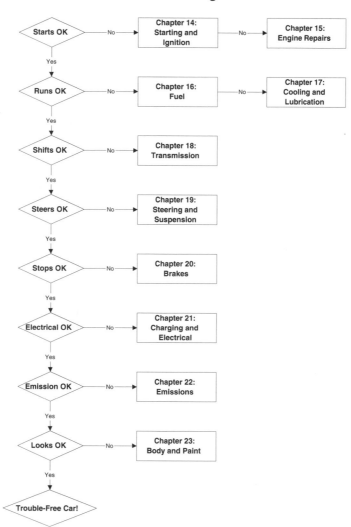

145

Ya Gonna Fix It or Pass the Buck?

Okay, you've identified the problem. Is the solution to replace a part or to repair it? With all the firmness I can muster, I respond: That depends. Read on.

Repairing many car components requires tools you probably don't have or want. Why buy a $2,000 tool to fix a $50 part? Okay, maybe you won Lotto America! Otherwise, don't bother. The total cost of starter parts, for example, is greater than the cost of a rebuilt starter—as long as you give them your old starter in exchange so that it can be rebuilt. The same goes for engines, transmissions, and many other parts: Buy and replace them as a unit, making sure the new parts are the same model numbers as the old ones.

An exception is any part that is difficult to replace. Just try to find a generator for a 1956 Continental Mark II! In such cases, take the old part to a specialized repair shop and give them joint custody of your wallet.

How long will the repair take? Chapter 7, "Finding a Good Mechanic: Who Can You Trust with Your Car?" introduced you to the flat-rate manual. Available through larger libraries, a *flat-rate manual* estimates the amount of time required by a trained mechanic to perform defined jobs on specific cars. By doubling the time, you can probably estimate how long it will take an untrained owner to do the same job—maybe more, maybe less.

The Least You Need to Know

➤ A simple diagnostics test can help you define your car's problem.

➤ Troubleshooting charts are useful for translating symptoms into solutions.

➤ Sometimes the solution is to *not* fix a problem or to pay someone else to do it.

Chapter 16

Non-Nerd's Guide to Understanding Your Car's Computer

> **In This Chapter**
>
> ➤ How your car's computer works
>
> ➤ Sensors and actuators do the real work
>
> ➤ The ECM does the thinking
>
> ➤ You can actually troubleshoot your car with its computer

Cars have changed dramatically over the past few decades. For example, my 1956 Continental has no computer, no transistors, no electronic control module. It's electronically naked! But my 1995 Honda probably has more computing power than the original, room-filling ENIAC computer of the 1950s. It's wired!

The good news is that computers do a lot to help your car run smoother and more efficiently. The bad news is that if the computer fails, most car owners haven't a clue what to do about it. The other good news is that *you* can outsmart your car's computer.

No, you're not going to be able to plug your kid's computer into the car's wiring maze and quickly diagnose the problem. However, understanding how the computer on your car works can help you figure out where to start—or at least who to ask.

It may simply be out of fuel!

Who's in Control Here?

Okay, so what are we dealing with? A computer is simply a machine. It computes. On or off? It just does it so fast that it can check the condition of millions of things before you finish this sentence.

Computers are found throughout modern cars. They check fuel, spark, heat, speed, emissions, electrical signals, internal engine parts, and much more. Most of what car computers do is control the fuel and ignition systems. You've already learned about these systems, and coming chapters will offer specific information on repairing these systems. So for now, let's consider how to use your car's computer to troubleshoot.

Computer control systems have only three stages: input, processing, and output. That's simple enough. Input checks to see how a part is doing, processing compares it against what it should be doing, and output makes any needed changes.

For example, the temperature of coolant is checked and compared against what engineers have told the computer it should be. Then an adjustment is made to the flow of coolant to correct the temperature. The same is true for engine speed, manifold heat, exhaust emissions, and bunches of other systems throughout your car: test, verify, correct.

Did You Know?

The idea for the computer has been around for a few hundred years. It was the need to calculate trajectories. The invention of solid-state electronics after World War II finally made computers both practical and achievable.

The boss is the Electronic Control Module, or ECM. (Some folks call it an Electronic Control Unit or ECU just to be contrary.) It knows what conditions should be, and it's what can tell you—or your mechanic—if things aren't going well.

Getting a Sense of Things Automotive

So what does the testing? Sensors.

Sensors monitor the various conditions throughout your car. They check temperature, electricity, heat, movement, and other physical things. Sensors then turn that information into an electrical signal that is sent back to the ECM.

Let's get more specific.

An oxygen (O_2) sensor tests the oxygen level in the engine's exhaust gasses. It then turns this information into an electrical signal and sends it to the ECM: "Yeah, things are fine here. How's by you?"

Now, sensors don't work all the time. They are off when your car isn't running, of course, but they may also be off until certain things happen. For example, the oxygen sensor might be programmed to not wake up until the exhaust temperature reaches 600° Fahrenheit. A temperature sensor says, "Hey, wake up!" and the oxygen sensor grabs its lunch-pail (just kidding!) and goes to work testing the oxygen.

Remember this: Until the sensor goes to work, the circuit is considered "open," and once it starts working, the circuit is "closed." Think of the circuit as a loop that must be closed to work.

There are many other types of sensors that live peacefully in your car. An engine speed sensor sends information about engine speed (revolutions per minute, or rpm) to the ECM. Smart ones even tell the ECM the position of the individual pistons and the crankshaft! Pretty smart, eh?

A vehicle speed sensor does just that: measures the speed of the car. It senses the rotations of the car's transmission parts and does some quick calculating to tell you the speed in miles per hour (mph).

A knock or detonation sensor measures abnormal engine vibrations caused by advanced ignition timing. The signal is used to retard the timing and correct the condition.

Some sensors in your car aren't as smart. The only answers they can send back to the ECM are yes or no. But they, too, serve. Common passive sensors measure the coolant temperature, engine air flow, manifold air temperature, and throttle position sensor.

In addition, there are numerous switching sensors throughout your car. Is the door open or closed? Is the transmission in reverse or not? Et cetera.

In days of yore, all the wires for these sensors made the car's engine compartment and dashboard look like electric spaghetti. Fortunately, automotive designers have since figured out a way of carrying most of these sensing signals over just one or two wires.

"Okay, let's now go live to the radiator where the coolant sensor is standing by. How's it goin', Carl?"

"Things are fine here, Bob."

"Glad to hear it. Let's switch to a report from Mary at the manifold. Come in, Mary."

"Well, temperature has risen two degrees since my last report, Bob, but we're still okay."

"Thank you, Mary. Now..."

You get the idea: A single wire can carry many sensor reports. This is called (as it is in radio broadcasting) *multiplexing*, or *MUX*.

How does all this info get from the radiator, manifold, and other places to the control center? By bus! The wire with all these reports is the *data bus*. Each sensor gets a specific amount of time, and in a particular order, to make his/her/its report. Electronic signals move so fast that many hundreds of reports can be made in a second.

Some cars use fiber optics rather than copper wires to carry all these sensor reports. Fiber optics eliminate interference from other electrical devices.

The Boss: ECM

The electronic control module, or ECM, is where all the decisions are made. That's why it's a good idea to know how it works and what to do if it doesn't. No, you won't be able to fix it yourself, but you will be able to help your mechanic maintain honesty.

"We'll have to replace the ECM so I'll need a co-signer."

"Before you do that, Mr. Mechanic, show me a test of all the sensors so we can rule them out as the problem."

"I, er, uh…"

The ECM has five easy-to-understand sections:

➤ The *input section* converts the sensor's signals to a form the computer can use.

➤ The *memory section* stores data until it is needed by the computer.

➤ The *logic section* does the arithmetic calculations ("Let's see, where'd I put that formula?").

➤ The *control section* manages everything.

➤ The *output section* converts the computer's output signal to a form that the control section can use to do the job.

That's pretty well it.

The ECM remembers what sensors tell it as well as what the car's designer taught it at ECM school. Think of it as short-term and long-term memory. What's really cool about today's cars is that the long-term memory (PROM or EPROM, for you acronym nuts) can be changed after the car has left the factory. In fact, you can have your car's ECM reprogrammed to have more power or more efficiency. Some restrictions apply. Void where prohibited.

The Slaves: Actuators as Employees

We've been introduced to the tattlers (sensors) and the boss (ECM), but who does all the work? It's the slaves, the actuators. An *actuator* simply converts the electrical signal from the ECM to physical movement.

Typical movement includes opening, closing, pushing, or pulling. For example, a fuel injector is an actuator that opens up to allow the fuel into the throttle body or cylinders.

If the car has a carburetor, a mixture control solenoid adds air as needed to make the optimum fuel-air mixture.

In some cases, the car needs to recycle exhaust gases for cleaner burning of the fuel. The exhaust gas recirculation (EGR) valve opens and closes as mandated by the ECM.

There are other actuators throughout the modern car. In all cases, they convert an electronic signal into work. Some of them use vacuum power to move things. Others, like the electric fan relay, pass along a signal to another part that does the actual work.

Shooting Trouble

So today's computerized car is really quite simple in principle. Sensors check things, the ECM makes a decision based on what it knows should happen, and actuators make it happen.

Did You Know?

The story is told that Bill Gates, president of Microsoft, compared the computer industry with the auto industry, saying "If General Motors had kept up with technology like the computer industry has, we would all be driving $25 cars that got 1,000 miles to the gallon of gas."

In response, General Motors reportedly issued a press release that said if GM had developed technology like Microsoft, we would all be driving cars with these characteristics:

➤ For unknown reasons, would crash twice a day.

➤ Each time GM introduced a new model, car buyers must learn how to drive all over again because none of the controls would operate in the same manner as those on the old car.

➤ Occasionally, executing a maneuver such as a left turn would cause your car to shut down and refuse to restart, in which case you would have to reinstall the engine.

➤ The airbag system would say "Are you sure?" before deploying.

But what can you do if things don't work as they should? What can the car's owner do without a gazillion gadgets to test the computer?

Lots!

First, the service manual for your car will probably tell you many things. It will probably give you a logic diagram to follow for figuring out who the culprit might be.

Using this, you might decide that the problem is in the idle speed motor. Tightening a loose connection or a gentle whack to the unit may fix it, or you might decide to go ahead and replace it.

Sometimes you don't even know there's a problem until a dashboard light goes on: Check Engine. What's happened is that the ECM saw a problem it couldn't fix. It sent a message, called a *trouble code*, to its memory. If you had one of those new-fangled diagnostic tools, you'd be able to find out what the code is. The car's service manual would then tell you what the code means.

So where can you get one of these handy-dandy diagnostic checkers? Many large auto parts stores carry a consumer version that interprets the less obscure codes for you. The checkers aren't cheap, but they can save you money. Make sure the one you buy reads and interprets the codes for your make and model of car. It can't fix your car, but it can translate what the ECM wants to tell you.

Also, some cars have a self-diagnostic system that you can use. For example, your car's service manual may have you turn the ignition switch on and off a set number of times within five seconds to release the code. Really! The trouble code could be communicated by a specific number of flashes of a warning light or a digital dash readout. Trouble code 4, for example, might produce four flashes or display a digital "4" on the dash.

I'm not making this up.

You then refer to the service manual to learn what trouble code 4 means. Digital displays, obviously, are the easiest to decipher. A trouble code 17 may mean that the engine coolant temperature remains below normal operating temperature. A display of "17" is easier to recognize than 17 flashes of a warning light!

Fixing Things Without Going Broke

After you know where the problem is, you can begin trying to solve it. Here's a tip: Most mechanics don't spend a $50-an-hour hour trying to fix a $20 part. You shouldn't either. Call your favorite auto parts store to find out what the replacement part costs before deciding whether you should try to repair it yourself.

Of course, some parts are beyond repair. They are built to be disposable and really don't make it easy to fix them.

You can test some electrical devices using a volt-ohmmeter (VOM) purchased from an auto parts or hardware store for less than $20. The car's service manual may even tell you what the part's reading should be, or it will tell you, as in the case of oxygen sensors, to *not* test it with an ohmmeter.

In some cases, the solution is obvious: Reinstall a loose wire, wipe the gunk off the contact, push the sensor back into the hole, wipe the unit with solvent, or whatever. These things you can do. It's especially satisfying when you think that your mechanic would have charged you 75 bucks to reconnect a loose vacuum hose.

Moving On with Your Life

If you've learned something about your car as you poked among the wires and counted flashing lights, write it down. Make notes in the car's service manual, owner's manual, or even in this book. Draw a diagram, scribble comments, note the part number of the replacement, write an obscene note to the manufacturer. Then next week or next year you'll have a reference point from which you can troubleshoot your car's fun-loving computer system.

The Least You Need to Know

➤ Car computer sensors continually check the condition of components (for alliteration).

➤ The electronic control module (ECM) is the brains of your car's computer system.

➤ Actuators do the work, opening and closing as needed to allow the passage of fuel, air, water, or electric signals.

➤ Many modern cars have self-diagnostic systems that can be interpreted with your car's service manual.

Chapter 17

Do-It-Yourself Repair Without Major Medical

In This Chapter

➤ How to reduce repair costs by doing it yourself

➤ Finding the right tools for the job

➤ Repairing your car safely

The tool's the thing.

The correct tool can save you many hours of work and many dollars of mechanics' labor charges. The wrong tool can help you create a sailor's vocabulary and test your major medical plan.

Chapter 6, "Do-It-Yourself Maintenance, or Getting Your Hands Dirty," guided you through the toolbox looking for items you needed for maintaining your car: wrenches, sockets, screwdrivers, and lubrication tools. Fortunately for you, they are some of the same tools you use for repairing your car.

But there's more—and yes, these tools will cost you some bucks to buy or rent. Consider it an investment. Buying the right tool can not only save you money, it can keep you from getting hurt.

Let's get started revamping your toolbox.

Tap! Tap!

So what's a tap and why might you need one? If you're a klutz like me, you'll probably ruin a perfectly good bolt hole by stripping the threads. Yes, it happens, and the best way to fix the threads is to use a tap.

My Mechanic Says. . .

One of the most useful tools I have in my toolbox is one a son gave me for Christmas one year (with some hints, of course). It's a lighted mirror probe. A 1 × 2-inch mirror is at the end of the handle. Rotating a small wheel on the handle moves the mirror. Pushing a button turns on a tiny light that reflects against the mirror. So? I can insert the probe under my car's dashboard (or underneath the car), turn on the light, adjust the mirror, and see things like loose wires, lost parts, and other useful stuff. It's less than 20 bucks and makes a great gift!

A metal tap looks like a boltshaft with threads on it. Fortunately, it's made of much stronger metal that a bolt or the metal the bolt went into. By carefully threading a tap into the hole, you are recutting the threads.

Of course, make sure the tap you use is the correct one for the hole. There are different widths, threads, and chamfer. Some taper toward the end and others don't. Instead of getting into a diatribe about short chamfer bottoming plugs and other boring stuff, here's the rule: Buy what you need and when you need it.

If you have a big repair job coming up and you have some bucks you want to invest in tools, go ahead and buy a set of quality taps. Otherwise, wait until you really need a tap, and then talk with your friendly auto parts person about what you need for the job.

What kind of taps should you buy? The options are, as with other tools, standard or metric. Standard tools are measured in inches and metric tools are measured in, well, metrics.

But there's more. The threads are either coarse or fine, depending on how many there are to the inch or other measurement. UNC stands for Unified National Coarse and UNF means Unified National Fine. UNC used to be called U.S. Standard and UNF was SAE, if that helps.

So what can you do if the threads on the bolt hole are fine but those on the bolt are damaged? First, of course, find a replacement for the bolt. But if you cannot or it really isn't a bolt but some convoluted object to which you could never find a sister, *die* it!

A die is used for cutting external threads on bolts and screws. A die looks like a big, thick washer with a threaded hole in the middle. As you might imagine, the bolt is placed in the hole and either the die or the bolt are turned to cut the new thread. So you want to make sure the die is the correct one for the bolt: metric or inch, coarse or fine.

One more thing about having a quality tap and die set: it looks great in your toolbox. Tim "The Tool Man" Taylor has one! (with a 400 hp hemi-block and dual quads!)

Pull!

Some car parts are attached with pressure—lots of pressure. For example, a gear is placed on the end of a shaft and then pressed into place. Pressed-on parts include gears, pulleys, bearings, axles, shafts, rings, and sleeves—parts you'll meet in coming chapters.

So how can you get these parts off? Certainly not with a screwdriver and hammer! You've probably guessed that there are special tools, called *pullers*, that can do the job.

There are two types of pullers: manual and hydraulic. Manual pullers can tackle most jobs and are less expensive, so that's what do-it-yourselfers typically buy and use. Hydraulic pullers can be rented as needed for special jobs.

In fact, you can probably rent rather than buy a set of manual pullers at a nearby rental store. It's the cheaper way to go, unless you're rebuilding your car's engine and transmission.

Where do pullers come in handy?

➤ Removing a transfer case

➤ Removing an axle

➤ Pulling a bearing

➤ Removing a gear from a shaft

➤ Removing a steering wheel from a steering shaft

Money Saver

Some auto parts stores have professional mechanics tools that they will rent or loan if you buy auto parts from them. Ask!

Your car's service manual can tell you which puller is needed for the job and when it's needed.

A caution: Puller sets have dozens of Rube-Goldberg–looking parts. Jaws, claws, bolts, disks, shafts, and thingamarammers. The point is that, without a diagram and instructions, pullers are difficult to assemble and safely use. Buy or rent only pullers that include illustrated instructions. Using an incorrectly assembled puller can be dangerous to your health.

Let's Get Precise

Infernal combustion engines are actually precision machines. They run like a Swiss watch. Tolerances (fit) between parts are exact. That's why today's engines run 100,000 miles or more before major work is needed. With smart car care, they can run even longer.

But what if they quit running or start making clanky noises when they run? Or what if the brake disks wear down? And what if you decide you want to make the repairs yourself (or know what the mechanic is talking about when he mentions "inside mike")?

You already know about measurement tools such as rulers and gauges, but many parts must be measured even more accurately than, say, $1/8$ inch. There are other parts—bolts and shafts, for example—that are difficult to measure with a straight-edge ruler.

So, for your amazement and amusement, here are some useful tools and equipment for precise measurement of your car's innards. They include outside micrometer, inside micrometer, digital micrometer, depth gauge, calipers, dividers, and other gauges.

157

Hello, Mike!

A micrometer or mic (or mike) measures a part at the outside edges (outside micrometer), inside edges (inside micrometer), or depth (depth gauge).

For example, you've removed the pistons from your car's engine and want to know how much wear there is. You use an outside mike to measure the distance between the outside edges. You then compare that number to the original dimension found in the car's service manual. The difference is the amount of wear, such as 0.010", or 10 thousandths of an inch.

You then want to measure the wear of the cylinder the piston came from. You use an inside mike to measure the distance between the inside edges of the cylinder. You can also measure the distance at various points around the cylinder to make sure wear is even.

So how do you read a micrometer? An outside mike is used by placing the part between the mike's inside edges (the anvil and the spindle), and then turning the thimble (corrugated surface) until the part edges are touched. Read the numbers on the sleeve. On some units, "1" means 100-thousands of an inch (0.100"), for example. Add this number to the minimum range of the micrometer, such as 2 inches for a 2- to 3-inch micrometer. (Make sure you get a set of instructions with the micrometer you buy or rent.)

An inside mike is used similarly except that it measures the distance between inside surfaces.

Fortunately, for those of us who hate trying to do the math or see those tiny numbers, there are digital micrometers. As you might expect, a digital mike works about the same way as a mechanical one, except you don't have to read the fine print.

As with other measurement tools, micrometers come in two flavors: inches and metrics. Make sure you get the correct one for your car. If the car's spec book gives dimensions in inches, use the inches mike. If in metrics, get metric.

For the final word in measurements, a vernier micrometer can help you determine the width of a hair, if so required. It measures to one ten-thousandths of an inch (0.0001").

Accurate readings are critical, so make sure you know how to read and interpret your micrometer before buying new parts based on mic measurements.

How Deep Is My Love? Get a Micrometer!

There's also a thing called a depth micrometer or micrometer depth gauge. It can measure to 0.001" and is usually used to measure valve lift, cylinder taper, camshaft end play, and other fun stuff. It works something like an outside micrometer, but without the horseshoe-shaped anvil.

Fortunately for us trifocal folks, depth mikes also come in a digital-readout version.

As with other expensive measuring tools, make your decision to buy or rent based on how much you can save now and in the future. For a small, one-time job, it may be smarter to rent a set of mics. But if you have a couple of clunkers to fix, you might want to buy it once. Be careful, however, of so-called combination mics. They are typically not as accurate as individual mics. The comparison is like that between a standard wrench and an adjustable wrench. Adjustable wrenches shouldn't be used for precise work, but they can be handy for less-critical jobs.

Calipers, and Rules, and Gauges—Oh My!

There are many other types of measurement tools available to the do-it-yourselfer. They include calipers, dividers, gauges, rules, scales, and other more-than-fun stuff. Learning about them does two things:

➤ Expands your knowledge of automotive tools and, thus, your cerebrum.

➤ Puts off the moment when you'll have to use them.

A caliper is a poor person's micrometer. It costs less than a micrometer and it isn't as accurate. However, for many jobs, such as measuring brake wear, it's close enough.

As you might expect, an outside caliper measures the outside diameter of objects and an inside caliper measures the inside. An outside caliper looks something like the tongs the ice man used to deliver blocks of ice—but I date myself by that analogy.

There are also depth calipers that work about the same way to measure the depth of a hole.

Outside, inside, and depth calipers are adjusted by a knob on the side. You simply turn the knob until the caliper points touch the object edges, and then read the number on the knob's shaft.

Dial calipers are cool, too, because they can measure the outside or inside diameter of objects with numbers on a dial or digital readout. Some can also measure depths. In fact, they are a best-buy in the automotive measurement tool world. If this is your choice, get the most accurate digital multi-caliper you can afford.

So what other measurement tools can you buy for your toolbox?

Thickness gauges (also called *feeler gauges*) are strips of hardened metal of a specific thickness. Each strip is marked in thousands of an inch or millimeters (and sometimes both). You use a feeler gauge to check the gap on spark plugs or piston rings. Some thickness gauges use wire rather than metal strips.

A steel rule is handy for measurements that don't have to be within thousandths of an inch. You can use a steel rule or a steel tape measure to measure the length of a bolt or the distance between two parts. They are not expensive, so consider getting assorted lengths.

Some quality steel rules can also serve as a precision straight edge. You can check to see if an engine head or a flywheel is warped by laying a precision straight edge across it and looking for high or low spots.

A compression gauge measures the pressure developed in an engine cylinder. A vacuum gauge measures vacuum produced by the engine intake manifold. An oil pressure tester measures what you might expect: engine oil pressure. A fuel pressure tester measures pressure in the fuel pump.

And there are electrical testers that measure resistance, volts, amps, or all of the above.

Whether you buy any of these gauges or testers depends on the complexity of the repair job. If you're simply tuning up your car, an oil pressure tester isn't needed. If you are rebuilding the engine, however, both a compression and vacuum gauge are pretty important. The manufacturer's instructions for each of these measurement tools show you exactly how to use them.

Avoiding Ouchies!

We've all heard horror stories about the guy who was crushed while working on his car. I think the story is perpetuated by mechanics who need more work. Yes, it can happen. You can be injured while working on your car. You can also be injured while driving your car, but that doesn't stop you from doing so. You just make sure you're as safe as possible.

Did You Know?

Most injuries that occur while working on a car are the result of not using the correct tool.

Here are some common-sense rules for safely working on and around your car:

➤ **Cars roll.** When you work on your car, make sure the parking brake is set. If it isn't reliable or if you'd rather be safe than sorry, wedge a rock or piece of wood in front of and behind one tire. Test it by pushing on one or both ends of the car to verify that it doesn't move.

➤ **What goes up must come down.** If you use a jack or other device to lift your car off the ground, place something under the car to ensure that it will not fall from its perch. The best device for this is a set of two car stands, purchased at an auto parts retailer for about $25. Buy ones that are rated high enough to safely hold your car. Follow directions on the box. Of course, make sure the jack you're using is placed on a flat and firm surface. If you can't, don't!

➤ **Avoid accidental charges.** Your car's battery uses the chemistry of lead and acid to store electrical energy. Older batteries had caps that could be removed, which enabled you to let the acid out. Today's maintenance-free batteries are sealed. Even so, they can develop a leak or vent gases that can explode. This isn't meant to scare you, but to help you develop a healthy respect for the power of your car's battery. Wear eye protection *and rubber gloves* when working around a battery. Respect the electrical current the battery stores. If it can start your car's engine, it can speed up your heart.

➤ **Coils (even those not on snakes) are dangerous.** The battery furnishes 12 volts of electrical power, but your car needs higher voltage to produce sparks in the engine. The coil converts low voltage to high voltage—as much as 50,000 volts! Be careful when working around coils and spark plug wires when the ignition is activated.

➤ **Electronics have feelings, too.** Sensitive automotive computers operate on just a few volts of electricity. Some use less than one volt. So if they come into contact with 12 volts from the car battery, they can be damaged. In Chapter 18, "Starting and Ignition System Repairs for the Clueless," you'll learn how to jump-start your car to minimize potential damage to your car's electronics and yourself.

Safety First

Don't forget to wear safety goggles or safety glasses when working with any moving part or powered tool.

➤ **Make sure gas burns only inside the engine.** Inside your engine, gas and air combine with a spark to make an explosion. Outside your engine, the same thing can happen. Make sure you store fuels in an enclosed container. Oily or fuel-soaked rags must be stored in vented, enclosed containers. *Also, make sure you work in a well-ventilated area.*

➤ **Don't let the engine bite you.** A running engine has belts and blades and other moving parts that can grab you or clothing you're wearing. The best rule is not to work on a running engine. If you must, identify hot surfaces and moving parts—and stay the heck away from them. Don't wear loose sleeves or a scarf or tie that could get caught easily by a fast moving fan or belt. Also, don't work on a running engine inside a building because carbon monoxide gas can literally take your breath away. If you think mechanics are expensive, wait 'til you get the doctor's bill!

The Least You Need to Know

➤ Repairing your car requires more tools than you may have, but you can buy or rent them as needed.

➤ Look for quality all-in-one tools that will do many tasks safely and accurately.

➤ Work safely!

Starting and Ignition System Repairs for the Clueless

The starting and ignition systems are vital to your car. They both require electricity to operate. The ignition system is your car's heartbeat. The starting system, then, must be the first cup of coffee in the morning. And we all know what some people are like if they don't get their coffee fix!

This chapter guides you through common repairs to starting and ignition systems. Reading over the instructions can help you decide whether you want to tackle the project yourself or hire someone to do it. Remember that although you don't know as much about your car as a trained mechanic, you have a greater need to make sure the job is done right and at a reasonable cost.

The repair procedures in this chapter are typical for most modern cars. Refer to the manufacturer's manual or an aftermarket service manual for specific instructions and details for your car.

An automotive starting system.

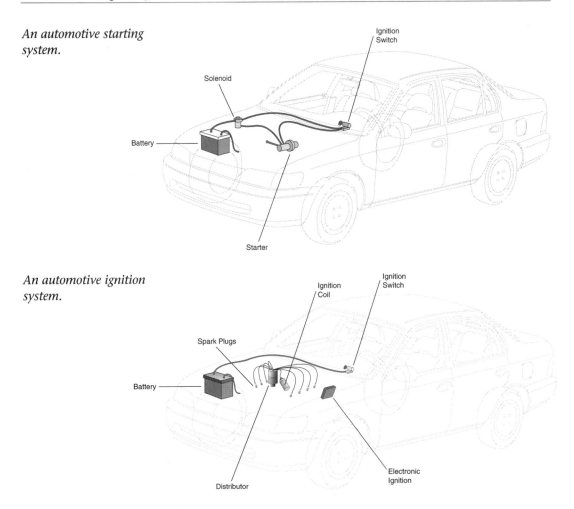

An automotive ignition system.

You Can't Get 'Em Up in the Morning

Here's where the job of the starting system is like the task of your first cup of coffee. The starting system turns the engine quickly enough to enable it to start—at least, that's what it does when it operates properly. Components of the starting system include the battery, the starter motor, the starter solenoid, and all the wires that connect these parts.

How does the starter system work? As you turn the ignition key to the start position, an electric signal runs along the wire to the starter solenoid. The solenoid is told to deliver electricity from the battery to the starter motor. It does so until the ignition key is released from the start position. The end of the starter motor has a small gear that meshes with the teeth around the edge of the engine flywheel. The gear rotates the flywheel. At the same time, the ignition system is delivering a spark and the fuel system is supplying a fuel/air mixture to the engine. The engine starts...in theory, and if everything is in good working condition.

If the engine doesn't start, the cause could be one of many things, including the starter or solenoid. Before you consider repairing the starter, however, check one more thing: the interlock. An interlock stops something from happening if all conditions are not met. Most cars now have an interlock that must be operated before the signal to start is sent to the solenoid. The interlock on cars with manual transmissions requires that the clutch pedal be pushed in before the car is allowed to start. On automatic transmissions, the interlock requires that the gear selector be in the park or neutral position.

So, before you begin to repair your car's starter or solenoid, find and test the interlock, fuses, and battery. *Finding* the interlock may be the operative term here because some are mounted near the clutch pedal, and others are in the steering column or mounted near the starter. Testing an interlock means using an ohmmeter to see whether the circuit is open or closed (read the ohmmeter's instructions) when it's activated.

One more tip before we (that's like the nurse asking how we feel today) get our hands dirty: Have someone turn the ignition key to the start position. If, standing near the engine, you hear the solenoid click, it's working. If you don't, it's not working, assuming that you've already checked the battery and any starter system fuses.

A starter motor should give your car 75,000 to 100,000 miles of trouble-free service—and more with proper maintenance.

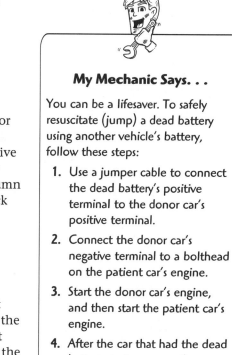

My Mechanic Says. . .

You can be a lifesaver. To safely resuscitate (jump) a dead battery using another vehicle's battery, follow these steps:

1. Use a jumper cable to connect the dead battery's positive terminal to the donor car's positive terminal.

2. Connect the donor car's negative terminal to a bolthead on the patient car's engine.

3. Start the donor car's engine, and then start the patient car's engine.

4. After the car that had the dead battery starts, remove the jumper cable in the reverse order of how it was installed.

When Your Car Won't Wake Up: Troubleshooting Electrical Problems

Here are some guidelines for troubleshooting starting and ignition systems:

➤ Make sure the automatic transmission is in the correct gear or that the clutch on a manual transmission is fully depressed (or at least morose).

➤ If your car won't even make a noise when you try to start it, first check the battery terminal connections. Then look for other loose connections in the starting and ignition systems.

My Mechanic Says. . .

Before disconnecting the battery cables on cars with alarm systems, make sure you have the manufacturer's code. Otherwise, your alarm system or radio won't work after you've reconnected the battery. If you don't know the code, your dealership should be able to help get it.

Car Speak

Your car's *starter* is a wondrous invention that operates without caffeine; it's an electric motor that engages, spins, and disengages the engine's flywheel to start the engine.

➤ If your car won't start, causes may be a discharged battery, loose or broken wires, a faulty starter or solenoid, or a faulty ignition switch or neutral interlock, mentioned earlier in this chapter.

➤ Dirty battery connections can cause fuel-injection systems to hesitate or surge. Keep those connections clean!

What tools will you need for repairs in this chapter? The car care toolbox described in Chapter 6, "Do-It-Yourself Maintenance, or Getting Your Hands Dirty," will have most of the necessary tools. I'll mention any special tools as we go along.

Using Caffeinated Coffee: Replacing Your Car's Starter

To replace the starter motor and/or starter solenoid, follow these steps:

1. Remove the negative or ground cable from the battery (see Chapter 9, "CAR Quarterly Check Up," for tips on identifying cables).

2. Find the starter. No, it doesn't look like a coffee cup. It's a round motor about three inches across located at one side or the other of the flywheel. The flywheel is located between the engine and transmission. The solenoid is probably mounted on the side of the starter. If not, trace the wire to the solenoid, which is probably mounted nearby on the firewall.

3. Disconnect the battery cable and any other wires to the starter or solenoid.

4. Remove the starter and solenoid. This usually means removing two bolts that mount the starter on the side of the engine or the *bellhousing* (clutch cover). The starter weighs a few pounds, so be careful not to drop it when the last bolt is loosened. If the solenoid is not attached to the starter, remove it from the firewall.

5. Repair or replace the starter and solenoid. Unless you have the equipment and knowledge to repair or rebuild a starter (it's a specialty, so I'm assuming you don't), buy a replacement at an auto parts store or automotive electrical shop. A helpful counterperson at either place should be able to test your starter and solenoid before you buy a replacement.

6. Reinstall the starter and solenoid. Tighten and check all connections before trying to use the starter.

Diagnosing and Treating Ignition Ills

An automotive ignition system has a pretty simple job: to supply a spark to the engine at the time it's most needed. To do so on today's fuel-efficient cars requires nothing short of a computer, however. That's why cars have become so difficult for the owner to repair. Fortunately, the technology has stabilized somewhat and the newest cars at least have some logic to them.

In addition, cars are using more modularized systems. No one, not even mechanics, repairs ignition systems. They replace components that test bad. So can you. Using a simple volt-ohmmeter (VOM) and the car's service manual, you can probably track down and solve many ignition system problems, saving yourself many dollars.

As you learned in Chapter 1, "How Cars Run: What Makes Them Go?" high-voltage electricity comes from the *ignition coil*, and is passed to the appropriate cylinder by the distributor. All distributors, in both older and newer cars, are driven by the engine's camshaft. The distributor is advanced or retarded as engine speed changes by electronics (newer cars) or a vacuum/mechanical advance system (older cars). Computerized ignition systems also sense and respond to changes in engine speed, coolant temperature, throttle, vacuum pressure, and, seemingly, the manufacturer's daily stock value.

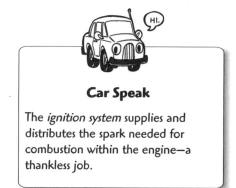

Car Speak

The *ignition system* supplies and distributes the spark needed for combustion within the engine—a thankless job.

Switching Switches

The ignition switch in a car used to be a simple, three-position switch: Off, On, and Start. Today, it's become more complex, as so many other automotive components have. The ignition switch is now linked to sensors, anti-theft devices, interlocks, and the bank where you have your car loan.

Fortunately, failure of an ignition switch typically is traced to a loose wire. That's something you can fix—if you can find it.

To repair an ignition switch and wiring, follow these steps:

1. Find an electrical schematic for your car's ignition system. It's usually printed in the car's service manual or in an aftermarket service manual. If not, you might have to order one through the dealer. The schematic tells you what's in the ignition wiring system, such as interlocks and sensors, besides the switch. It might also identify their locations.

2. Visually trace and inspect the ignition switch and wiring for loose wires, burn marks, or other damage. Reconnect or replace as needed.

3. Use an ohmmeter to test continuity of the ignition switch and wiring. Replace defective parts as needed.

It's Coiled, But Is It Ready to Bite?

The coil converts low voltage (12 volts) from the battery into high voltage (30,000-plus volts). It either works or doesn't. There are two electrical circuits within a coil, and both must work. If they don't, replace the coil as a unit.

To test and replace an ignition coil, follow these steps:

1. Find the coil. On some cars, it's installed in the distributor, which requires you to remove the distributor cap. In other cars, it's mounted on the engine block or on the firewall. Coils located outside the distributor are typically cylindrical, with two small wires and one large one.

2. Use an ohmmeter to test continuity. Your car's service manual identifies the coil's primary and secondary circuits. Measuring continuity across two points in a circuit shows whether the circuit is letting electricity pass through it (a closed circuit) or not (an open circuit). Verify that both coil circuits are not only closed, but also have the resistance (in ohms) recommended by the manufacturer.

3. If the coil is defective, replace it, following instructions in the car's service manual. If not, spend the money on sugar donuts.

Replacing Sensors and Control Modules and Distributors, Oh My!

There are many other electrical components in your car's ignition system: sensors, a control module, and a distributor. Each can be tested using a volt-ohmmeter (VOM) and replaced as needed. It's critical that you compare the test results to those from the car's manufacturer.

To test and replace electronic ignition components, follow these steps:

1. Locate your car's distributor and electronic ignition, also called an ignition control module (ICM). The distributor operates from the camshaft, so it is mounted on the upper half of the engine. The ICM controls the ignition system and is mounted either within the distributor or nearby. Breaker-point ignitions are mechanically rather than electronically controlled.

2. Remove the distributor cap or ICM cover as necessary. Inspect the unit for obvious problems, such as a cracked cap or rotor, loose wires, or debris. Clean or replace as needed.

3. Following manufacturer's recommendations, use an ohmmeter to test continuity for each component. Find and test sensors as well as the ignition control module.

4. If necessary, remove and replace the distributor as a unit. Make sure you note the rotor's exact position so that you can reinstall the new distributor with the rotor in the same position.

5. Carefully document the steps required for easy reference at your next (and last) party.

Car Speak

An automotive ignition system that uses electronic signals to interrupt the electrical voltage within the distributor is called an *electronic ignition*. They are common in cars built since 1976.

The Least You Need to Know

➤ Your car's electrical system can be tested using an inexpensive volt-ohmmeter and some common sense.

➤ Starters and solenoids are simple devices that can be replaced by most folks.

➤ You don't have to be an electronics wizard to replace ignition components.

Chapter 19

Performing Engine Surgery

In This Chapter

➤ Learn to repair an engine head without removing the engine from the car

➤ How engines are overhauled and deciding whether you want to do it or hire someone to do it for you

➤ Understand how the engine's internal organs work—and what to do if they don't

I can't repair my car's engine!

Sure you can!

In fact, engine repair is often easier than other repairs. Why? Because you're working with more information. Service manuals typically include step-by-step instructions, often with photos or drawings, to walk you through every procedure for most engine repairs.

And you're working with physical parts that are easier to find and replace. They're not some micromicrocomponent that requires a microscope to assemble. The functions of these parts are easier for most folks to understand because they follow the laws of physics rather than the black magic of electronics.

Another option you have is to let a pro do some of the engine repair work for you. Many folks take this road. You remove the engine head from the block (sounds gory), and then take the head into an automotive machine shop for work, saving yourself

Car Speak

Internal combustion is the combustion or burning of fuel in an enclosed area, such as an engine's combustion chamber. Spontaneous combustion occurs when you get the repair bill.

some money. Or you remove the engine yourself and then buy and install a replacement ordered from your handy-dandy auto parts store.

Sold yet?

Not yet, eh? Well, even if you decide to have someone else do your car's engine repairs, learning how and why they are done will help you keep the mechanic honest and his or her bill fair.

You like saving money, don't you?

So grab your car care toolbox (see Chapter 6, "Do-It-Yourself Maintenance, or Getting Your Hands Dirty") and let's look busy. I'll let you know if there are any special tools or parts you need.

An engine on a front-wheel-drive car.

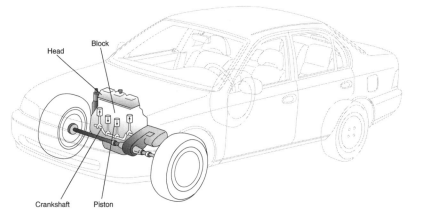

Diagnosing Your Car's Sick Engine

This chapter offers solutions for many common engine ailments, such as:

➤ If your car lacks power, the valves or piston rings could be worn.

➤ If your car uses excessive oil, the piston rings or valve guides could be worn. First, check under the car to see whether oil is leaking and from what. Tightening a bolt or two might solve the problem.

➤ If your car makes a light clicking noise, the valves are probably the culprit.

➤ If your car will start but won't run, the problem could be a loose or broken timing chain.

➤ If you hear sharp metallic knocks when your car is running, the cause could be the bearings at either end of the connecting rods.

➤ If your car swerves all over the place, there's probably a loose nut behind the wheel. It's a joke!

Testing Your Car's Heart Through Compression

How can you learn whether your car's engine is ticking properly? There are many tests you can do yourself. One of the most useful is a compression test.

Pistons move up in the cylinders to compress the fuel/air mixture. A spark ignites the mixture and the resulting explosion pushes the piston down. Rings around the edge of the piston (*piston rings*) keep the mixture and the exhaust gases from leaking out of the combustion chamber. The gasket between the cylinder block and the engine head also seals the chamber from leaks. Low compression in the cylinder can keep the engine from running. It often means the engine head needs repair, covered later in this chapter.

Car Speak

Piston rings fit around the side of a piston and against the cylinder wall to seal the compression chamber.

Knowing that, if you could find a way of checking the amount of compression within each cylinder, you could learn whether the rings and gasket are doing their jobs—without having to disassemble the engine.

To the rescue: a compression tester you can buy for about $25. Here's how to test your car's engine compression with that nifty tool. There will be no bloodshed.

To test engine compression and identify needed repairs, follow these steps:

1. Disconnect all spark plug wires from the spark plugs, labeling the wires as necessary to make sure they are reinstalled properly.

2. Use a spark plug socket wrench to loosen each spark plug about one-half turn. Don't remove the plugs yet.

3. Disconnect the large wire at the center of the coil and place it over an unpainted bolt on the engine to ground the wire. If necessary, use a *jumper* (a short wire with clips at each end) to ground the coil wire to the engine.

4. Use a clean paintbrush to sweep debris away from the spark plugs where they enter the engine block. Remove all spark plugs using a spark plug socket wrench, placing the plugs in sequence on a table so that you can reinstall them in the same order.

5. Remove the air-filter housing. Block the throttle open so that air can easily get into the carburetor or fuel-injection system. For fuel-injected systems, remove the fuel pump fuse, typically located on or near the fuel pump. If in doubt about location, refer to your car's service manual.

6. Tightly screw the tip of the compression tester into the spark plug hole at the front of the engine. That's the one closest to the radiator on rear-wheel-drive cars or closest to the driver's side on front-wheel-drive cars.

7. Turn the ignition switch to the start position and hold it there until the engine has turned at least four revolutions. That's about three to five seconds. With the spark plugs out and the coil wire off, the car won't start. You just want the piston to compress the air in the chamber so that you can read the resulting pressure on the compression gauge. Write down the reading.

Car Speak

The *compression ratio* compares the difference between the area when a piston is at the top of its travel to the area when it is at the bottom. Engines must adequately compress the fuel/air mixture or the engine won't run smoothly or at all.

8. For four-cylinder engines, repeat steps 6 and 7 at the other spark plug holes, in order from the front of the engine to the back. If the engine is a V-6 or V-8, check compression from front to back on one bank or side, and then repeat the process on the other bank. Make sure you zero or clear the previous reading by pressing the button on the side of the compression tester.

9. Compare the results of the compression test with the manufacturer's specification, found in the car's service manual or an aftermarket manual. Standard compression for a newer car may be 180 psi (pounds per square inch), for example, and minimum compression may be 135 psi. An older car might have a standard compression of 150 psi and a minimum compression of 130 psi.

10. Finally, compare compression ratios between cylinders. On newer cars, the maximum variation should be about 25 psi; for older cars, it should be about 15 psi—not because they're old, but because compression was designed lower on earlier cars. If compression is lower than these tolerances, the cylinder could have a defective valve or piston ring. To figure out which, put a teaspoon of motor oil into the spark plug hole of the cylinder with the low reading and repeat the compression test on that cylinder. If the reading increases, the piston's oil ring is defective and the engine should be overhauled. If the reading doesn't increase, the valve is the problem and the head(s) should be rebuilt. Both procedures are covered later in this chapter.

11. If no repairs are necessary, reinstall the coil wire, air-filter housing, spark plugs, plug wires, and any other parts you removed for this test.

12. You've earned a break. Pop open a soft drink, kick back in the shade, and watch your neighbor mow the lawn.

Automotive Head Injuries and Brain Surgery

As you would guess, the *cylinder head* or *head* is the top of the engine (see the figure illustrating the engine head and block). It's the area above the combustion chamber. Really old cars (pre–mid-'50s) must have been pretty dumb because there was nothing in their heads. The head was just a flat piece of metal that formed the top of the cylinders above the engine block, so they were called *flathead engines*. Not very flattering.

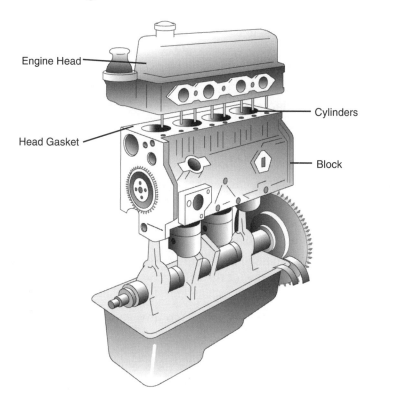

The engine head and cylinder block.

Engine Head

Head Gasket

Cylinders

Block

Today's cars must be smart. They have a lot in their heads: valves and sometimes camshafts. These are called overhead valve or overhead cam engines. An *overhead valve* (OHV) engine has valves in the engine's head above each cylinder, but the valves are operated by a camshaft in the engine block and a contraption called the *rocker arm and push rod assembly*. An overhead cam engine includes both the valves and the camshaft in the head. Defective valves and camshafts should be replaced or machined.

The point is that what you'll find in the engine's head depends on the design of the engine, so the following procedures for head repair are pretty generic. They give you a good idea of what's involved in head repair, but don't try taking the engine apart based on these sketchy instructions. Find a good manual with information about your car's engine. Look for one that has excellent illustrations to help you identify parts and their relationships, and review the following list to become familiar with some of the terms and parts you might encounter when performing surgery on the head:

➤ **Valve:** Part of an engine that opens and closes to control the flow of a liquid, gas, or vacuum; most commonly, the intake valve that lets fuel/air into the engine's cylinder and the exhaust valve, which lets combusted gases out.

➤ **Valve cover:** A metal covering encasing the engine's valves, keeping oil in and dust out.

➤ **Cylinder block or block:** Where cylinders live, also known as a cylinder 'hood; alternatively, the largest part of the engine, including cylinders, oil passages, water jackets, and some other components.

➤ **Rocker arm:** Movable part of a musician; alternatively, a part of an overhead valve system that transfers upward motion of the lifters and/or push rod to downward motion of the valves.

➤ **Lifter:** The metal part of a valve system between the cam lobe and the push rod or rocker arm.

➤ **Camshaft:** The rotating shaft inside the engine that opens and closes valves using cams or lobes.

➤ **Single-overhead cam (SOHC):** An unmarried engine that uses one camshaft to control both the intake valves and exhaust valves.

➤ **Double-overhead cam (DOHC):** An engine that uses two camshafts to control valves: one for the intake valves and one for the exhaust valves; also available as a latté.

➤ **Timing gears:** Gears that keep the camshaft (valves) in time with the crankshaft (pistons) using a timing chain or timing belt.

Some good news: Heads can be removed from most engines without removing the engine from the car. Too bad I can't do the same and leave my head at the dentist's for repair while I do other errands.

An engine head is typically repaired following these steps:

1. Remove the engine's valve cover, which is located on the top of the engine head. On some engines, you first need to remove the spark plugs and wires. You might also need to mark and remove other wires or vacuum hoses. Loosen nuts or bolts fastening the cover to the head. Clear away any debris that could fall into the engine as the cover is removed. Lift the valve cover off the engine and remove the gasket that seals the cover to the head.

2. As necessary, remove the engine head from the engine block. On most cars, this means removing the exhaust manifold and then removing the bolts that fasten the head to the block.

176

3. Using your car's service manual, determine what needs to be removed next and how to do so. To access the valves or cam assembly, most cars require that the rocker arm assembly be removed. This is done by removing bolts at each end and sometimes in the middle of the assembly. Then, depending on the engine, the cam or the valve stems may need to be removed.

4. Replace or repair parts as needed. Your car's service manual can guide you in figuring out which parts are worn and which aren't. A worn camshaft can be reground by a machine shop, but most folks buy and install a replacement. Valves can also be reground or replaced. Valve springs, lifters, and other components can be replaced. Overhead cam engines have a timing gear that can be replaced. If the engine head is cracked, it can be repaired or replaced through a large auto parts store. If the head is slightly warped, it can often be sent to a machine shop for repair. Let the manual be your guide.

5. Adjust the valves, following the instructions in the service manual.

6. Reassemble the engine head and reinstall the valve cover, cleaning and replacing parts as needed. Use a torque wrench to tighten bolts to the car manufacturer's recommendations.

Open Engine Surgery

Your car's engine could power you for 100,000, 200,000, or even more miles before it needs to be overhauled—or it might peter out within the first 50,000 miles. Much depends on how well it's maintained.

What's an engine overhaul? It's the replacement of worn parts in the engine block. That includes the crankshaft, pistons and rings, connecting rods, bearings, flywheel, and related parts. The engine block with the head(s) removed is sometimes called a *short block*. If you buy one at an auto parts store, that's what you'll ask for.

Actually, most mechanics typically don't overhaul an engine. They buy and install a new or rebuilt engine. Why? Because most garages don't have all the expensive machines needed to completely overhaul an engine.

The typical engine overhaul includes reconditioning the cylinder walls and crankshaft; installing new main, connecting rod, and camshaft bearings; and replacing other worn or damaged components. Engine overhaul kits can be purchased through larger auto parts retailers. If the engine cylinders have been enlarged to compensate for wear, oversized pistons and rings might be needed. If you're unfamiliar with any of the terms or parts you'll encounter during an engine overhaul, check out the following list:

➤ **Combustion chambers:** Where judges let off steam; alternatively, the area within an engine cylinder where combustion of a fuel/air mixture takes place.

➤ **Bore:** The know-it-all who doesn't need an auto repair manual, or the width of an engine's cylinder.

➤ **Stroke:** What you have when you see some auto repair bills; alternatively, the distance a piston moves up and down within an engine cylinder.

➤ **CID:** Cubic inch displacement, or the total volume of all combustion chambers in an engine measured in cubic inches. To translate engine size in liters to cubic inches, multiply liters by 61.027.

➤ **Connecting rod:** The rod that connects an engine's crankshaft to a piston.

➤ **Crankshaft:** A grumpy mechanic; alternatively, the main rotating part of an engine that turns the piston's up-and-down motion into a circular motion that can be used by the transmission and, eventually, the wheels.

➤ **Rod bearing:** A dissimilar metal part between the crankshaft and individual connecting rods for reducing wear.

An engine is typically overhauled following these steps:

1. Remove the engine from the car. Depending on the car's design, this may require removal of the hood, the radiator, the back seat, three tires, and the glove compartment lock. Mark disconnected wires and hoses so that you can easily replace them when done. The engine should be disconnected from the clutch housing or torque converter. Finally, remove bolts from the engine mounts and lift the engine out of the car using a rented engine puller, available at any large rental center or auto parts store.

2. Place the engine on a sturdy workbench where it can be disassembled. Turn the engine upside down and remove the oil pan cover by removing bolts around its perimeter. Remove the oil-pan gasket. Remove the flywheel cover at the same time. Depending on its location, you might need to remove the oil pump next.

3. Remove the bolts holding the main bearing caps on the block, marking the location of each cap. Remove the caps and main bearings. Remove the bolts holding the connecting rod caps, marking the location of each cap, and then remove the caps and bearings. Push the piston and rod assemblies out of the cylinders. Remove the crankshaft from the engine block. Remove the flywheel from the end of the crankshaft.

4. Remove any other parts necessary to completely dismantle the engine block.

5. Clean, inspect, measure, and repair or replace parts as needed. Your car's service manual shows you how. Wear is measured with a micrometer that can be rented or purchased, depending on whether you got a tax refund this year. They're $50 to $150 to buy. Because of the work needed to remove and dismantle an engine, most mechanics replace all parts that can wear out instead of just those that have already worn out. The parts are inexpensive in relation to the labor cost.

6. Carefully reassemble the engine to ensure that everything fits as designed and is within manufacturer's tolerances.

7. Reinstall the engine in the car. Reattach all those loose things. Aren't you glad you marked them? Check to make sure you have no leftover parts.

The Least You Need to Know

➤ A compression test can tell you much about the condition and needs of your car's engine.

➤ Many engine repairs, including valve and head repairs, can be made without removing the engine block from the car.

➤ Whether you supervise or actually perform an engine overhaul, knowing the process can make the job easier and probably save you some money.

Chapter 20

Fuel System Repairs: Fill 'Er Up!

In This Chapter

➤ Safely repair your car's fuel-injection or carburetion system

➤ How to safely repair the fuel tank and lines

➤ Replacing a defective fuel pump in four easy steps

Where would your car be without a fuel system? Stranded! And so would you.

Before you find yourself in this situation, you might want to learn how repairs are done to an automotive fuel system. If not, at least read this chapter before you hire a mechanic to do the needed (or unneeded) repairs. You might decide to do it yourself. Or you might want to make sure the mechanic doesn't treat you like a complete idiot.

Your car's fuel system is based on either a carburetor or a fuel-injection system. One or the other. Which one? If your car was built in the past 10 years, chances are it uses a fuel-injection system. If it was built more than 10 years ago, it probably uses a carburetor. The car's owner's manual and certainly its service manual can tell you which one you have.

In this chapter, you also learn about repairs to fuel pumps, fuel tanks, and fuel lines (see the figure illustrating the fuel system components). All internal combustion engine cars have these parts.

Unless you're Superman or Wonder Woman, you'll need some tools to do these repairs. Chapter 6, "Do-It-Yourself Maintenance, or Getting Your Hands Dirty," covers basic repair tools, and I'll try to identify special tools as we go along.

Components of an automotive fuel system.

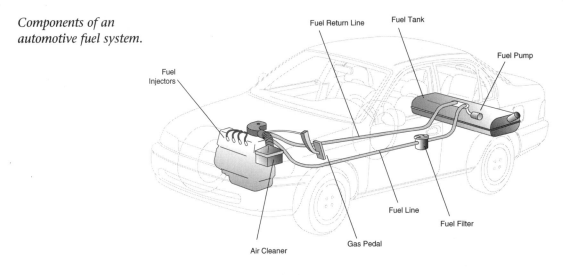

Are You Starving Your Car?

This chapter offers solutions to many common fuel system problems. Here are some additional tips:

➤ Are you sure that your car has gas? If you don't trust the fuel gauge, carefully lower one end of a cotton rope through the fuel filler pipe to test the depth of the fuel in the tank. A clean stick is better if it will negotiate all the turns in the filler pipe.

➤ If your car's engine starts okay but dies when you put it in gear, the carburetor (if it has one) might need the fast idle speed adjusted (see Chapter 10, "CAR Semiannual Adjustments").

➤ If your car seems starved for fuel, remove the air filter. If the engine then runs smoothly, replace the air filter with a new one. If the engine still does not run smoothly, use a vacuum tester to test the fuel pump and fuel lines as covered later in this chapter.

➤ A vacuum leak in a fuel-injection system, intake manifold, or vacuum line can cause all sorts of weird problems. Check vacuum hoses for leaks before repairing other parts (see Chapter 9, "CAR Quarterly Check Up").

➤ If your car runs erratically or even not at all, check the fuel filter; if it's clogged, replace it.

➤ If your car sounds like a diesel engine when going uphill, buy a higher octane fuel or add an octane booster to your fuel tank (see your friendly auto parts retailer).

➤ If your car is difficult to start but finally does so, check the automatic choke as described in this chapter.

Painless Carburetor Surgery

The carburetor has been a vital part of a car's power system since cars first drank, or guzzled, gas. The carburetor mixes fuel with air and sends it (through the intake manifold) to the engine cylinders for burning.

A carburetor is a mechanical device; it's not electronically controlled. That means it's subject to wear. Small jets get clogged with junk from the fuel tank. The float inside the carburetor's bowl or reservoir wears out or breaks. But, most often, poor fuel and too many gas additives take their toll on the carburetor, requiring that it be replaced. How can you tell? Troubleshooting tests (see Chapter 15, "Don't Shoot! Troubleshoot") can help determine the source of the problem. If it's the carburetor, keep reading.

You have options. Sometimes, all your car needs is an adjustment or two (see Chapter 10). Because your carburetor is a mechanical device, you can rebuild it for less money than it costs to buy a rebuilt or new one. Or you can whip out your wallet and plunk your money down for a new one, but before you do, make sure you've considered the other options.

Is rebuilding a carburetor difficult? Not particularly. In fact, the most difficult part may be selecting the right parts from the carburetor rebuild kit. These kits, available at auto parts stores for nearly all carburetors, are typically sold for more than one carburetor model. That means you're going to have some parts left over when you're done (leftovers are okay in this case). Instructions in these kits are generic, too. One solution to this problem is to stay away from the low-price leaders at automotive superstores. If you're going to rebuild your car's carburetor, get a kit from the dealer's parts department or the original equipment manufacturer (OEM). It costs more, but it saves you time—and time is money.

A carburetor is replaced following these steps:

1. Open your car's hood and look for the carburetor. In most cars, it's beneath a round metal part called the *air-filter housing*. Disconnect the large hose leading into the air-filter housing (if there is one) and remove the nut on top of the housing. Disconnect any other parts and hoses needed to remove the air-filter housing.

2. You should now be able to see the carburetor. Disconnect the throttle linkage and the fuel line to the carburetor. You'll probably need the car's service manual as a reference so that you don't remove the wrong parts. Remember, the carb cops are watching you!

3. Remove the carburetor. For most cars, this means first removing the two or four nuts at the edges where the carburetor sits atop the intake manifold.

4. Remove the gasket between the carburetor and intake manifold. If the gasket lifts off easily, you're done. If it's stuck, you must scrape it off. To do so, first plug the holes on the manifold with rags so that bits of gasket don't fall in, making life

183

more difficult. Then use a putty knife or other flat edge to remove all gasket material. (Don't forget to remove the rag from the manifold holes when you're done!)

5. Buy or rebuild the carburetor. You can buy a new or rebuilt unit or you can rebuild it yourself with a carburetor kit. In general, rebuilding a carburetor means taking it apart, soaking parts in a carburetor cleaner, reassembling the parts, and adjusting them following the instructions in the kit.

6. Install the new or rebuilt carburetor in the reverse order of how you took it out. Install the new gasket, the new carb, attach lines and linkage, a new air-filter housing gasket, and then the old housing.

7. Finally, adjust the carburetor (if the manufacturer has provisions for adjustment) following instructions in the car's service manual or in Chapter 10.

Don't Choke Your Car to Death

A choke has a strangle-hold on the carburetor. Pretty graphic, huh? The *choke* limits the amount of air going into the carburetor. Why? Because as a car starts, it needs a richer (more fuel, less air) mixture than when it's tooling along the highway.

The automatic choke system knows that the car's engine isn't warm enough yet (because it's measuring the temperature of the exhaust gas), so it uses a butterfly valve to keep some of the air from flowing into the carburetor. A *butterfly valve* is a shaft with a "wing" on each side that chokes or blocks air flow through the carburetor's throat when the shaft is turned. This butterfly doesn't fly, however, and it isn't very pretty.

How do you know whether your car's carburetor choke isn't working? Common sense. Is your car "cold-blooded" and difficult to keep running the first time it's started? Among other things, the automatic choke might not be working automatically. Some cars get help from a vacuum or electric assistant that reduces excessive choking. Sounds gruesome, doesn't it? If your car sends out black exhaust smoke when it starts, the automatic choke's assistant is probably not working.

An automatic choke is replaced following these steps:

1. Find the automatic choke. On some cars, it's located on the side of the carburetor; on others, it's mounted nearby on the manifold. Unfortunately, some systems have choke parts under the carburetor. Follow the instructions (in the previous section) for digging your way down to the carburetor by removing the air-filter housing.

2. Using your car's service manual, figure out what type of automatic choking system it has and where the components are located. Without starting the car and while the engine is cold, put your ear near the carburetor while your lovely assistant presses the gas pedal. You should see and hear the choke butterfly valve move. If it doesn't, try moving the butterfly by hand and checking the attached

parts for smooth movement. If something seems stuck, try to free it. The cause is often a loose connection or something in the way.

3. Depending on the type of choke system, you can use a carburetor choke cleaner spray to clean and free up mechanical parts. Don't spray any electronic parts with this stuff. How can you tell the difference? If in doubt, wires leading to a part identify it as electrical.

4. If your automatic choke system's thermostat needs an adjustment, follow the service manual's instructions for adjusting it. In most cases, you loosen the choke cover and turn it to the next index mark on the cover's body, and then retighten the screws. If the thermostat doesn't respond to adjustment, it's probably broken and needs replacement.

5. To replace an automatic choke system component, identify and remove the defective component, and then take it to a full parts house for an exact replacement. Some choke systems are an integral part of the carburetor and cannot be replaced easily. In this case, you're stuck with buying a new or rebuilt carburetor.

6. To adequately test your car's rebuilt carburetor, start the car and drive it by your favorite mechanic's garage, honking.

If Your Car Injects Itself: Fuel-Injection Repairs

As you learned in Chapter 1, "How Cars Run: What Makes It Go?" fuel-injection systems are more efficient and more trouble-free than carburetion systems. Even so, they may need periodic repair or replacement.

Most cars built since 1986 use fuel injection rather than carburetion. Some cars used it even before that.

The two most common types of fuel-injection systems today are throttle-body and multiport. There will be a quiz later, so pay attention—and drop that spitball!

A *throttle-body* fuel-injection system is similar to a carburetor, except that the amount of fuel is controlled electronically rather than mechanically. The fuel/air mixture is then distributed by the intake manifold to the cylinders. A *multiport* fuel-injection system electronically controls the distribution of fuel through one or more fuel rails (like pipes) to each cylinder's fuel injector. Multiport fuel injection (MPFI) is also called *multiport injection*, *port fuel injection*, and other creative names. Same thing.

Still awake?

So what can go wrong with a fuel-injection system? The system is controlled by the electronic control module (ECM) or the computer, which makes all the major decisions. So if the ECM is damaged, problems begin showing up in components it controls, including the fuel-injection system. Fortunately, these things don't fail very often, especially on newer systems in which the design bugs have been worked out.

Unfortunately, when they do go awry, they go extremely awry—and Einstein can't fix them. The solution then is to have a qualified and honest mechanic (I knew one once, but he died—broke!) test and replace as needed.

My Mechanic Says. . .

The best way to maintain your car's fuel-injection system is to make sure it drinks only quality fuel. Brand-name fuels today include additives specifically formulated to keep fuel injectors clean. If you suspect that your car's injectors are gummed up, try switching gas stations for a tank or two. Use fuel additives only if the gasoline you buy doesn't have them.

How can you tell if your car's fuel-injection system is sick? That's a toughie. Much depends on the type of fuel-injection system your car has, and whether other causes have been ruled out. Your car's service manual is the best source for specific ailments and cures, but to understand them, let's look at typical fuel-injection system repairs.

I reiterate: Fuel-injection systems are complex. Tackle repair at your own risk. They can be repaired successfully by mechanically inclined car owners with a good service manual and the right tools. Really they can. Plan on spending some time scratching your head, however. A well-written service manual with lots of illustrations specific to your car's engine really makes the job easier.

Fuel injectors should last about 50,000 miles, and other parts in the system should last about twice as long.

Fuel-injection systems are repaired following these steps:

1. Relieve pressure in (depressurize) the fuel system. Fuel-injection systems are pressurized, so working on the fuel system requires that you first relieve system pressure. Your car's service manual or an aftermarket manual shows you how. Typically, you remove the filler cap on the fuel tank and then loosen the specified pressure reliever (a bolt or fitting).

2. Follow manufacturer's directions for testing and repairing or replacing components. Typical components include the air intake system, throttle body, fuel rail (MPFI), fuel pressure regulator, fuel injectors, and electronic control module. Sometimes you can fix a system simply by tracing down all the wires and hoses, attaching those that have worked themselves free or are damaged. Sometimes not.

3. If you are able to repair your car's fuel-injection system within a reasonable time and cost, try not to act smug.

All Tanked Up: Fuel Tank and Fuel Line Repairs

A fuel tank is simply a reservoir for your car's fuel. Fuel tanks typically hold from 10 to 20 gallons of fuel, depending on the car's fuel efficiency. (My 40-year-old Continental has a 25-gallon fuel tank, accurately suggesting a low number of miles to the gallon. My Honda acts very smug about its small tank and efficient mileage.) Cars are designed to travel 300 to 400 miles before running out of gas. Unfortunately, human bladders are smaller and need more frequent pit stops.

What can go wrong with fuel tanks and fuel lines? They can spring a leak. A small point of rust can become a hole in a few years. If the hole is in a tank or line housing fuel, the fuel can leak out and cause more problems than just low fuel efficiency. If you find puddles of fuel under your car, you know that the tank or line needs repair. Do it before the leak becomes a fire hazard.

The best insurance against such leaks is a full undercoating of the underside of your car to minimize rust. Depending on the size of your car, undercoating can cost about $25 in materials plus your labor, or about $100 to $150 if a shop does it for you. Make sure a rust inhibitor is applied first.

Fuel tanks and fuel lines can be repaired following these steps:

1. Visually inspect your car's fuel tank and fuel lines, looking for small wet spots. Touch the spot with a finger and then sniff it to see whether the liquid is gasoline. If so, look for other leaks and repair or replace the part as needed.

2. To repair a fuel tank, purchase and apply an internal or external fuel tank sealer. Internal sealers are poured into the fuel; external sealers are applied to the holes on the outside of the tank. Internal sealers find and seal all holes, seen and unseen, but might not be recommended by the car's manufacturer because they can clog a system. External sealers are easy to apply, but can't ensure that unseen holes are sealed.

3. To replace a fuel tank on a fuel-injected car, first depressurize it, as described in the preceding section. This isn't necessary on a carbureted car. Then drain or siphon the fuel from the tank into one or more large gas cans. Detach the fuel tank from the inlet pipe and the output fuel line. Find and remove the straps or hangers that attach the fuel tank to the car. Carefully lower the tank to the ground and remove it from underneath the car. Replace it with a new or rebuilt replacement tank. Don't try to make one fit that doesn't.

4. To repair a fuel line, first determine whether the entire line or only one spot needs replacement. A damaged line can be repaired, but a rusted fuel line will soon spring another hole and should be replaced. A rubber fuel line that has developed a leak is probably old and needs to be replaced entirely. If your car is fuel-injected, depressurize the fuel system before working on it. Larger auto parts stores have fuel lines cut to length and bent for many newer cars. Otherwise, you might need to buy a straight fuel line along with some bending and flaring tools to make it fit your car.

5. Realize that, once done with this job, you're a better person for the experience. And if you believe that...

Minor Heart Surgery: Fuel Pump Repair

Fuel pumps use suction to pull fuel from the tank and deliver it to the carburetor or fuel-injection system. Older cars used mechanical fuel pumps that were operated by the engine's camshaft. Newer cars use electromechanical or solid state fuel pumps. An electromechanical pump uses electricity to power the mechanical suction diaphragm. Solid state fuel pumps rely on electronics to do the job and have no mechanical parts.

One more time: If your car has a fuel-injection system, make sure you depressurize the fuel system before working on it. See the instructions provided earlier in this chapter.

To replace a fuel pump, follow these steps:

1. First, find the darn thing. Your car's fuel pump could be mounted on the side of the engine, somewhere in the engine compartment, near the fuel tank, or even inside the fuel tank. Your car's service manual helps you pinpoint it.

2. Test the fuel pump. Some fuel pumps can be tested without taking them off the car, but others must be removed (see step 3). To test the pump, you first need to remove the fuel lines from the pump. Before disconnecting the input line, find a way of blocking it so that fuel from the tank doesn't spurt out. For a rubber input line, use Vise-Grip pliers to clamp the line. For a metal line, use a cap or a wad of putty to block flow after the input line is disconnected. Check input vacuum pressure with your finger or a vacuum gauge over the input. The car's service manual tells you what the input vacuum should be, but your finger over the input can give you a good idea as to whether the fuel pump is working. Check the fuel pump output pressure and volume in the same way.

3. To remove the fuel pump, remove the mounting bolts that attach it to the engine block, frame, or tank. Fuel pumps inside a fuel tank typically can be accessed through a cover underneath a back seat or a trunk mat. Disconnect any electrical wiring. Drain any gas in the fuel pump or bowl into a gas can. Remember: Smoking while you're working on the fuel system can really be hazardous to your health and to those within a wide range of your location!

4. Replace the fuel pump with one of the same output. Your car's specifications tell you what pressure and volume the fuel pump should be able to produce.

The Least You Need to Know

➤ If your troubleshooting efforts suggest that the carburetor needs repair, the easiest solution is to buy and install a replacement.

➤ Fuel-injection systems are complex and each one is slightly different, but the car's service manual can help you isolate and replace sick parts.

➤ Fuel line and tank leaks are easily seen and nearly as easy to repair by using sealants or replacing parts.

Chapter 21

Cooling and Lubrication System Repairs: Fixing a Hot Car

In This Chapter

➤ Repairing or delegating repair of the cooling system

➤ Replacing your car's water pump with basic tools and instructions

➤ Passing air conditioner repair off to experts who have the specialized tools and knowledge for the job

Most modern cars have a pressurized engine-cooling system (illustrated in the first figure in this chapter) that uses a thermostat to control the flow of coolant throughout the engine. The thermostat stops coolant from flowing until the engine is warm and then regulates the coolant temperature.

Why is the cooling system pressurized? Because the boiling point of a pressurized liquid is higher than that of a nonpressurized one. So the engine can safely operate at higher temperatures without boiling over. Unfortunately, a pressurized system means that all parts, including hoses, must be strong enough to withstand the higher pressure.

The procedures in this chapter are typical for most modern cars. Refer to the manufacturer's manual or an aftermarket service manual for specific instructions and details.

As with other repairs, grab your handy-dandy car care toolbox. I'll let you know if there's anything special you need to make the repairs in this chapter.

An automotive cooling system.

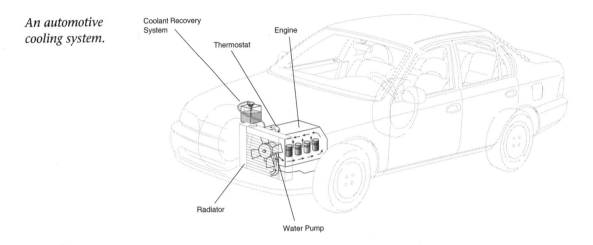

Coolant Recovery System

Thermostat

Engine

Radiator

Water Pump

What to Do with a Hot Car

Relax—I'm not going to tell you how to get rid of a stolen car, but your car may occasionally get too hot in other ways. To make life somewhat easier, here are a few guidelines for troubleshooting cooling and lubrication systems:

➤ If your car always seems to run hot, first look for debris blocking the front of the radiator. Also check the seal on the radiator cap, test the radiator hoses (see Chapter 9, "CAR Quarterly Check Up"), and then consider replacing the thermostat or water pump (covered later in this chapter).

➤ If your car warms up slowly, the thermostat may be stuck open.

➤ If you must remove the radiator from your car to have it rebuilt, consider buying a replacement unit instead. It might be cheaper.

➤ Check the sides of the engine block for signs of coolant leaking through round metal parts called *freeze plugs* or *core plugs*. Refer to the service manual for instructions on replacing core plugs.

➤ If you car's heater doesn't work after not being used for a while, find the heater under the hood or dashboard and check to see if the hose to it has a spigot or valve that's closed.

If Your Car Is Radiating Too Much Heat...

...chances are you don't have the specialty tools needed to repair your car's radiator. If it needs repair, the best you can do is remove it and reinstall it. Radiators for most modern cars are a commodity; you can order a new one through an auto parts store and pick it up on Tuesday. The price is cheaper if you bring your old radiator in for an exchange. Until you do, most auto parts stores or radiator shops require a deposit called a *core charge*.

To remove and reinstall a radiator, follow these steps:

1. Drain the car's cooling system as described in Chapter 12, "CAR Biannual Replacements." If the coolant is relatively new and clean, save and reuse it. Some coolants can be poisonous to your pets.

2. If your car is equipped with an automatic transaxle, disconnect the coolant lines from the radiator.

3. Loosen the hose clamps on the radiator and detach the hoses. Some hose clamps require you to unscrew them; others require you to use a special pair of pliers to squeeze the wires until the clamp opens.

4. Remove the engine cooling fan if it's attached to the radiator.

5. Loosen and remove the bolts holding the radiator to its frame.

6. Look around for any other components that are attached to the radiator and remove them. Mark their locations and sources to make reinstallation easier.

7. Lift the radiator from the frame, being careful not to spill coolant or to damage paint. Drain any coolant left in the radiator before taking it to the radiator shop or auto parts store.

8. Reinstall the radiator in the reverse order in which you took it out.

9. Refill the system with coolant, a 50/50 mixture of water and antifreeze.

10. Start the engine. As it's warming up, look for leaks.

11. To adequately test the new radiator, drive to an ice cream parlor at least 25 miles away, park and check for leaks, and then go in and order while the system is cooling. When you system is cool, check it again, get a quart to go, and drive home. Warning: Rocky Road is a bad omen!

My Mechanic Says. . .

Car coolant contains antifreeze that can be poisonous to pets. Some antifreeze products use toxic ethylene glycol and other ingredients that taste sweet. Newer antifreeze uses less-toxic propylene glycol, but check with the car's manufacturer to make sure using it doesn't void the car's warranty. Dispose of old antifreeze by sealing it in a leakproof container and taking it to a local recycling center.

A Fever of How Much?

If you suspect that the cooling system's thermostat needs replacement (because the engine is overheating), test some other options first before you start tearing into the engine. Check the coolant level in the reservoir or radiator (see Chapter 8, "CAR Weekly Check Up"). Check the tension on the engine drivebelts (see Chapter 10, "CAR Semiannual Adjustments"). Make sure the temperature gauge or warning light (see Chapter 15, "Don't Shoot! Troubleshoot") is not the culprit.

To check the thermostat, let the engine run 15 minutes or more and then carefully place your hand on the hose that runs between the high side of the radiator and the engine. If the engine is hot but the hose isn't, the thermostat isn't doing its job. It needs to be replaced.

A thermostat can be replaced following these steps:

1. When the engine is cool, drain the cooling system. If the coolant is relatively new and clean, save and reuse it.

2. Find the upper radiator hose. Remove the clamp that attaches the hose to the engine.

3. Remove the thermostat housing from the engine block. It's typically attached to the block with two bolts.

4. Remove the thermostat from the housing, noting which way it's installed. Scrape away any gasket material on the housing or engine block using a screwdriver tip.

5. Install a new gasket, placing it exactly where the old gasket was. Make sure all bolt holes line up.

6. Install a replacement thermostat in the same way that the old unit was removed. Make sure any pins or holes are lined up correctly.

7. Replace the thermostat housing.

8. Replace the upper radiator hose and clamp. If the hose will soon need replacement, save some trouble and do it now. Install a new clamp.

9. Refill the system with coolant.

10. Start the engine. As it's warming up, look for leaks. When the engine is warm, test the upper radiator hose for heat, as described earlier.

11. As needed, repeat step 11 in the preceding section for removing and reinstalling a radiator.

My Mechanic Says. . .

Don't run your engine without a thermostat. Bad things happen—and none of them are cheap to fix.

When Your Water Pump Doesn't

The water pump's job is to pump coolant through the engine and radiator. A water pump is actually a pretty simple part. A belt wrapped around the crankshaft pulley also turns the water pump shaft. Inside the pump, the shaft has a bunch (technical mechanic's term) of blades. As the shaft rotates, the blades go around, moving the coolant forward. Pretty slick!

The most common problem with a water pump is that the shaft wears out. On newer cars, there's a sealed bearing on the shaft. On older cars, the water pump has a zerk or lubrication fitting that needs a shot of grease once in a while. A water pump that is going out tells everyone so, making lots of racket and leaking coolant all over the place. It's a pretty effective warning system.

To replace a water pump, follow these steps:

1. When the engine is cool, drain the cooling system. If the coolant is relatively new and clean, save and reuse it.

2. Remove the drivebelts and, if necessary, the timing belt (see Chapter 10).

3. Remove any other parts attached to the water pump.

4. Remove the bolts holding the water pump in place. If one bolt is longer than others, make sure you remember which hole it's from. Clean away any gasket or O-ring material on the housing or engine block.

5. Install a new gasket and/or O-ring.

6. Install the replacement water pump. Hand-tighten all bolts and then use a torque wrench to tighten them to the manufacturer's specifications.

7. Reinstall all parts removed to get to the water pump.

8. Refill the system with coolant.

9. Adjust the drivebelt tension as described in Chapter 10.

10. Just kidding. There's no step 10. You're finished.

Turning Up the Heat

A car's heater simply circulates some of the hot coolant from the engine through a device that looks like a small radiator and then blows the resulting warm air to heat the interior of the car (see the figure illustrating this process). By this description, you can identify the main parts of a car's heater: the heater core (radiator), blower motor (fan), and hoses.

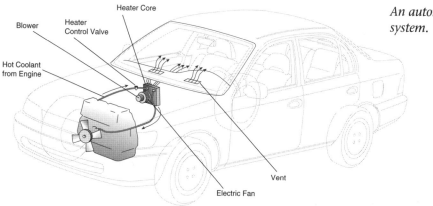

An automotive heating system.

The first step to repairing a car's heating system is to describe the problem ("Doctor, it hurts when …"). This helps define the solution. If the heater is leaking coolant into the car's interior, for example, you know that replacing the blower motor is probably not the solution. Chances are the problem involves a hose or the heater core. Knowing that makes your repair job easier. Common sense will probably dictate the cure. Coolant leaking into the passenger compartment suggests there's a leak in the heater or an attached hose. If you don't hear the motor or feel air movement with the heater switch on, the blower should be checked.

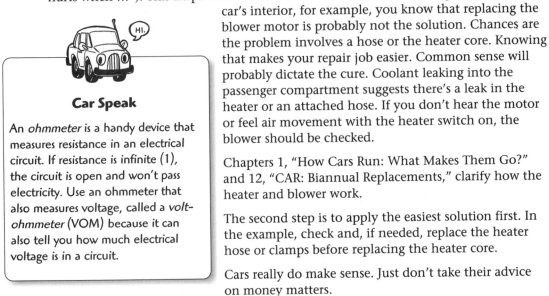

Car Speak

An *ohmmeter* is a handy device that measures resistance in an electrical circuit. If resistance is infinite (1), the circuit is open and won't pass electricity. Use an ohmmeter that also measures voltage, called a *volt-ohmmeter* (VOM) because it can also tell you how much electrical voltage is in a circuit.

Chapters 1, "How Cars Run: What Makes Them Go?" and 12, "CAR: Biannual Replacements," clarify how the heater and blower work.

The second step is to apply the easiest solution first. In the example, check and, if needed, replace the heater hose or clamps before replacing the heater core.

Cars really do make sense. Just don't take their advice on money matters.

A car's heater can be repaired following these steps:

1. Inspect the heater system for blockages and broken parts. Make sure the heater hoses are in good condition. If your car has a *summer* valve on the engine block (which lets you shut off circulation to the heater core), make sure the valve is open.

2. If necessary, check the blower circuit and motor. If the blower motor isn't operating, check the fuse and all switches and wire connections. Some blower motors also have resistors that can burn out and need replacement; you can check them with an ohmmeter.

3. If the blower motor needs to be replaced, follow the instructions in the service manual for doing so. In some cases, the dashboard must be partially disassembled. In all cases, you must first drain the cooling system.

4. If the heater core needs to be replaced, again, follow the instructions in your car's service manual. There are just too many ways of doing so to cover them all here. The heater core is typically found in a housing unit under the dashboard or in the engine compartment against the firewall. Disconnect, disassemble, replace, and assemble.

5. To test your car's heater, repeat the earlier procedure for purchasing ice cream. If it melts before you get back home, the heater works fine.

Why You Can't Cool It

Stop! There are so many federal and state regulations limiting what a car owner can do to repair an automotive air-conditioning system that about all you can do is stare at it. The reason is that most older systems use a fluorocarbon-based refrigerant to cool the car's air (actually, it removes the heat from the air). None of us want nasty fluorocarbons escaping into the atmosphere and eating up the ozone layer, so laws have been passed to make sure only trained folks with approved equipment can work on automotive air conditioners.

Sorry.

But for you folks who want to know how it works anyway, the next figure might appease you.

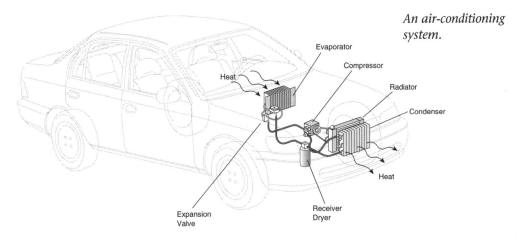

An air-conditioning system.

You Own an Oil Pump

Unfortunately, you probably don't own an oil well under your oil pump. Your oil pump, like mine, is probably in your car. Your car's lubrication system is simple. Oil held in the oil pan is pumped through the engine's oil passages. The oil pump does the work. If it doesn't, you've got a problem. Without lubricating oil, your car's engine soon becomes expensive scrap metal. So it's important to replace an oil pump that doesn't work as it should before the engine is damaged.

So where the heck's the oil pump?

Good question! On some cars, the oil pump is located on the side of the engine. On others, it's in

Car Speak

The *oil pump* pumps lubricating oil from the oil pan throughout the engine as needed to minimize wear and to maximize our need for peace in the Middle East. The *oil pan* is the removable part of an engine below the block that serves as a reservoir for the engine's oil.

the oil pan (see the figure showing the lubrication system). After the oil pump is found and removed, you can repair it using a rebuild kit available from a parts store, or you can buy a new or rebuilt one.

And why would you need to replace an oil pump? Because the car's idiot light or oil gauge says oil pressure is low, suggesting that the pump isn't working efficiently. Your car's owner's manual will tell you what normal operating pressure should be.

A lubrication system.

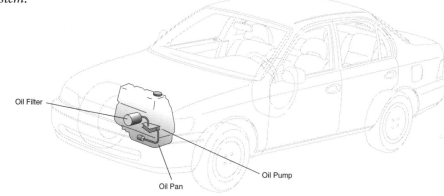

Oil Filter

Oil Pump

Oil Pan

Car Speak

Sludge was a popular rock band of the '70s. It's also a pasty compound of oil, water, and debris that accumulates in the oil pan and around rocker arms, reducing the flow of oil through the engine.

An oil pump is typically replaced following these steps:

1. Check the service manual to locate the oil pump.

2. If the oil pump is in the oil pan, drain the oil, remove the pan and its gasket, and then remove the pump. If the oil pump is mounted on the side of the engine block, remove the bolts holding the pump in place, and then remove the pump.

3. Rebuild, repair, or replace the oil pump by following the manufacturer's instructions.

4. Replace the oil pump in the reverse order in which you removed it. If oil was drained from the oil pan, clean out any built-up sludge in the bottom of the pan, replace the gasket, and reinstall the oil pan.

You're ready to begin pumping oil again. Well, at least your car is.

The Least You Need to Know

➤ You can keep your car's cool by watching its operating temperature and using common sense to replace defective parts.

➤ The water pump is the cooling system's heart. Fortunately, you can perform open-heart surgery on your car's water pump without a license.

➤ Most repairs to your car's air-conditioning system must be done by licensed folks with expensive equipment that you help pay for—like it or not.

➤ A car's oil pump is critical to operation. You can replace it yourself or be a knowledgeable consumer as you have it replaced for you. Your choice.

Chapter 22

Transmission Repairs: Those Troublesome Trannys

In This Chapter

➤ How to replace your car's manual transmission and clutch

➤ How to replace an automatic transmission and torque converter as a unit

➤ Repairing the transaxle, differential, universal or CV joints, and other useful parts of your car

---

As you learned in Chapter 1, "How Cars Run: What Makes Them Go?" a transmission uses gears to transmit the engine's power to the wheels. A manual transmission lets the driver select the gears, and an automatic transmission selects gears based on the car's speed and weight.

So what can you do if the transmission decides not to transmit? You can repair it yourself or knowledgeably have it repaired for you.

This chapter offers basic instructions on repairing manual and automatic transmission systems, drivelines, and differentials. Refer to the car's service manual or an after-market manual for specific instructions on repairing your car's transmission (but you knew that).

Technically, most front-wheel-drive cars don't have transmissions. They have transaxles. A *transaxle* combines the transmission and differential into one unit. So, as you read this chapter, translate *transmission* to *transaxle* if you have one. Otherwise, whistle silently.

Car Speak

The *transaxle* is a transmission and differential axle combined into one unit. It's named for the Transaxle Highway.

Car Speak

A *manual* transmission allows the driver to manually select the operating gear.

Do me a favor? Work safely! Please don't try working on your car's transmission or related parts without first safely jacking up the car and installing safety stands. Or use a heavy-duty ramp. Place blocks on the ground behind other tires to keep the car from rolling. I really don't like sending get well cards to readers.

It's Test Time!

Get your pencil out. Here are some tips for troubleshooting troublesome transmissions:

➤ If the car won't go into any gear, trace the shifting linkage from the steering column or floor to the transmission. It might simply be loose.

➤ If your car's clutch doesn't operate smoothly, check to see whether it has a booster that requires hydraulic fluid. It's located near the power brake booster and probably uses the same fluid. Check the car's owner's manual or service manual.

➤ If your car has a manual transmission and the engine sounds like it's speeding up when it really isn't (especially on a hill), the clutch might be slipping and need adjustment or replacement.

➤ If you hear rattling from your car's transmission, first make sure it has lubrication. Then look for loose mounting bolts.

➤ If the clutch pedal stays on the floor, check for a broken release bearing or fork.

➤ If you hear a knocking noise at low speeds or during turns, check the constant velocity (CV) joints.

Shifting for Yourself

Manual transmissions (see the first figure) that have been regularly serviced might not need repair for 100,000 miles or more. And when they do, most mechanics and do-it-yourselfers replace the transmission as a unit. They don't tear the transmission apart and start replacing components. They leave that up to specialists.

So if your car's manual transmission needs repair, you simply remove it from the car and reinstall a new or rebuilt unit. The job requires bigger tools, but it isn't particularly difficult—in most cases. The disclaimer is offered because some automotive designers have the transmission wedged into the car so deep that the engine and transmission must be removed together and then separated. Nice of them!

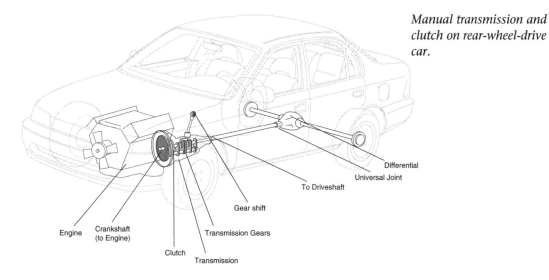

Manual transmission and clutch on rear-wheel-drive car.

Differential

Universal Joint

To Driveshaft

Gear shift

Transmission Gears

Engine

Crankshaft (to Engine)

Clutch

Transmission

Chapter 15, "Don't Shoot! Troubleshoot," describes some common transmission problems. More specific symptoms and solutions are included in your car's service manual.

Fortunately, most manual transmission problems aren't caused by the transmission, but by the linkage and switches attached to it. The *linkage* translates the movement of the gearshift to the movement of the appropriate gears within the *tranny* (what transmissions let friends call them). Manual transmissions have one, two, or three levers on the side that slide the appropriate gears around inside. Adjusting the linkage can solve many manual transmission problems.

If the service manual says the problem is the overdrive unit, check to see whether your car's overdrive is mounted in or on the transmission case. Some overdrives are external and can be replaced without removing the entire tranny.

A manual transmission is typically repaired following these steps:

Car Speak

The *overdrive* transmission gear reduces engine speed and increases fuel economy when the car is operating at more than 50 miles per hour; some cars use a fifth gear instead of an overdrive gear. Caution: Police radar is tuned to a little-known transmitter in your car's overdrive.

1. Locate and identify your car's manual transmission and linkage. It's behind the engine and below the firewall on rear-wheel-drive cars and either to the right or left of the engine on front-wheel-drive cars. Identify the transmission and check it against instructions in the service manual.

2. Adjust the shifting linkage. The linkage is composed of rods or cables between the shifter and transmission. Typically, the linkage is adjusted by moving adjustment nuts on a linkage rod or at the end of the linkage cable. If instructions aren't available, some staring and thinking will probably tell you what the adjustments do. Move—or have someone move—the shift linkage slowly through the gears to help you figure out what's needed. In many cases, a bent rod or a loose nut suggests an easy solution. (*Note:* Studying the transmission is another term for taking a nap.)

3. If adjusting the linkage doesn't solve the problem, consider replacing the transmission. On many cars, this means disconnecting the driveshaft at a U-joint or CV joint (described at the end of this chapter) and removing bolts that hold the front of the transmission to the bellhousing. Remove all linkage and drain the lubricant from the transmission first. The transmission must be slid away from the engine to remove it from the clutch. Depending on the weight of the transmission, you might need help or a jack to safely lower the unit after it's unbolted. Your car's service manual will probably tell you the transmission's weight.

4. If necessary, replace the old transmission with a new or rebuilt unit. Of course, make sure it's an exact replacement and that the bolt holes are in the same position so that it easily remounts. Check this even if you had your old transmission rebuilt because the shop might have replaced the case or given you the wrong unit. It can happen!

5. As needed, reinstall and adjust the linkage, and then check the transmission for lubricant (see Chapter 9, "CAR Quarterly Check Up"). Test the transmission for correct operation. If you're getting tired of ice cream runs (and runny ice cream), go for pizza. Hold the anchovies on my half.

My Mechanic Says. . .

Mechanics suggest that when replacing a transmission, you also replace the clutch and related parts (see the instructions for these repairs later in this chapter). They all get about the same amount of wear, so if one goes out, chances are the others will soon follow—requiring that you do the job again.

Clutch Repair

The engine and transmission work together with the help of the clutch. A *clutch* connects and disconnects an engine and manual transmission. It does so by friction, pressing the clutch plate against the engine's spinning flywheel. When you push down on the clutch pedal, you are forcing the clutch release bearing and fork to release the clutch plate from the pressure plate's clamping force against the flywheel. That disconnects the transmission from the engine. You then move the gear shifter to select the next gear and release the clutch pedal to reconnect the transmission to the engine.

If you've performed clutch adjustments described in your car's service manual and it still doesn't work smoothly, consider replacing the clutch.

So what can go wrong with the clutch system? The linkage can be out of adjustment because of wear. The bearing or clutch plate (also called a *friction plate*) can be worn out, or other components can be damaged.

Some clutch systems use a hydraulic booster to make engaging and disengaging the clutch easier on the driver. The clutch booster works similarly to a power brake booster. If your car has a clutch booster, refer to the service manual for more specifics.

To repair a clutch system, follow these steps:

1. Adjust the clutch linkage to see whether that solves the problem. The adjustment is located between the clutch pedal and the clutch fork that does most of the work. The linkage may be a rod or a cable. Follow the service manual for specifics. In most cases, the linkage is adjusted until the pedal *freeplay* (the movement of the clutch pedal before the clutch bearing moves) is $^1/_2$ or $^3/_4$ inch. The adjustment is made by turning the adjustment nut until freeplay is correct and then tightening a locking nut to make sure it doesn't change.

2. If adjustment doesn't solve the problem, you might need to replace some clutch components. To disassemble the clutch, first disconnect the driveshaft at a U-joint or a CV-joint, disconnect the shift linkage, remove the bolts holding the front of the transmission to the bellhousing, slide the transmission away from the bellhousing, and then remove the bellhousing to expose the clutch components. Whew!

Car Speak

The *clutch* connects and disconnects the engine from the transmission. The *flywheel* is a round, metal wheel at the end of the engine's crankshaft that collects and passes the engine's power to the transmission. The *bellhousing* is a metal shroud that covers the engine's flywheel and the transmission's clutch or torque-converter mechanisms.

3. Replace clutch components as needed. Typically, the only parts replaced during a clutch repair are the clutch release bearing, the pilot bearing, and the clutch plate. They can be purchased at larger auto parts stores or through the dealer's parts department. On many cars, remove the fork and bearing, the clutch pressure plate, the clutch plate, and then the pilot bearing. Cussing is discouraged because clutches are notoriously sensitive.

4. Reinstall the clutch components in the reverse order in which you installed them, making sure that the bearing and linkage are lubricated. Keep lubricants off the clutch plate or they won't get the traction needed to rotate. Finally, adjust the clutch (as described in step 1).

Your Automatic Transmission Does It Better

An automatic transmission (see the next figure) is designed not only to shift gears for you, but to do it more smoothly and accurately than you can. Sorry. However, automatic transmission parts—and there are hundreds of them—wear out and need adjustment or replacement. You can adjust an automatic transmission, but even most mechanics don't fool with tearing them apart. If an automatic transmission is worn, mechanics pull out the old one and install a new or rebuilt one. You too can have that fun.

Chapters 14, "Why Cars Don't Run: The Little Car That Couldn't," and 15, "Don't Shoot! Troubleshoot," offer common symptoms for automatic transmission troubles. Automatic transmissions typically live to be at least 100,000, with many seeing 150,000 miles before retiring to the old transmission home—without their teeth.

Automatic transmissions weigh up to 300 pounds, so please be careful. Follow smart safety rules. I said *please*.

An automatic transmission, torque converter, and differential—together called a transaxle unit— on a front-wheel-drive car.

Transaxle

CV Joints

An automatic transmission is repaired following these steps:

1. Adjust the automatic transmission linkage following the car's service manual. This may solve the problem. A loose bolt or bent linkage can make the difference between cruising and cursing. Older cars may require that the bands be adjusted to hold gears in place. If so, follow instructions in the service manual. This typically means removing the transmission pan, removing the fluid and filter to access the bands, and then tightening them to specifications (see Chapter 12, "CAR: Biannual Replacements").

2. Depending on the symptom, check the neutral safety switch. It's a switch typically located on the steering column near the floor. The switch won't let you start the car while it's in gear. If the switch is defective or the gear selector is misadjusted, the car might not start. The car's service manual tells you how to find, test, and replace the unit. In most cases, follow instructions in Chapter 18, "Starting and Ignition System Repairs for the Clueless," for testing electrical continuity on switches.

3. If the automatic transmission's problems cannot be adjusted, it needs to be replaced. To do so on most cars, you must disconnect the linkage, disconnect the driveshaft at a U-joint or CV joint, and remove bolts that hold the front of the transmission to the bellhousing. Remove all linkage and drain the lubricant from the transmission first. You must slide the transmission away from the engine to remove the input shaft from the torque converter. You will probably need help or a jack to safely lower the unit, which can weigh up to 300 pounds, after it's unbolted.

4. If necessary, replace the old transmission with a new or rebuilt unit. Reinstall and adjust the linkage, and then check the transmission for lubricant (see Chapter 9). Test the transmission for correct operation.

5. Congratulate yourself on a job well done.

Car Speak

An *automatic transmission* automatically selects gears based on the car's weight and speed, automatically ignoring your advice.

What Your Converter Converts and What to Do When It Doesn't

Manual transmissions have manual clutches, so automatic transmissions should have automatic clutches. Good guess. They do! They are called by assorted names, most commonly *torque converter* or just plain *converter*. Like an automatic transmission, the converter is hydraulic and complicated. If your car's service manual suggests that the converter be replaced, don't try rebuilding it yourself. Replace it as a unit, typically at the same time the automatic transmission is replaced.

A converter is typically replaced following these steps:

1. Disconnect the driveshaft at a U-joint or CV joint, remove bolts holding the front of the transmission to the engine, slide the transmission away from the converter, and then remove the converter from the engine.

2. If necessary, replace the old converter with a new or rebuilt unit. Reinstall and adjust the linkage, and then check the transmission for lubricant (see Chapter 9).

3. Test the converter with a visitation to your favorite fast food franchise or the zoo.

Separating Good Joints from Bad Joints

The joints on a *driveline* (the shaft and joints that connect the transmission with the differential) serve the same purpose as those on your body: They increase flexibility.

Rear-wheel-drive cars need a driveline from 3 to 6 feet long to deliver power from the transmission to the differential and rear axle. They use U-joints to compensate for flex in the driveline.

Front-wheel-drive cars have short drivelines, but they must be more flexible than those in rear-wheel-drive cars. Front-wheel-drive cars use CV joints.

With proper lubrication and maintenance, U-joints last 60,000 to 80,000 miles or more. CV joints, used in front-wheel-drive cars, typically last about 40,000 to 60,000 miles. However, if they get noisy or make a clunking sound as you put the car in gear, it may be time to replace them.

Technically, when you replace a U-joint, you are replacing only the bearing unit at the middle of it, an X-shaped part called the *trunnion*. CV joints have a Y-shaped part called the *tri-pot assembly*, which serves as the joint.

> ### Car Speak
>
> A *U-joint* (universal joint) is a public establishment where everyone is welcome without regard to automotive marquee. Or, in the car world, it's a joint in a car's driveshaft that allows the shaft to pivot. A *CV joint* (constant velocity joint) is a joint in a car's driveshaft that allows the shaft to pivot without vibration.

Universal joint for a rear-wheel-drive car.

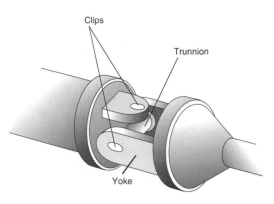

206

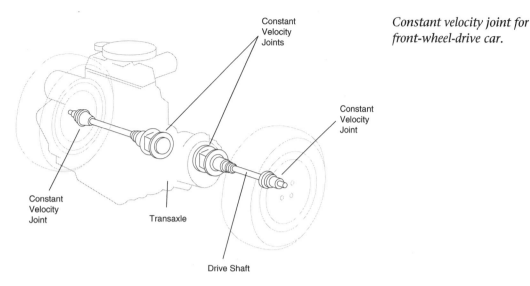

Constant
Velocity
Joints

Constant
Velocity
Joint

Constant
Velocity
Joint

Transaxle

Drive Shaft

Constant velocity joint for front-wheel-drive car.

To replace U-joints, follow these steps:

1. Test U-joints for looseness. Under the car, identify the U-joints on the car's driveline. They are at the joint between the transmission and the driveline (front), maybe somewhere along the driveline (intermediate), and at the end of the driveline where it attaches to the differential (rear). Some cars have double U-joints, two-in-one. With the car in neutral and the parking brake on, turn the driveline back and forth by hand. A clunking sound or lots of movement, called *play*, in the joint means that the U-joints should be checked and, if necessary, replaced.

2. To replace the universal joint, first use chalk, tape, or the end of a nail to mark the current position of each component in the driveline, making reassembly easier. After it's loosened, the driveline will fall, so have one hand on it or tie a sling around it and to the frame to keep it from falling. Remove the bolts on the center or yoke. Use a large screwdriver to carefully push the two halves apart.

3. Remove the clips holding the X-shaped trunnion in the yoke. Be careful not to remove any of the four caps on the ends of the trunnion because they contain small bearings.

4. Depending on your car, you might need to replace other U-joints. Follow the same instructions. The front U-joint is typically attached to the transmission through a sliding shaft called the *slip yoke* and may need a seal removed first. If so, place a pan under the seal to catch transmission fluid or lubricant. The rear U-joint is attached to the differential through a sliding pinion shaft.

5. Reinstall the driveline.

207

A CV joint.

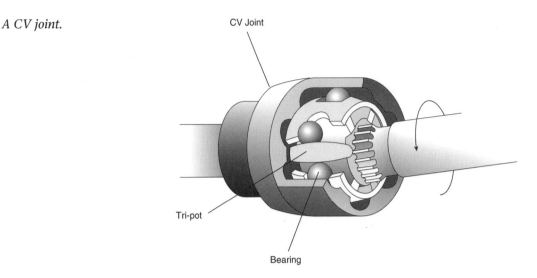

To replace CV joints, follow these steps:

1. Test the CV joints by listening for front-end clicking noises as the car turns or for vibrations as the car accelerates. The CV joints are located between the transaxle unit and the front wheels. Inspect the CV joint's rubber cover called a *boot*. If the boot is damaged but the CV joint isn't making noise, replace the boot. If the CV joint is noisy, replace the entire unit.

2. On most front-wheel-drive cars, the CV joint is replaced as a unit. Follow instructions in the service manual for removing and replacing CV joints. Typically, this means removing the drive axle and then removing the boot clamp and boot to access the CV joint. Parts to the CV joint include the housing, internal tri-pot assembly with roller bearings, and the boot. Replace any part that shows damage or wear.

3. Reinstall the CV joint on the drive axle. Then reinstall the drive axle on your car.

Rear End Problems (Your Car's)

The differential (illustrated in the next figure) on a rear-wheel-drive car is pretty simple. The end of the driveline is attached to a pinion gear. The pinion gear turns a larger ring gear that, in turn, passes power to gears within the differential case. It's these differential case gears that decide which wheel gets how much of the power.

So what? Let me tell you.

The rear wheels must rotate at different speeds during turns. The outside wheel in a turn travels farther than the one on the inside of the turn. The differential tries to give wheels the power they need in turns, which means you can navigate the turn accurately and safely.

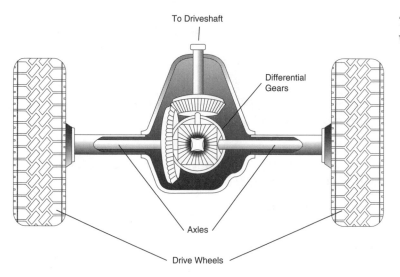

To Driveshaft

Differential Gears

Axles

Drive Wheels

The differential on a rear-wheel-drive car.

How do you know when your car's differential needs repair? If you noticed bits of metal in the bottom of the differential when you last lubricated it, the gears are wearing out. Jack the rear end of the car up and rotate the wheels one direction and then the other, listening for clanking sounds. If you hear them, the differential may be ready for replacement—or at least a closer look.

To replace a differential, follow these steps:

1. To inspect the differential gears, place a pan under the differential to catch lubricant. Then remove bolts on the rear side of the differential case. When the case is open, lubricant flows out of it. Carefully touch the lubricant and the bottom of the case with your fingers or a magnet to check for small metal bits that indicate worn gears. Visually inspect the gears for wear, broken teeth, or other damage.

2. If repair is necessary, refer to your car's service manual or an aftermarket manual for instructions. Some differentials are quite easy to repair by replacing one or more gears. Limited-slip or other differentials are more complex. In many cases, the axle or at least the wheels must be removed to replace differential gears.

3. Reinstall the differential and test it.

Your rear end problems should be resolved—or at least your car's rear end problems should be resolved.

Car Speak

The *differential* in a rear-wheel-drive car uses gears to transfer the single driveline's power to two wheels as needed.

The Least You Need to Know

➤ Replacing a manual transmission requires that you safely jack up the car, unbolt the driveshaft, and carefully remove the transmission.

➤ An automatic transmission is heavier and usually requires that the torque converter be removed at the same time, so rent a transmission jack or stand to help hold it.

➤ Universal and constant velocity joints in automotive driveshafts can wear out, but are usually easy to replace with basic tools.

➤ The differential in a rear-wheel- or all-wheel-drive car can be replaced if gears become noisy or fail to turn rear wheels.

Chapter 23

Steering and Suspension System Repairs: No More Swerves or Bounces!

> ### In This Chapter
>
> ➤ How repairs are made to automotive steering and suspension systems
>
> ➤ How the car's front wheels are aligned for smooth steering and less tire wear
>
> ➤ How to replace shocks and struts yourself—or what to watch for when a mechanic does it

Your car's steering system enables the car to turn; its suspension system smoothes out the ride. It's that simple—and that important. Things can go wrong, however, making the ride rough or steering difficult or dangerous. In either of those cases, it's time to repair.

Many types of steering and suspension systems have been used to control cars. Until recently, most cars used *pitman-arm steering*, which passed the steering wheel's rotation to a lever (pitman arm) that moved side to side. Many of today's cars rely on *rack-and-pinion steering*, which uses meshed gears to control steering. Older cars use mechanical suspension that relies on springs and shock absorbers, but newer cars use hydraulic cylinders called *struts*.

All these components are covered in this chapter. Whether you do these repairs yourself or have them done for you, understanding what's involved will make you a more savvy car owner.

With proper care, your car's steering system should give you 80,000 to 100,000 miles of smooth turns.

Why Won't My Car Turn Where I Want It To?

Chapters 14, "Why Cars Don't Run: The Little Car That Couldn't," and 15, "Don't Shoot! Troubleshoot," outlined common car problems and how to troubleshoot them. To add to your list of conversation starters, here are some guidelines for troubleshooting steering and suspension systems. Don't worry if you're not sure what all the terms mean; they are covered later in this chapter and in the glossary.

➤ If your car's power steering growls when you try to turn, first check the power steering booster fluid level. Then, if necessary, repair the power steering unit.

➤ If your car makes a high-pitched squeal, check the drivebelt on the power-steering unit for slippage.

Car Speak

The *steering system* parts transfer the driver's guiding movements to the appropriate wheels; antonym: steering committee. The *suspension system* parts (springs, shock absorbers, and so on) suspend the car's frame and body above the wheels.

➤ If your car shimmies, check tire pressure and inspect the tires to make sure they are all the same size and aren't damaged. Then check for worn tie-rod ends and lower balljoints in the steering system. That should control your car's urge to dance down the street.

➤ If it's difficult to steer your older car, lubricate the steering system's zerk fittings to see whether that solves the problem before replacing parts.

➤ If your car leans hard on corners, check the stabilizer and struts for loose parts and wear.

➤ If your car shakes, shimmies, rattles, rolls, and gyrates, you have the Elvis Presley model.

Stopping Arguments Between Your Wheels

All right you wheels, let's get some cooperation going. It has to hurt if the left wheel always wants to go right, and the right wheel always wants to go left. Teamwork!

Grab your car care toolbox (see Chapter 6, "Do-It-Yourself Maintenance, or Getting Your Hands Dirty"). Chances are you don't have the tools and equipment in your garage to accurately align your car's wheels. You'll probably take it to a specialist who can do the job for you. Even so, understanding why and how wheels are aligned can help you better understand your car and help keep you from getting ripped off. And it will motivate you to keep them aligned. You can also check tire wear to discover whether your car's wheels are aligned properly.

Wheel alignment is necessary to keep the four wheels traveling in the same direction. You don't want the right wheel going straight ahead and the left one trying to make a turn. Think how quickly you would trip if your feet didn't aim in the same direction. Front wheels must be moved to steer, so they must be aligned. Rear wheels on cars built since about 1980 also may require alignment. Most cars need wheel alignment every 30,000 to 60,000 miles. That's a lot less often than your kid's braces need realigning.

Maybe you've heard the terms *toe in* and *toe out* regarding wheel alignment. No, it's not a dance. The *toe* is the front edge of the wheel. *Toe in* means that the front edges of the two wheels are a little closer to each other than the heels or backs of the wheels. *Toe out* means the front edges are farther apart than the back edges.

Caster is the tilt of the steering connection to the wheel. *Camber* is the inward or outward tilt of the wheel's top.

The point to wheel alignment is that each car was designed to operate best with specific alignment tolerances. If the wheel alignment isn't within its tolerance, tires wear unevenly, the car can be harder to steer, and stress can be put on steering components, making them unsafe and causing fuel mileage to suffer. Sounds expensive.

Car Speak

Alignment is an adjustment to keep parts in the correct relative position, such as the alignment of a car's wheel and suspension system.

Front-wheel-drive cars have different wheel-alignment specifications than rear-wheel-drive cars. The same is true of front-engine and rear-engine cars. Your car's owner's manual and service manual will give the manufacturer's wheel-alignment specs.

Here are some tests you can make to ensure that your car's wheels are aligned properly:

➤ Run your hand over the tire tread from the outer edge to the center and then to the inner edge. The surface should feel equally smooth in both directions. If the surface is rougher moving from the inner edge to the center, the wheel may have too much toe out. If the surface is rougher moving from the center to the outer edge, the wheel may have too much toe in.

➤ Wear on the outside edge of tires usually means that the camber isn't set properly.

➤ Wear on both inside and outside edges of tires usually means that the tire is underinflated.

➤ Wear in the center of tires usually means that the tire is overinflated.

Toe is corrected by adjusting the tie rod or rear lower arm. Newer vehicles might have caster and camber set at the factory, with no adjustments available to the mechanic or car owner.

Suspension and Your Car

Your car's suspension system (see the first figure in this chapter) includes a shock absorber, a stabilizer bar, leaf springs, a suspension arm, and/or MacPherson struts.

These parts wear out with use and need to be replaced. Here's the lowdown on what each of them does:

➤ **Shock absorber:** A tranquilizer; alternatively, a mechanical cylinder that dampens a wheel's up-and-down movement caused by bumps in the road.

➤ **Coil spring:** A circular steel spring used to minimize up-and-down motion.

➤ **Leaf spring:** A group of flat steel springs used to minimize up-and-down motion.

➤ **MacPherson strut:** A Scottish dance; alternatively, a component of most front-wheel-drive cars that combines the coil spring and shock absorber into one unit; named for an engineer at Ford in England—really!

➤ **Stabilizer bar:** A tavern with seat belts on the bar stools; alternatively, a bar linking the suspension systems on two wheels (front or rear) to stabilize steering or turning.

➤ **Independent suspension:** A suspension system that allows two wheels on the same axle to move independently of each other.

A suspension system.

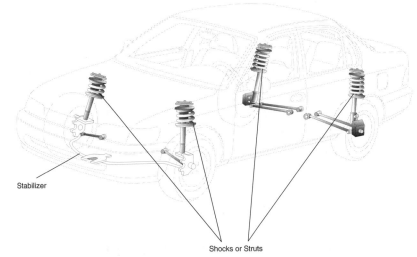

Stabilizer

Shocks or Struts

How often do the parts in your suspension system need to be replaced? Older cars may need new parts every 25,000 miles, but newer cars could go as many as 100,000 miles before needing parts replacement. Much depends on the car's design as well as how it is driven. Heavy loads and rough roads wear down suspension parts faster.

Because wear to suspension parts is gradual, you might not notice how far components have deteriorated. Steering becomes more difficult. The car doesn't corner as smoothly. Lots of passengers or heavy packages make the car sag more than it did. You can replace parts as recommended by the manufacturer, or you can test and visually inspect them using your car's service manual.

To replace suspension parts, follow these steps:

1. Find out what suspension parts your car has. A stabilizer bar buffers side-to-side motion. Shock absorbers and coil springs dampen up-and-down motion. A strut combines the shock absorber and coil spring. Front-wheel-drive cars have suspension arms on the rear wheels.

2. Jack up the car and place safety stands under the wheels.

3. Cars with independent front suspension have a stabilizer bar. Stabilizer bars don't wear out; the rubber mountings, called *bushings*, do. The stabilizer bar and bushings are bolted to the underside of the vehicle between the right and left wheel suspension systems. Replace the bushings by removing the brackets holding the bar in place, removing the bushings, and replacing them. Stabilizer bar bushings are sold in sets at larger auto parts retailers.

4. Shock absorbers are installed inside the coil spring at each wheel. Shock absorbers can be replaced by removing the bolts at the top and bottom that connect them to the suspension system. Be sure to follow the manufacturer's instructions because shock absorbers and springs are under tension and can injure you if they are not removed properly.

5. Struts are shock absorbers integrated into the coil spring. Remove the fasteners at the top and bottom that connect them to the suspension system. Your car's service manual or an aftermarket manual tells you exactly how. Don't try to disassemble a strut. Replace it as a unit.

6. Many cars have upper and lower suspension arms that allow the wheels to move up and down independently of each other. These arms typically don't need replacement, but the rubber bushings on which they are mounted do. To replace them, first locate and inspect them using the service manual. Most require that you loosen and remove a bolt on which the bushing is mounted.

7. Tell at least two people on the street about your experiences repairing your car's suspension system until tears come to their eyes.

The Steering Committee

A steering system (see the figure showing steering systems) uses a steering gear and rods to transfer the turning of the steering wheel to the front wheels. Steering gears usually last as long as the car, but some of the connecting components need replacement along the way.

Chapters 14 and 15 offer troubleshooting tips. Also refer to your car's service manual for specific information on fixing your car's steering problems.

As always, make sure you install safety stands under your car before working there. Refer to your car's service manual for specific information on making repairs to the steering system.

Pitman-arm and rack-and-pinion steering systems.

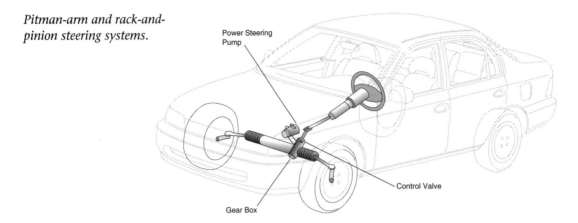

Power Steering Pump

Control Valve

Gear Box

Steering systems are typically repaired following these steps:

1. Inspect, adjust, and, if necessary, replace tie-rod ends. Tie rods connect the wheels to the steering unit. The ends of these rods must be free to move with the movement of the steering system. They wear out. If they are worn or damaged, replace the tie-rod ends with ones from an auto parts retailer. Mark the exact location of the old ones so that the new ones can be installed in the same position and require little or no adjustment.

2. Check, adjust, and, if necessary, replace the steering gear unit. Many steering gear systems offer adjustments that can be made with a wrench and screwdriver while following instructions in the service manual. If replacement is needed, the steering wheel and column may need to be removed first. Each car is different, so check the manual for specific instructions.

Car Speak

Pitman-arm steering was popular for 50 years and used a gear to transmit the driver's steering motion to the pitman arm. In *rack-and-pinion steering,* meshed gears make steering more responsive than pitman-arm steering. A *tie rod* is a jointed rod that ties the steering gear to the wheels.

3. Test the repaired steering system by driving to some friends' houses to tell them all about your repair experiences. It helps if they're trying to watch a big football game.

When the Steering Needs a Boost

Some cars have a booster that uses hydraulics to make turning the steering wheel easier. Most power steering booster systems use a pump turned by the engine's crankshaft to circulate the hydraulic oil or fluid.

To repair power steering systems, follow these steps:

1. Check the power steering hoses for leaks or damage. A small leak can slowly drain the system

of hydraulic oil and make turning the steering wheel difficult. Find the steering gear box (near the end of the steering column) and the power steering pump (on the front of the engine, driven by a belt). Locate the hoses running between the two units and check them for leaks and loose fittings. Replace them as needed with identical replacement parts.

2. If the power steering pump leaks or is noisy and must be repaired, loosen the bracket that maintains belt pressure, remove the drivebelt, siphon fluid from the reservoir, and then remove the pump and reservoir. Have the unit rebuilt or replaced and reinstall it.

Car Speak

Power steering is a hydraulic unit that magnifies the driver's motions to more easily steer the car.

3. If power steering fluid must be replaced or the reservoir is dry and fluid must be refilled, make sure you remove air from the brake system. Otherwise, air in the brake lines can make braking more difficult. Check your car's manual for specific instructions. In many cases, air can be removed from the power steering system by running the engine to operate the pump, removing the reservoir cap, and then turning the steering wheel fully to the left and then to the right a few times. Remember to replace the reservoir cap.

The Least You Need to Know

➤ You probably don't have all the tools needed to align your car's steering system, but knowing the process will help you be a smarter car consumer.

➤ Troubleshooting your car's steering and suspension systems is a matter of paying attention to small changes in how the car handles and learning what you can do about it.

➤ You can replace many worn steering and suspension components with basic tools and instructions offered in this chapter and in Chapter 8, "CAR Weekly Check Up."

Chapter 24

Brake System Repairs: Stop Ahead!

In This Chapter

➤ Repairing your car's disc and/or drum brakes and saving yourself a hundred dollars or more in labor costs

➤ Learning to replace your car's master brake cylinder

➤ How to repair your car's power brake booster, if it has one

➤ Adjusting your car's parking brake

Brakes are an obviously important part of your car. Although many car owners leave brake work to a specialist, it doesn't have to be so. Brake parts are commodities, easily found at larger auto parts stores. The steps to repairing or replacing brake parts are easy to follow. The job requires few special tools beyond those in your car care toolbox (see Chapter 6, "Do-It-Yourself Maintenance, or Getting Your Hands Dirty").

Can you do the job as well as a brake specialist? Maybe not. But you can do it adequately—and sometimes better than a poorly trained employee who last week was grilling hamburgers. Specialists know more; you know less. They have a hundred brake jobs to do this week; you have just one.

Most cars today use a hydraulic brake system (see the figure showing a brake system) with drum brakes on the rear, disc brakes on the front, and each with a brake cylinder that's controlled by the master cylinder. A hydraulic system uses brake fluid to force the brakes against moving parts in the wheels. Some cars have a proportioning valve that keeps the rear brakes from locking up when you slam on the pedal. Antilock brake systems (ABS) have a built-in proportioning valve and some electronics to control skidding.

An automotive braking system.

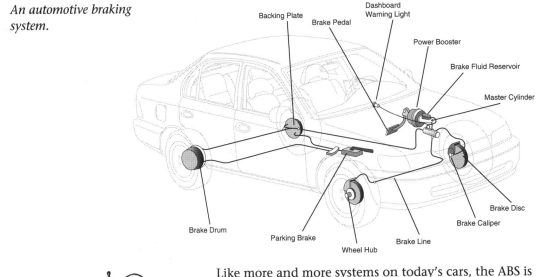

Backing Plate
Brake Pedal
Dashboard Warning Light
Power Booster
Brake Fluid Reservoir
Master Cylinder
Brake Disc
Brake Caliper
Brake Line
Wheel Hub
Parking Brake
Brake Drum

Car Speak

Brakes convert kinetic energy into heat energy, slowing down the car. In an *antilock brake system (ABS)*, an electronic system controls hydraulics to evenly distribute a car's braking power to avoid skidding.

Safety First

A word of caution is due. To work on your car's brakes, you'll have to jack up one or both ends of the car. Make sure you place safety stands in the correct spots under the car (see the owner's or service manual). Be safe, please! I need to keep all my readers!

Like more and more systems on today's cars, the ABS is controlled by an electronic computer. Each brand is just a bit different to service. If your car has an ABS, find and follow the service manual. ABS systems usually can tell you what's wrong with them through trouble codes. Deciphering these codes requires the service manual.

Avoiding Skids on the Road

As promised, here are some useful tips for troubleshooting automotive brake systems. Don't worry if you're not familiar with all the terms used here. You'll learn about them later in the chapter, and you can find them in the glossary. Troubleshooting in general is covered in Chapters 14, "Why Cars Don't Run: The Little Car That Couldn't," and 15, "Don't Shoot! Troubleshoot."

➤ If your car pulls to one side during braking, first check tire pressure and front-end alignment. Then check for malfunctioning drum or disc brakes.

➤ If disc brakes squeal when applied, the brake pads are probably worn out and need replacement.

➤ If the brake pedal pulsates when pressed, brake pads or shoes might be worn unevenly and need adjustment or replacement.

➤ If drum brakes make a grinding noise, the brake shoes are probably worn out or the wheel cylinder is stuck.

➤ If the brake pedal seems mushy, there's probably air in the hydraulic brake lines. Bleed the brake system of air.

➤ If the brakes automatically apply when you see a police car, check your foot for lead content.

When Your Car Needs New Shoes

Most modern drum brakes (shown in the next figure) are self-adjusting (see Chapter 10, "CAR Semiannual Adjustments"). When the brakes are worn, the drum brakes need inspection and possibly replacement of key parts. Brake shoes need to be replaced about every 30,000 miles. You can do it.

A drum brake system.

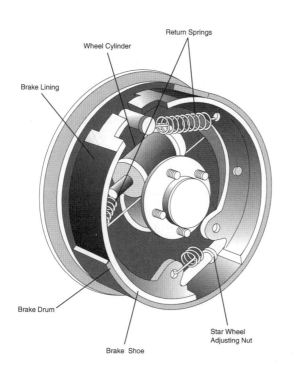

You need to be familiar with several parts of a drum system:

➤ **Brake drum:** The part on a drum brake system that receives pressure from the brake shoe.

➤ **Brake shoe:** The movable part of a drum brake system that applies pressure against the brake drum. The replaceable surface of a drum brake system is the friction lining, which typically is replaced with the shoe; alternatively, what brakes step on as they're dancing.

➤ **Wheel cylinder:** A hydraulic cylinder at each wheel that magnifies the master cylinder's pressure to evenly operate the wheel's brake system. Disc brake systems have wheel cylinders, too.

➤ **Parking brake:** A hand- or foot-operated brake that applies brake shoes or brake pads against the braking surface on a car's rear wheels; also called an *emergency brake.* All cars have an emergency brake.

What tools do you need for repairs in this chapter? The car care toolbox described in Chapter 6 will have most of the necessary tools. I'll mention any special tools as we go along.

To repair drum brakes, follow these steps:

1. Safely jack up your car and place stands under the axle.

Car Speak

A *drum brake* system applies brake shoes against the inside of a brake drum to stop or slow a car. A *disc brake* system applies pressure against a disc on the wheels to stop the car.

My Mechanic Says. . .

To adjust a parking brake, press or pull the brake level until it first clicks (about 1 inch). Then adjust the parking brake cable so that the brakes just start to drag on the rear wheels. The adjustment may be at the wheels or somewhere along the cable between the parking brake and the rear wheels.

2. Remove the wheel covers and then the wheel from the car as you would when changing a tire (see Chapter 8, "CAR Weekly Check Up").

3. Remove the cap at the center of the axle using large pliers and/or a screwdriver. Remove the cotter pin by straightening the bent end and pulling the pin out from the round end. Remove the nut and washer.

4. Carefully pull the brake drum toward you, wiggling it from side to side if necessary to loosen it. The wheel bearings and washers will come off the axle first, so catch them in your hand and set them aside. Continue pulling on the drum until it comes off the axle, and then carefully set it aside.

5. Clean parts as needed with an old brush or compressed air so that you can see what you're doing. Caution: Older brake shoe linings use asbestos, so wear a filtering face mask when cleaning.

6. Inspect the inside of the brake drum for deep scratches, and the brake shoes and other parts for wear or damage. If in doubt about wear or damage, remove the part and show it to an experienced auto parts clerk.

7. To remove brake shoes, first install a wheel cylinder clamp (from the auto parts store) to hold the cylinder together. Then remove the large return springs using a brake spring tool (from the auto

parts store, of course). Remove the self-adjusting unit as needed to free the brake shoes. Finally, remove any other fasteners or components holding the brake shoes in place.

8. Remove the wheel cylinder by disconnecting the brake line and removing fasteners holding the cylinder in place. If the cylinder is leaking or if you're completely replacing your brake system, replace the wheel cylinder with a new one. You can rebuild it yourself or buy a rebuilt unit.

9. Replace the brake shoes, wheel cylinder, springs, and other components as needed by reversing the earlier instructions.

10. Reinstall the drum, repack the wheel bearings (see Chapter 12, "CAR: Biannual Replacements"), and replace the wheel and tire. When done repairing all brakes, refill the master cylinder with brake fluid and bleed the brake system, as described in your car's service manual. Finally, adjust the brakes (see Chapter 10).

11. Brag! You've earned the right.

Car Speak

The *brake caliper* part in a disc brake system squeezes the disc to make the car slow or stop. Calipers have a replaceable surface called *brake pads*. The *pad wear indicator* on the pad shows you when brake pads are worn to the point of needing replacement. Your car's service manual will tell you how to read the indicator.

Replacing Your Car's Brake Pads

Disc brakes (see the figure showing the disc brake setup) stop your car by applying lots of pressure to both sides of a spinning disc (rotor) on which the wheels are mounted. The brake pads are held and operated by the caliper, which squeezes the pads against the disc when you press your foot on the brake pedal.

Brake pads should give you at least 25,000 miles of service before needing replacement.

To repair disc brakes, follow these steps:

1. Safely jack up your car and place stands under the axle.

2. Remove the wheel covers, and then remove the wheel from the car as you would when changing a tire.

3. Inspect the brake caliper, brake pads, the wear indicator, the disc, and other components of the disc brake system. If the brake pads are worn, replace them with new pads. They should be no thinner than $1/16$ inch. If the brake disc (rotor) is scored (has grooves in it), take it to a brake shop for resurfacing (turning) or replace it with a new disc.

4. To replace brake pads, use a C-clamp (which you can get at a hardware store or auto parts store) to push the piston back in the caliper. Remove the bolt(s) holding the caliper in place and move it aside. Don't disconnect the caliper from

the brake fluid line unless you plan to replace the caliper. If you remove the caliper, brake fluid will leak out. Remove the brake pads and shims from both sides of the disc. Install new pads and shims following the instructions that come with the parts.

5. Reinstall the disc and hub assembly, repack the wheel bearings (see Chapter 12), replace the caliper and other components, and replace the wheel and tire. When done repairing all brakes, refill the master cylinder with brake fluid and bleed (remove any air from) the brake system, as described in your car's service manual or in the next section. Finally, adjust the brakes (see Chapter 10).

6. A go-for-your-favorite-treat test drive is optional, but highly recommended.

A disc brake system.

Masters of the Brake Universe

A brake system's master cylinder usually doesn't need replacement, except as an entire brake system is being rebuilt. You don't want a 15-year-old master cylinder trying to operate new wheel cylinders or calipers. If you replace wheel cylinders (done in pairs), consider replacing the master cylinder at the same time.

On most cars, the master brake cylinder is located on the firewall on the left (driver's) side of the engine compartment. Your car care toolbox (see Chapter 6) has all the tools you need for this job.

To replace a master cylinder, follow these steps:

1. Remove fluid from the master cylinder using a siphon. Cover painted parts near the master cylinder with rags because brake fluid can damage paint.

2. Disconnect the brake lines from the master cylinder and plug the end of the lines to prevent leakage and contamination.

3. Disconnect the electrical wires from the master cylinder, marking them for later identification if it's not clear where they should go.

4. Remove the bolts holding the master cylinder in place and remove the unit from the car.

5. Replace the master cylinder with a new unit, reconnecting lines and wires. Refill the master cylinder with approved brake fluid.

6. Bleed the brake system following the manufacturer's instructions. Typically, this means having one person press on the brake pedal while another opens the bleed fitting on each wheel cylinder or caliper, in turn. Close the bleed fitting once brake fluid flows instead of air. Repeat the process at each wheel to remove air from the brake lines because air in the hydraulic system can reduce braking efficiency, and that can mean the difference between stopping in time and calling your insurance agent with another claim.

Car Speak

The brake system's *master cylinder* is a hydraulic cylinder that magnifies the driver's foot pressure to evenly operate the four wheel brakes.

Boosters for Brakes

Power brake boosters make braking easier because they boost the driver's foot pressure on the master brake cylinder. Some power brake boosters offer adjustments that can be made as needed. Such adjustments can be made at the top end of the brake pedal before the brake pushrod goes through the firewall to the booster. Visually check your car's system for adjustments before replacing the booster. The car's service manual can tell you more—if there's more to tell.

Before replacing the power brake booster, test it to find the cause of the problem. Boosters that use a vacuum might simply have a hole or break in the vacuum line to the booster. Use a vacuum gauge to test the line following the manufacturer's instructions.

In addition, many power brake booster systems have an adjustable pushrod between the booster and the master cylinder. If your car has one of these, check the manual for information on this adjustment. You can save yourself some valuable time and money.

To replace a power brake booster, follow these steps:

1. Locate the power brake booster on your car. It typically is installed on the engine firewall between the brake pedal lever and the master cylinder.

2. If necessary, remove the master cylinder from the power booster. Depending on the system, you might not need to disconnect brake lines or drain the master cylinder; just remove the bolts mounting the cylinder to the booster.

3. Remove vacuum and hydraulic lines from the power brake booster unit, marking them for easier reinstallation unless you like jigsaw puzzles.

4. Disconnect the power brake booster unit from the brake pedal arm. This typically means removing a nut or a cotter pin.

Car Speak

The *power brake booster* is a hydraulic and vacuum unit that helps the brake's master cylinder magnify the driver's foot pressure to evenly operate the four wheel brakes.

5. Remove the power brake booster unit from the firewall. On most cars, mounting bolts fasten the unit to the firewall.

6. Replace the power brake booster unit with an exact replacement, following the instructions that come with the part or in the service manual. Some units require adjustments before installation; others are adjusted in place.

7. Be careful when you test your brakes. If your brakes were tired, you might find yourself kissing the windshield the first time or two you apply the refreshed brakes.

The Least You Need to Know

➤ Cars today use a hydraulic braking system with disc and/or drum brakes. As parts wear out with use, you can repair them yourself with basic tools—or hire someone to do it for you.

➤ Most brake components aren't repaired, but replaced with parts available at larger auto parts retailers.

➤ Your car's brake system can get air mixed in with the hydraulic fluid, reducing the braking efficiency. Removing air from a hydraulic brake system is called bleeding. It isn't painful.

➤ Power brake systems use a brake booster that can be replaced as a unit if it isn't working efficiently.

Chapter 25

Electrical System Repairs: You'll Get a Charge Out of This!

In This Chapter

➤ How to safely test and replace a car battery and cables

➤ Installing a new alternator

➤ Checking out and replacing other components in your car's electrical system

Your car both produces and consumes power. Part of the engine's power is used to produce electrical power, which then is consumed by the computers, spark plugs, lights, radio, and other paraphernalia. The battery is the power storage room (yes, it's a small room). Repairing or replacing these components is what this chapter is about.

Your car's charging system includes the alternator, voltage regulator, battery, cables, wires, and fuses. (Don't sweat it yet if you don't recall what these are; I describe each of them later in the chapter.) Some alternators have the voltage regulator built into them; others require a separate component to regulate the alternator's voltage output. Some of us with geriatric cars have generators instead of alternators. Same difference.

If troubleshooting (see Chapters 14, "Why Cars Don't Run: The Little Car That Couldn't," and 15, "Don't Shoot! Troubleshoot," or your car's service manual) says you need to repair electrical components, this chapter will show you how. Most components in the charging and electrical system of your car are replaced rather than repaired. In fact, they are another commodity item. You can find them on the shelf of most auto parts stores or through mail-order suppliers and replace them yourself. You'll be able to make these repairs with your car care toolbox (see Chapter 6, "Do-It-Yourself Maintenance, or Getting Your Hands Dirty") and special tools noted as we go along.

An automotive charging system.

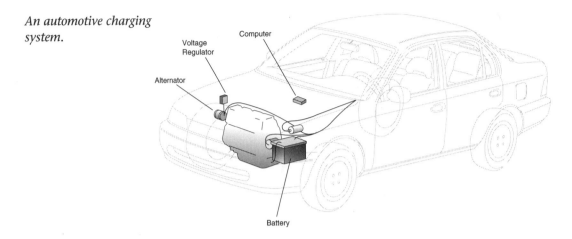

When the Automotive Power Goes Out

I know you've been waiting anxiously for these. Here are a few useful tips for trouble-shooting charging and electrical systems. Solutions are offered later in this chapter.

➤ If the battery tests okay but won't hold a charge, make sure the alternator drivebelt is adjusted tight. If the drivebelt is okay, test the voltage regulator using a volt-ohmmeter.

➤ If turn signals work only on one side, check the bulb and wiring on the side that isn't working. If they don't work at all, check the fuse.

➤ If you suspect that your car's battery is weak, pull your car up to a garage door or other wall, turn off the engine, and turn the headlights on for a moment. If they are bright, the battery and voltage regulator are okay. If they are dim but brighten after you start the engine, the battery is bad. If they are bright but the engine turns slowly when you try to start it again, the starter is bad (see Chapter 18, "Starting and Ignition System Repairs for the Clueless").

Energize Me!

A car battery is an electrical storage device. It receives electricity from the alternator/regulator and passes it on to other electrical components on demand. As the battery's electricity is used up, it is replaced. Problems occur when a battery isn't strong enough to keep a charge because the electrolyte is weak. This typically occurs a few days after the warranty expires.

To replace a battery, follow these steps:

1. Find your car's battery. It's usually under the hood and typically on the passenger's side of the car.

2. Disconnect the cable from the negative side of the battery first and then the positive side (see Chapter 9, "CAR Quarterly Check Up").

3. Remove the hold-down clamp or frame that keeps the battery in place. Typically, this means removing nuts from the end of two long bolts. Grasp the bolts as you loosen the nuts, making sure the released bolts don't fall out of reach.

4. Use a battery strap (from the auto parts store) attached to the two terminals to lift and remove the HEAVY battery. Set it aside for a moment.

5. Inspect the battery tray for corrosion and damage. If the tray is rusted or damaged, replace it. Wearing rubber gloves, clean the battery with baking soda and water to neutralize the battery acids.

6. Test the battery or have it tested to make sure it will hold a charge. If it will, recharge the battery or have it recharged by a mechanic. If it won't, replace the battery with one of the same voltage, size, amperage rating, and cold-cranking rating. Consider replacing the battery cables at the same time (see the following section).

7. Reinstall the battery, hold-down clamp, positive cable, and then negative cable.

8. Lift your right hand over your head, bend your elbow to 120°, and then move your wrist repeatedly, patting yourself on the back. You done good.

Money Saver

A more expensive battery can be worth the extra expense. A 60-month battery is built to hold a charge longer than a 48-month battery. So is a 60-month battery worth the extra money? Yes, it is—if you plan on keeping your car that long. If you plan to sell your car in the next year, a 36- or 48-month battery will do just fine at less cost.

Car Speak

Your car's *battery* produces and stores direct current (DC) by converting chemical energy into electrical energy. *Electrolyte* is the dietetic version of Electro. It's also the sulfuric acid and water solution within a car battery that produces electricity.

Your Battery on Cable

The battery cables play a vital part in delivering electricity to and from the car's battery. Battery cables are simply heavy-duty coated wires with terminals on the ends to make attaching them to the battery and other components easier.

So what can go wrong with battery cables? They can become corroded by the electro-chemical process that's going on inside the battery. *Corrosion* is a buildup of powdery substance on the cable ends. The ends can also be damaged by mishandling or become brittle with age. Unfortunately, I understand that all too well.

To replace your battery cables, follow these steps:

1. Find your car's battery. It's under the hood and typically on the passenger's side of the car. There are two cables attached to two terminals on the top or side of the battery. One is probably red and the other black.

2. Disconnect the cable from the negative side of the battery and then the positive side. The negative cable is usually black and smaller than the red, positive cable (see Chapter 9).

3. Disconnect the cables at the other end. The negative ground cable (usually the black one) is probably connected to the engine. The positive cable (red) is probably connected to the starter solenoid.

4. Inspect the cable wire and ends for damage. Even if you can't see it, there might be damage to the wires within the cable, reducing the flow of electricity through it. Battery cables are just a few dollars each, so replace them every few years whether or not you can see damage. The easiest time to replace cables is when you replace the battery, every four or five years.

5. To find replacement cables, clean the old cables and take them to your favorite auto parts retailer for an exact match. You want the new ones to match the old ones in length, circumference, and ends. If you have a choice, spend a couple of extra bucks and buy ones with better quality wires to transport electricity more easily. Cheap is cheap. Pick up some battery terminal corrosion inhibitor (or petroleum jelly) while you're at the store—and a candy bar for me.

6. Reinstall the ends of the cables to the ground and the starter solenoid or wherever they came from, applying corrosion inhibitor to the bolt threads.

7. Apply corrosion inhibitor to the positive battery terminal. Reinstall the positive (red) cable to the positive terminal on the battery.

8. Apply corrosion inhibitor to the negative battery terminal. Reinstall the negative (black) cable to the negative terminal on the battery.

What to Do When You Can't Charge Any More

An alternator produces electricity from a car's engine. If your car's battery is in good condition, but isn't getting recharged, the charging system may be the culprit.

An alternator should give you at least 50,000 miles of service, and up to twice as much. Before you replace an alternator, check its drivebelt and pulley to make sure they aren't the cause of the problem (see Chapter 11, "CAR Yearly Replacements").

To test and replace an alternator, follow these steps:

1. To test the charging system's fuse, first locate the fuse by using the car's service manual. It may be a fuse box or it could be on the wire between the starter solenoid and the alternator. Make sure the engine and ignition are off. Use an ohmmeter, placing one probe on one side of the fuse or wire and one on the other. If the fuse or wire has infinite resistance (1), the circuit is open and the fuse should be replaced.

2. To test the alternator, refer to the car's service manual for instructions on how to do so without removing the alternator from the car. One way of testing the system is by checking the battery's voltage with a volt-ohmmeter (VOM). With the engine off, the battery should give a reading of about 12 volts. With the engine on, the battery should give a reading of 14–15 volts on the VOM. If it registers lower, replace the alternator. If it's more than 15 volts, replace the voltage regulator (see the next section).

3. To replace the alternator, first disconnect the cable from the negative terminal of the battery. Then identify and remove all wires from the alternator. Loosen the alternator adjusting bolt, and then remove the drivebelt. Remove the alternator from the adjusting bracket and the engine. Replace the alternator with one of the exact same size and rating.

4. When done, test the alternator to make sure it's doing its job. If not, sell your car and take the bus.

Car Speak

Your car's *alternator* converts mechanical energy into alternating current (AC), which then must be changed (rectified) into direct current (DC) for use by the car's electrical system; also known as an AC generator.

A *generator* is a device that converts mechanical energy into direct current (DC) for use by the car's electrical system; also known as a DC generator.

My Mechanic Says. . .

If you replace your alternator, make sure the replacement has drivebelt pulleys. If not (often not), remove them from the old alternator and install them on the new one before returning or recycling the old alternator.

Regulating Those Volts!

The voltage regulator plays an important role in your car's charging system: It manages the alternator's output voltage.

How can you tell if the regulator isn't working as it should? By checking the voltage of the battery with the engine running. If the battery voltage is less than 12 volts or more

231

than 15 volts, the regulator is probably not working. Although you can replace the regulator without replacing the alternator, you should consider doing both at once.

Don't forget to disconnect the negative battery terminal when working on your car's electrical system, and be prepared to reenter alarm codes if necessary, after the battery cable is reattached.

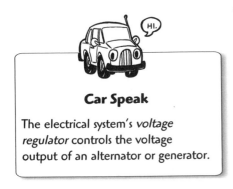

Car Speak

The electrical system's *voltage regulator* controls the voltage output of an alternator or generator.

To replace a voltage regulator, follow these steps:

1. Find the darn thing. Your car's service manual helps you locate it. Otherwise, older cars have the voltage regulator mounted on the firewall or a *cowl* (a wheel cover inside the engine compartment), and newer ones use a solid state regulator installed on the front side of the alternator behind the pulley wheel.

2. Loosen mounting screws and remove the regulator. Don't attempt to repair it. Replace it.

3. Take the regulator to your auto parts retailer along with model numbers from the alternator on which it was installed. Make sure the replacement is the same size, shape, and rating as the unit it's replacing.

4. Install the voltage regulator, making sure that all wires are connected correctly.

5. When done, test the voltage regulator to make sure it's working as it should. If it's now working properly, you have just passed the "Regulating Those Volts" final exam.

Other Auto Electrical Devices to Play With

Many other electrical devices in your car can also go awry at the least convenient time. They include lights, instruments, controls, radio, clock, and wiring (see the figure illustrating this system). Most have two wires; some have more. You can easily test these devices by checking the circuit to make sure electricity has a closed path through it.

A volt-ohmmeter (VOM) can measure either the voltage in a live circuit or the resistance in a dead circuit. A *live* circuit is simply one with electricity flowing through it (with the ignition on and/or the engine running), and a *dead* circuit is one without power applied to it.

So how is a dead circuit measured? The ohmmeter applies a small amount of electricity to the circuit using internal batteries, and then measures the output to see whether any of it made it to the exit. If so, it's a closed circuit; if not, it's open. An ohmmeter can also measure how much resistance the signal faced trying to get to the exit. Resistance is measured in ohms; more ohms means more resistance.

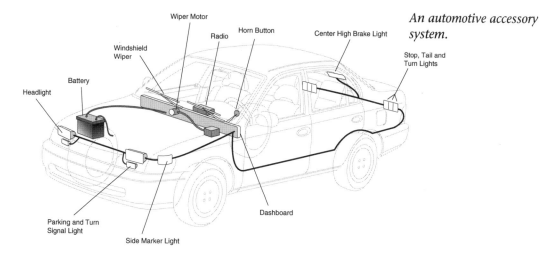

An automotive accessory system.

To test continuity of an electrical device, follow these steps:

1. Isolate the device by marking and removing any wires attached to it. You won't keep it isolated long enough for it to get lonesome.

2. Decide what ohmmeter reading you should be getting (open, closed, low resistance, or high resistance). The owner's manual can help you determine the appropriate reading.

3. Test the device using the ohmmeter. If the reading isn't what it should be, replace the device or have it repaired. A turn signal light should be replaced, for example, but an analog clock often can be repaired.

To test voltage of an electrical device, follow these steps:

1. Make sure the device has power coming to it: fuses okay, ignition on.

2. Learn what volt-ohmmeter (VOM) reading you should be getting (2 volts, 12 volts, and so on). The owner's manual may help. Otherwise, estimate output voltage by what the device is designed to do: Use voltage to do a task (lower output) or multiply voltage (higher output).

Money Saver

Blame the fuses! Whenever anything in your car's electrical system goes out, find the fuse box (identified in the car's owner's manual) and look for a blown fuse. Some fuse boxes are under the hood near the battery. Others are under the dashboard near the driver. Some cars have fuses in both locations. A blown fuse will have a visible break in the wire that runs through it.

3. Test the device using the VOM. If the reading isn't what it should be, replace the device or have it repaired, as necessary.

4. Use your experiences with a volt-ohmmeter to bore others.

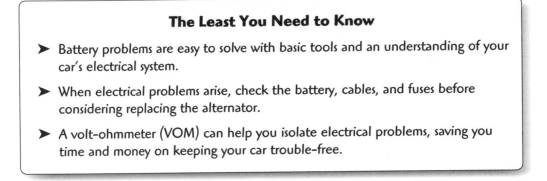

The Least You Need to Know

➤ Battery problems are easy to solve with basic tools and an understanding of your car's electrical system.

➤ When electrical problems arise, check the battery, cables, and fuses before considering replacing the alternator.

➤ A volt-ohmmeter (VOM) can help you isolate electrical problems, saving you time and money on keeping your car trouble-free.

Chapter 26

Exhaust System Repairs: Fixing an Exhausted System

In This Chapter

➤ How to safely repair exhaust manifold and pipe problems

➤ Learn to replace your car's muffler and catalytic converter with basic tools

➤ How to repair your car's emissions control system

Where there's fire, there's smoke. The controlled explosions within your car's engine also produce "smoke," or emissions. Your car's exhaust system is supposed to remove these emissions from the engine and clean them up as much as possible before dumping them into the atmosphere. When your car's exhaust system doesn't do its job, you need to replace it.

Components in your car's exhaust system (illustrated next) include some or all of the following: exhaust manifold, exhaust pipe(s) and hanger(s), muffler, resonator, catalytic converter, and exhaust gas recirculation parts.

What tools will you need for repairs in this chapter? The car care toolbox described in Chapter 6, "Do-It-Yourself Maintenance, or Getting Your Hands Dirty," has most of the necessary tools. I'll mention any special tools as we go along.

About replacing exhaust system components: Some can be replaced with simply a wrench, but others require welding equipment. Assuming that you probably don't have an arc welder in your household (I could be wrong on this one), you can use clamps to cinch down joints between components. It's doable.

Working on your car's exhaust system typically means getting it up on safety stands or ramps, blocking the wheels, and crawling underneath. Sorry, it can't be helped.

An exhaust system.

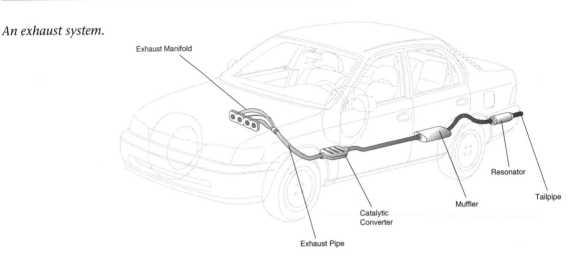

Exhaust Manifold

Resonator

Tailpipe

Muffler

Catalytic
Converter

Exhaust Pipe

Troubleshooting Tips for Tailpipes

In an effort to reduce noise and air pollution, here are a few tips for troubleshooting your car's exhaust system:

➤ If your exhaust system is loud, the muffler might need replacement. If the noise sounds more like hissing, it's probably a hole in an exhaust pipe.

➤ If the engine overheats or lacks power, the culprit might be a damaged muffler or tailpipe causing backpressure on the engine.

➤ If the exhaust system is noisy, visually inspect the pipes, muffler, catalytic converter, and other parts for obvious holes and broken hangers.

➤ If you can smell burning oil around the engine, the emissions-control system might be clogged and need cleaning or parts replacement.

The Manifold Life of an Exhaust System

The exhaust manifold collects burned exhaust gases as they leave the engine's cylinders. The collected gases are then piped to the catalytic converter through the exhaust pipe. Cars with all cylinders in one row (2, 4, or 6) have one exhaust manifold. Cars with cylinders in a V-shape (V-6, V-8) have two exhaust manifolds. Exhaust manifolds are pretty simple in concept and construction.

So what can go wrong with an exhaust manifold? Not a whole heck of a lot. It can become cracked or warped from excessive engine heat. Look and carefully feel for exhaust escaping from places it didn't before. If exhaust is escaping, the exhaust manifold may need to be replaced, although there are some aftermarket products that claim to repair manifold cracks. More often, repairing an exhaust manifold means replacing the gasket seals between the manifold and the engine block or the manifold and the exhaust pipe(s).

To repair an exhaust manifold, follow these steps:

1. When the engine is cold, locate the exhaust manifold on your car. The best way to do so may be backward: Find the exhaust muffler and pipe under the car and trace it into the engine compartment where it attaches to the exhaust manifold.

2. If necessary, remove the bolts that connect the exhaust pipe(s) to the output of the exhaust manifold. You will need a long $1/2$-inch socket wrench driver to loosen the bolts. If they won't budge, spray WD-40 or a penetrating lubricant on the nuts and let them sit for a while before trying again. After you have removed the bolts, check the gasket between the pipe and the manifold; if necessary, replace the gasket. Hold off on gasket replacement if you're also going to remove the manifold.

Car Speak

The *exhaust manifold* is a piping system that collects exhaust gases from the cylinders and delivers them to the exhaust pipes.

3. To remove the exhaust manifold, find and remove the bolts (or nuts) that attach the manifold to the engine block. There are typically two bolts per exhaust port or cylinder. Use a long $1/2$-inch socket wrench driver to loosen the bolts or nuts. Carefully remove the exhaust manifold and gasket from the engine block.

4. Replace the gasket and/or exhaust manifold if either is damaged, making sure that the old gasket material is removed from the engine and manifold. Then reinstall the exhaust pipe to the manifold output, replacing the gasket.

5. Take a rest after your exhausting work.

Don't Let Your Pipes Get Exhausted

Exhaust pipes are simply round pipes that transport exhaust gases from the manifold to the catalytic converter and/or muffler, but they aren't pipes you can buy at a plumbing shop. Exhaust pipes are bent to fit specific cars. You can buy prebent exhaust pipes for most modern cars, or you can hire a muffler shop to bend the pipes.

To repair an exhaust pipe that has a hole in it, purchase and use a muffler repair kit by following the package's instructions. Most kits include a tape or adhesive that can temporarily plug the hole. Of course, don't bother repairing a pipe that has numerous holes and really should be replaced.

To replace an exhaust pipe, follow these steps:

1. If you are replacing the entire exhaust pipe, loosen and remove the bolts holding the exhaust pipe to the exhaust manifold, as described in the preceding section. If you are not replacing the entire pipe, loosen and remove clamps on the section(s) you will replace.

My Mechanic Says. . .

Apply anti-seize lubricant on threads when reinstalling bolts to make future removal easier.

2. Carefully loosen and remove hangers holding the exhaust pipe to the underside of the car, making sure that the unit doesn't fall. You might need to grow or borrow an extra hand or two.

3. Replace the exhaust pipe(s) and reconnect to the system. If you are also replacing the catalytic converter, muffler, and/or resonator, do so as you replace the pipes, starting at the exhaust manifold and working toward the back of the car.

4. You deserve a treat for such a nice job. Sorry, I don't have one for you, but you deserve it.

Let There Be Silence!

A muffler minimizes exhaust gas noises. So what does a resonator do? The same thing. Some cars have both a muffler and a resonator in the exhaust system to reduce noise. Other cars can get by with just a muffler.

To repair or replace a muffler or resonator, follow these steps:

1. Find and inspect the muffler/resonator for damage. A small puncture can be repaired using a muffler repair kit found at most auto parts stores. A rusty or damaged muffler/resonator should be replaced.

Car Speak

A *muffler* is one who muffs; alternatively, it is a part that reduces the sound of automotive exhaust by passing it through small interior chambers.

2. To replace a muffler/resonator, figure out how the old one was installed: by welding or by clamping. If welded, the exhaust pipe may need to be cut with a hacksaw or replaced. If the muffler/resonator's joints are clamped together with metal connectors, remove the nuts holding the clamp in place and remove the muffler from the pipe. You might have to remove one or more hangers from the pipe to free the muffler or resonator. Replacement parts are available at larger auto parts retailers.

3. Make sure all clamps and hangers are tight before test-driving your quiet car. You can now come in at 3 a.m. without waking all the neighbors.

TLC for an Aging Catalytic Converter

If your car was born in the past 20 years, it probably has a catalytic converter. There are two types: Older ones reduce carbon monoxide and hydrocarbons; newer ones reduce nitrogen oxides as well.

How long should a catalytic converter live? It should give you at least 50,000 miles of service and, with care, up to 100,000 miles.

If you suspect that the catalytic converter isn't working well, take it to a mechanic who has emissions-testing equipment. If your converter needs replacement, do so yourself or have it done. Don't even think about repairing a catalytic converter.

Also, make sure your car hasn't been operated in at least eight hours, allowing the catalytic converter to cool down completely.

To replace a catalytic converter, follow these steps:

1. Find and inspect the catalytic converter. On most cars, it's located between the exhaust manifold and the muffler or resonator. Inspect it for obvious damage or simple solutions such as a loose clamp. A piece of wood can be carefully banged on the casing to test it for rust.

2. Remove the catalytic converter from the exhaust system. If the converter is welded, the exhaust pipe might need to be cut with a hacksaw or replaced. If your converter is clamped, remove the nuts holding the clamp in place and remove the catalytic converter from the pipe. You might have to remove one or more hangers from the pipe to free the catalytic converter. Larger auto parts retailers and dealer parts departments can get you a replacement catalytic converter if you tell them the car's make, model, and engine size.

3. Install the new catalytic converter, replacing rusty exhaust pipes and hangers as needed.

4. Don't forget that converted catalysts must also be confirmed.

Car Speak

A *catalytic converter* is someone who converts those of the Catalytic religion (just kidding). It is an exhaust system component that changes pollutants into less harmful elements.

My Mechanic Says. . .

How can you keep your car's catalytic converter in top shape? Make sure your car uses only unleaded gasoline. Leaded gas and similar fuel additives can damage the catalytic converter and dramatically shorten its life. And you don't want to be responsible for that!

Keeping the Environment Clean of Auto Emissions

Your car probably has at least 1.625 scads of emissions-control devices hidden in its nooks and crannies (see the next figure), maybe more. What do these components do? The exhaust gas recirculation (EGR) system returns exhaust gases to the engine for reburning. The positive crankcase ventilation (PCV) system recirculates gases from the oil pan to the intake manifold. The evaporative emissions control (EEC or EVAP) system recycles fuel vapors.

An emissions-control system.

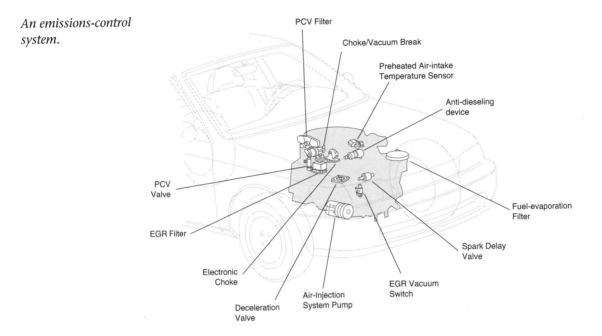

PCV Filter

Choke/Vacuum Break

Preheated Air-intake Temperature Sensor

Anti-dieseling device

PCV Valve

Fuel-evaporation Filter

EGR Filter

Spark Delay Valve

Electronic Choke

EGR Vacuum Switch

Air-Injection System Pump

Deceleration Valve

It's AC (Acronym City) under your car's hood.

How can you repair these systems when they go awry? When you suspect—or have been warned by a state emissions control officer—that your car's emissions-control system (ECS) isn't working efficiently, you can test and replace it. Your car's service manual or an aftermarket manual gives you specific instructions on how to test and replace these components. Here are some guidelines.

To replace an emissions-control component, follow these steps:

1. Test the ECS components in your car using a vacuum gauge or volt-ohmmeter (VOM), depending on the component's function. If it is a sensor, a VOM typically tells you whether it's working correctly. If it recirculates fuel, oil, or emissions vapors, a vacuum gauge can register vacuum pressure. Compare readings with those suggested by the manufacturer.

2. Inspect the component for obvious damage. Then clean it up and test it again. Vacuum-operated components can be cleaned with a solvent. Electronic components can be wiped clean and retested, but cannot be rebuilt. Instructions in the service manual overrule anything said here.

3. To replace a defective component, remove it from the car and take it (along with vehicle

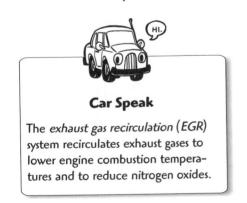

Car Speak

The *exhaust gas recirculation (EGR)* system recirculates exhaust gases to lower engine combustion temperatures and to reduce nitrogen oxides.

identification information) to your friendly auto parts professional. In most cases, the defective components are vacuum-controlled or electrically controlled valves that either work or don't.

4. Install the new part and test the system to make sure it works. Take your car to an emissions test center to verify that it works.

5. Feel good about doing your part to keep the environment clean and healthy.

The Least You Need to Know

➤ Exhaust manifolds don't frequently need repair, but when they do it's usually because of a leaky gasket or other easily fixed problem.

➤ Visually inspect your car's exhaust manifold, pipes, muffler, resonator, and catalytic converter to make sure there are no holes or loose clamps.

➤ A noisy muffler can be temporarily patched, but the best solution is to replace it with a high-quality replacement muffler. It's easy to do on most cars.

➤ Understanding your car's emissions-control system is half the battle of repairing it. Refer to the car's owner's manual and, as needed, the service manual, to minimize pollution and maximize power.

Chapter 27

Body and Paint Repairs: Giving Your Car a Makeover

In This Chapter

➤ Repairing windows on most cars using only a couple of special tools

➤ How to adjust your car's door so it closes smoothly and completely

➤ How to do minor body repairs for much less money than a paint shop will charge you

➤ Painting your car with rented equipment following simple instructions

➤ Making interior repairs using low-cost products found in any auto parts store or department

Whether you're trying to sell your car for the highest dollar, want to increase pride of ownership, or just want to boost your car's morale, you can make body and paint repairs. A window has a crack in it or is leaking. A door doesn't close tightly. The garage attacked your car's fender. A rock—or a boulder—whacked your car when you weren't looking. The upholstery has a tear or a cigarette burn on it. You can fix these and many other body and paint problems yourself.

Here's how.

Makeover Tips for Your Car

These are the last ones. I promise! Here are some guidelines for troubleshooting automotive body and paint problems that I'll cover in this chapter:

➤ If your car is parked overnight in a rough neighborhood and it isn't stripped, it probably needs body and paint work.

➤ Before spending big money on a new paint job, spend a little money on cleaners, rubbing compound, and polishes to see if elbow grease solves the problem (see Chapter 13, "Body and Interior Maintenance: Keeping Your Car All Spruced Up").

➤ Rust-neutralizing products like naval jelly really work to remove and stop rust. Follow the manufacturer's recommendations.

➤ Your auto parts retailer probably has bunches of aftermarket car-care products designed to tempt you to keep your car looking good. In this case, give in to temptation. Look them over, buy a few, and make your car feel better about itself.

What Kind of a Crack Is That?

Car windows are amazing. They allow you to see where you're going without letting the wind muss your hair. Windows keep the rain and snow from joining you inside the car.

So what can you do if car windows are cracked or leak? You can easily repair them using products you can buy from auto parts retailers and even many super-duper stores. Depending on what you're doing, you might also need one or two glass suction cups to lift and position larger pieces of glass.

To repair a car window with basic tools, follow these steps:

1. Identify the damage to the window. If it is a small chip or crack, it probably can be repaired using an automotive window repair kit. If possible, check the damage over a few days to learn whether it is stable or spreading. If it is spreading, a repair kit might not be able to stop the spread. New glass will be needed.

Safety First

Please be careful working around glass. Wear sturdy gloves that help you grasp glass, and make sure that any glass you buy for your car is automotive safety glass rather than household glass. Auto safety glass won't shatter and splinter into sharp fragments like ordinary glass.

2. To repair the glass, read the instructions on the packages of various window repair kits. Some are for cracks, others for chips, and some are for both. Find one that seems to best solve your car window's problem. Follow the manufacturer's instructions. Some kits require that you remove rough edges from a chip, install a retaining cup, and then inject plastic filler into the chip. For glass scratches, apply a glass abrasive and cleaner available from larger auto parts retailers or at a glass shop.

3. To replace the glass, first figure out how you're going to get it out. Even if it has shattered into a thousand pieces, you're going to have to remove glass at the edges before installing new glass. Door glass typically requires removal of door paneling

to access the mechanism that moves the window up and down (called the *lift channel*; call your local cable company for availability). The glass is attached at the bottom. Front and rear window glass requires that trim and a rubber gasket be removed. Replace the rubber gasket with a new one as you reinstall the glass. The car's service manual sure comes in handy for removing and replacing glass.

4. To repair a leaking window gasket, run water on the glass to identify how it's getting in. If it is getting in through a gasket, use a putty knife to lift the gasket away from the glass and then squeeze a little window sealer (from the parts store) behind the gasket. Clean away any excess. Let it dry, and then retest and repeat as needed.

Money Saver

Minor chips and cracks in car windows can be repaired by windshield repair services. Leave any minor chip or crack for a couple of days. If it doesn't spread, chances are it can be repaired. But don't have it repaired if it obstructs the driver's view, or costs more than your insurance deductible. Instead, have it replaced.

Sagging Doors Make Your Car Feel Old

There are few things more frustrating than standing at a car door in the rain trying to get it to close tightly. Bang! Slam! *%$#@!

To adjust doors using your car care toolbox, follow these steps:

1. Check for door sag. Open the door and slowly close it, stopping just as it touches the latch. Is the door too high or too low for the opening? Then lift the door from the bottom edge below the handle. Does the door move very much before it moves the car itself, indicating play? In either case, open the door fully and look at the hinges for loose bolts or obvious movement in the hinges.

   To move the door forward, back, up, or down, slightly loosen the hinge bolts on the body, move the door to the correct position, and then tighten the bolts.

   To move the door in or out, slightly loosen the hinge bolts on the door, move the door to the correct position, and then tighten the bolts.

2. When the door is aligned correctly, check for door latching. Carefully close the door to see how it catches. Either the striker bolt on the door or the latch on the door frame can be adjusted. By carefully opening and closing the door a few times, you can roughly estimate how much of an adjustment is needed. To guide you, look at the relative positions of the latch and striker on the opposite door. Once you've adjusted the door so that it's almost but not quite right, make small changes in alignment by adjusting the screw(s) on the top or bottom, but not both at the same time. When the door latches well, tighten the screws as much as

possible to make sure that the force of closing the door doesn't knock the latch out of alignment.

3. Inspect the rubber seal around the door's edge for cracks or stiffness that can keep the door from closing securely.

4. Let your kids or nephews test the door for you. They love slamming doors!

Un-Denting Unavoidable Dents!

Someone should offer a T-shirt that boldly exclaims "Dents Happen!" No matter how careful you are parking and driving your car, dents will happen, especially those little ones that no one knows anything about. Of course, you can call your insurance agent and let him or her take care of it—except that your policy has a $1 million deductible!

Here's what you can do to remove body dents. Repainting the car is covered later in this chapter.

You might need some specialized body tools for the following job. Read on. You can find them at larger auto parts stores.

To remove body dents, follow these steps:

1. Scrutinize it. Is it a deep scratch, a large indentation, a crease, or many of the above? A scratch might need only touch-up painting (see Chapter 13). Deeper damage means that you must move some metal.

2. Visit an auto parts retailer and ask to see the tools for body repair. There are bumping, pick, and slide hammers, and a variety of metal blocks called *dolleys*.

Car Speak

Body fillers include cookies and a hardening plastic material used to fill small dents and creases in an auto body.

3. To hammer out a dent, hold a dolly on the back side of the dent while you bang on the front side with a hammer.

4. To pull out a dent, drill a hole in the dent, screw the slide hammer into the hole, and then move the handle back and forth to pull it out.

5. To fill holes and finish repairing a dent, use a file or grinder to remove paint from the area, and then use filler to contour. Filler can be lead or plastic. Easier and more popular, plastic filler is sometimes called *Bondo*, the brand name of a popular filler product.

Permanent Makeup

Painting some or all of your car isn't really difficult—as long as you take your time. Much of it is common sense: Remove the old finish, cover the parts you don't want to paint, and then paint. You'll actually paint twice. The first coat, called the *primer coat*, gives the second or finish coat something to hold on to. Many cars also have a third coat, called a *clear coat*, to protect the color coat.

Touch-up painting is covered in Chapter 13.

Painting equipment you'll need includes an applicator and a respirator (for you, not the car). Applying paint by brush doesn't produce a smooth surface, so automotive painters spray on primer and paint. The spray can be powered by an air compressor or compressed air. An air compressor, in turn, can be powered by hydraulics or electricity. Hydraulic-pneumatic air compressors are expensive, but they can be rented. Electric air compressors are less expensive and can be purchased for less than $100. Paint in compressed air cans can be bought for a few bucks each, but is offered only in standard car colors.

A respirator is any device that keeps you from breathing paint fumes as you work—dangerous stuff. Your paint or auto supply store can help you pick out one that is both functional and fashionable. Maybe you can find one that matches the color you are painting your car.

To repaint your car, follow these steps:

1. Pick your equipment. Depending on the size of the job, your budget, and the value of your car, choose a paint application system. You can often rent what is too expensive to buy, such as a sprayer and compressor.

2. Pick your paint. Automotive paint supply stores are located in larger cities. Most sell to the public as well as to paint shops. Find one with helpful clerks who don't mind questions. They can help you choose between lacquer and enamel paints and select the right supplies and equipment, as well as offer techniques for easy application.

3. Pick your spot. Paint in a clean, dry, well-ventilated area. Follow paint and equipment manufacturers' recommendations.

4. Prepare the car. Make sure the body work is done and that rusty areas have been cleaned. Use masking tape and paper to cover any area you don't want to paint. If you're painting a small section, you need to mask off only the area around it. If you're painting the whole car, mask off windows, and mask or remove chrome and plastic parts.

5. Apply primer to the car. Spray primer on the areas to be painted. Some primers also include a filler to fill in small scratches. Follow the primer paint manufacturer's recommendations for sanding and second coats.

6. Paint the car. Lightly apply paint in long back-and-forth motions, overlapping edges. If you're repainting an entire car, start with an obscure part to build your skills. Don't get in a hurry. Follow the paint manufacturer's recommendations for sanding and second coats.

7. If you're painting a portion of a clear-coated car, make sure you apply a clear coat to the repainted section.

Beautiful on the Inside

Car interiors get lots of use—and abuse. If your car's interior looks like an emotionally disturbed gorilla lives in it, here are some things you can do to repair it (after you've carefully evicted the gorilla).

To repair vinyl upholstery, follow these steps:

1. Identify the damage. A few small tears can be repaired. If the damage is more extensive, consider seat covers.

2. Buy a repair kit. Most auto parts retailers and larger department stores sell vinyl repair kits that include a patch, glue, and filler of the same color as your existing vinyl.

3. Follow the kit manufacturer's instructions. The typical steps are to trim the tear, install the backing, cement the vinyl to the patch, and then fill the edge.

4. Stand back, look at the job, and repeat these words: "Good job!"

To remove stains, follow these steps:

1. Identify the stain. Typical stains include pen ink, food grease, automotive grease, and body fluids.

2. Apply the cleaner. If the stain is dry, use a brush to remove as much as possible without extending the stain. Pen inks require rubbing alcohol. Greases are removed with a cleaning fluid. Body fluids are removed with mild soap and water.

3. Reapply as needed. Some stains require heavy-duty upholstery cleaner.

The Least You Need to Know

➤ Before repainting your car, try cleaners and polishes to renew your car's finish (see Chapter 13).

➤ You can often fix a small crack or chip in a window or have it done before deciding to replace the window.

➤ Dents can be removed using auto body tools and filler products to make your car look like new at a reasonable cost.

➤ Automotive refinishing supplies, equipment, and advice are available at auto paint stores. You can often borrow or rent equipment as needed.

Glossary of Car-Care Terms

Advance   Setting the ignition timing so that a spark occurs earlier in the engine's cycle for more efficient operation.

Air bag   A restraint system that inflates a hidden bag (or bags) when a sensor at the front of the car is hit in a collision.

Air cleaner   A metal or plastic housing on or near the carburetor or fuel injection intake with a filter to remove larger particles from the air.

Alignment   An adjustment to keep parts in the correct relative position, such as the alignment of a car's wheels.

Alternator   A component that converts mechanical energy into alternating current (AC) that then must be changed (rectified) into direct current (DC) for use by the car's electrical system.

Ammeter   An instrument that measures and reports the flow of electric current.

Antifreeze   A liquid added to water and used to keep a car's engine cool when running; the antifreeze ingredient keeps the coolant from freezing in cold weather.

Anti-lock brake system (ABS)   An electronic system that controls hydraulics to evenly distribute a car's braking power to avoid skidding. See also *Hydraulic*.

Automatic choke   A device that reduces air flow into a carburetor when the engine is cold to increase the richness of the fuel/air mixture and help the engine start faster.

Automatic transmission   A device that automatically selects gears based on the car's weight and speed.

Balljoint   A ball and socket used as a joint in the steering arms, similar to a joint on a human body.

Battery   A device that produces and stores direct current (DC) by converting chemical energy into electrical energy.

Bearing   A part made of a metal and designed to reduce friction between surfaces.

Bellhousing   A metal shroud that covers the engine's flywheel and the transmission's clutch or torque converter mechanisms. See also *Clutch*, *Flywheel*, and *Torque converter*.

Bias tire   A tire with cords or layers set at an angle, found on older cars.

Body filler   A hardening plastic material used to fill small dents and creases in an auto body.

Bore   The width of an engine's cylinder.

Brake   A device that converts kinetic energy into heat energy, slowing down the car.

Brake caliper   The part on a disc brake system that squeezes the disc to make the car slow or stop.

Brake drum   The part on a drum brake system that receives pressure from the brake shoe. See also *Drum brake*.

Brake pads   The replaceable surface of a disc brake system's calipers. See also *Disc brake*.

Brake shoe   The movable part of a drum brake system that applies pressure against the brake drum; the replaceable surface of a drum brake system is the friction lining on the shoe.

Breaker-point ignition   An ignition system using two contact points that are moved to interrupt the electrical current within a breaker-point or mechanical distributor, common in older cars.

BTDC (before top dead center)   Any point during the upward movement of an engine piston between the bottom and top.

Camber   The inward or outward tilt of a car's wheel.

Camshaft   The rotating shaft inside the engine that opens and closes valves using cams or rotating high spots.

Carburetor   A device that dumps a stream of fuel into passing air for distribution to the engine's cylinders for burning.

Caster   The backward or forward tilt of a car's front wheel axle or spindle.

Catalytic converter   Someone who converts those of the Catalytic religion; also, an exhaust system component that changes pollutants into less harmful elements.

CID (cubic inch displacement)   The total volume of all combustion chambers in an engine measured in cubic inches. To translate engine size in liters into cubic inches, multiply liters by 61.027.

Clutch   A device that connects and disconnects the engine from the transmission, or an air conditioner compressor pulley from the compressor shaft.

Combustion chamber   The area within an engine cylinder where combustion of a fuel/air mixture takes place.

Compression ratio   The ratio of the area when a piston is at the top of its travel to that when it is at the bottom.

Connecting rod   The rod that connects an engine's crankshaft to a piston. See also *Crankshaft*.

Constant velocity (CV) joint   A joint in a car's driveline that enables the shaft to pivot without vibration. See also *Driveline*.

Coolant   A mixture of water and ethylene glycol in a car's radiator that helps transfer the engine's heat to the air.

Cooling system   The system that removes heat from the engine.

Crankcase   The lowest part of an engine, surrounding the crankshaft.

Crankshaft   The main rotating part of an engine that turns the piston's up-and-down motion into a circular motion that can be used by the transmission and, eventually, the wheels.

Cylinder block   The largest part of the engine, including cylinders, oil passages, water jackets, and some other components.

Cylinder head   The detachable part of the engine above the cylinders, sometimes including the valves or other components.

Differential   The part of a rear-wheel drive system that uses gears to transfer the driveline's power to two wheels as needed. See also *Driveline*.

Disc brake   A brake system that applies caliper pressure against a disc on wheels to stop the car. Typically used in the front wheels of many cars.

Distributor   A device that sends the coil's electricity evenly and at precisely the right time to the engine's spark plugs.

Double-overhead cam (DOHC)   An engine that uses two camshafts to control valves—one for the intake valves and one for the exhaust valves.

Drivebelt   The rubber and fabric belts that apply the crankshaft pulley's rotation to rotate an alternator, water pump, power steering pump, and air conditioning compressor, if so equipped. Some cars use a single belt, called a *serpentine drivebelt*, for driving many components.

Driveline   The shaft and joints that connect the transmission with the differential. See also *Differential*.

Drivetrain   All components that transmit power to a car's wheels, including the clutch or torque converter, transmission, driveshaft, joints, and the differential or driveaxle.

Drum brake   A brake system that applies brake shoes against the inside of a brake drum to stop or slow a car.

Electrical system   The components that start your car, replenish and store electricity, and operate electrical devices.

Electrolyte   Sulfuric acid and water solution within a car battery that produces electricity.

Electronic fuel injection (EFI)   A computer-controlled system that injects fuel into engine cylinders.

Electronic ignition   An automotive ignition system that uses electronic signals to interrupt the electrical voltage within the distributor—common in cars built since 1976.

Exhaust emission control   One or more devices for reducing the engine's contaminants before they go into the atmosphere.

Exhaust gas recirculation (EGR) system   A system that recirculates exhaust gases to lower engine combustion temperatures and reduce nitrogen oxides.

Exhaust manifold   A system that collects exhaust gases from the cylinders and delivers it to the exhaust pipes.

Filter   A replaceable part that attempts to keep contaminants out of the air, fuel, or oil used by an engine.

Flathead   An engine with the valves in the engine block so the engine's head is flat.

Flywheel   A round metal wheel at the end of the crankshaft that collects and passes the engine's power to the transmission.

Four-wheel drive   A drive system that distributes the engine's power to all four wheels.

Freon-12   A fluorocarbon refrigerant once used in automotive air conditioning systems; now banned as a hazard to the earth's ozone layer.

Front-wheel drive   A drive system that distributes the engine's power to the wheels at the front of the vehicle.

Fuel   Any combustible substance that is burned to provide power or heat—for example, gasoline, ethanol, methanol, diesel, natural gas, or propane.

Fuel/air mixture   The combustible mixture of gasoline fuel and air fed to an automobile engine.

Fuel filter   A replaceable part that attempts to keep contaminants out of the fuel used by an engine.

Fuel injection   Injects metered fuel into the intake manifold at each cylinder for burning.

252

Fuel pump A device that draws fuel from a tank and delivers it to the fuel system.

Fuse The weakest link in an electrical circuit, designed to fail first before an electrical overload damages other components.

Fuse panel A panel where electrical fuses are mounted for easy access.

Gap Typically, the distance a spark must jump between the center electrode and the ground electrode on a spark plug.

Gasket A thin, pliable material used as a seal between two metal surfaces.

Gasoline The most common fuel used to power automobiles; refined from petroleum.

Generator A device that converts mechanical energy into alternating current (AC) that then is changed to direct current (DC) for use by the car's electrical system.

Ground The neutral side of an automotive electrical system, typically the negative terminal, that is attached or grounded to the engine or frame.

Horsepower A confusing formula for determining the power generated by an engine.

Hydraulic A system that uses hydraulic oil to transmit or magnify power.

Hydrocarbons Any compound that has hydrogen and carbon molecules, such as in gasoline, diesel, or other petroleum products.

Idle system The system within a carburetor that maintains an even flow of fuel when the engine is idling.

Ignition coil An electromagnetic device in a car that converts low voltage into high voltage.

Ignition system The system that supplies and distributes the spark needed for combustion within the engine.

Independent suspension A suspension system that allows two wheels on the same axle to move independently of each other.

Intake manifold A system that distributes air (port fuel-injected systems) or fuel/air mixture (carbureted and throttle-body injected systems) to the appropriate cylinders.

Internal combustion The combustion or burning of fuel in an enclosed area, such as an engine's combustion chamber.

Kickdown A switch or linkage that moves an automatic transmission into a lower gear when the accelerator pedal is pushed down.

Leaf spring A group of flat steel springs in a car's suspension system used to minimize up-and-down motion.

Lifter The metal part of a valve system between the cam lobe and the push rod or rocker arm. See also *Cam*.

Liter   A measurement of volume equal to 61.027 cubic inches. To translate engine size in cubic inches to liters, multiply cubic inches by .0164.

Lubrication system   The engine passages, the oil pump and filter, and related parts that lubricate the engine to reduce wear on moving parts.

MacPherson strut   A component found on most front-wheel drive cars that combines a suspension coil spring and shock absorber in one unit. See also *Shock absorber* and *Suspension*.

Manual steering   An automotive steering system that doesn't use a power booster.

Manual transmission   A transmission in which the driver manually selects the operating gear.

Master cylinder   A hydraulic cylinder that magnifies the driver's foot pressure to evenly operate the four wheel brakes.

Millimeter   A metric measurement equal to .03937 of an inch. There are 25.4 millimeters to an inch.

Mixture adjusting screw   A tapered screw that regulates the fuel in a carburetor's airstream.

Motor   An electromagnetic device such as a starting motor; technically, a car's power source is an engine rather than a motor.

Muffler   A part that reduces the sound of automotive exhaust by passing it through baffles and chambers.

Octane   A unit of measurement for a fuel's tendency to detonate or knock.

Odometer   A meter that reports miles driven since the car was built or since being reset at the beginning of a trip.

OEM (original equipment manufacturer)   The maker of parts installed on the car when built.

Oil pan   The removable part of an engine below the block that serves as a reservoir for the engine's oil.

Oil pump   A part that pumps lubricating oil from the oil pan through the engine as needed to minimize wear.

Overdrive   A transmission gear designed to reduce engine speed and increase fuel economy when the car is operating at more than 50 miles per hour; some cars use a fifth gear instead of an overdrive gear.

Overhead cam (OHC) engine   An engine with the camshaft in the cylinder head instead of the engine block.

Overhead valve (OHV) engine   An engine with the valves in the cylinder head instead of the engine block.

Pad wear indicator   A device that indicates when brake pads are worn to the point of needing replacement.

Parking brake   A hand- or foot-operated brake that applies brake shoes or brake pads against the braking surface on a car's rear wheels; also called an *emergency brake*.

Passenger-restraint system   A system of seatbelts and interlocks or internal switches designed to protect passengers from injury in an accident.

Piston   The movable floor of an engine cylinder that is connected by a rod to the crankshaft.

Piston rings   The rings that fit around the side of a piston and against the cylinder wall to seal the compression chamber.

Pitman-arm steering   A steering system popular for 50 years that used a gear to transmit the driver's steering motion to the pitman arm.

Points   See *Breaker-point ignition*.

Positive crankcase ventilation (PCV)   A system of pipes and passages that recirculates vapors from the oil pan for burning by the engine.

Power brake booster   A hydraulic and vacuum unit that helps the brake's master cylinder magnify the driver's foot pressure to evenly operate the four wheel brakes.

Power steering   A hydraulic unit that magnifies the driver's motions to more easily steer the car.

Powertrain   See *Drivetrain*.

Rack-and-pinion steering   A steering system with one gear across another, making steering more responsive than pitman-arm steering. See also *Pitman-arm steering*.

Radial tire   A tire with cords or layers laid radially or across the bead; the most popular design today.

Radiator   A car part that reduces engine temperatures by transferring the heat in a liquid (coolant) to the air.

Rear-wheel drive   A drive system that distributes the engine's power to the wheels at the rear of the vehicle.

Rocker arm   A part of an overhead valve system that transfers upward motion of the lifters and/or push rod to downward motion of the valves. See also *Lifter*.

Rod bearing   A dissimilar metal part between the crankshaft and individual connecting rods for reducing wear.

Rotor   (1) A brake disc on a disc brake system; (2) A distributor part that rotates to transmit electricity to each spark plug wire through the distributor cap.

Shock absorber   A cylinder that uses hydraulic fluid to dampen a wheel's up-and-down movement caused by bumps in the road.

Single-overhead cam (SOHC)   An engine that uses one camshaft in the engine's head to control both the intake valves and exhaust valves.

Sludge   A pasty compound of oil, water, and debris that accumulates in the oil pan and around rocker arms, reducing the flow of oil through the engine. See also *Rocker arm*.

Spark advance   See *Advance*.

Spark plug   A metal-and-ceramic part that uses electricity to ignite the fuel/air mixture in the cylinder.

Speedometer   A meter that indicates a car's speed by measuring the driveline's turning or rotation.

Stabilizer bar   A bar linking the suspension systems on two wheels (front or rear) to stabilize steering turning.

Starter   An electric motor that engages, spins, and disengages the engine's flywheel in order to start the engine. See also *Flywheel*.

Steering column   The shaft from the steering wheel to the steering gear.

Steering system   A system of parts that transfers the turning movements of the steering wheel to the wheels.

Stroke   The distance a piston moves up and down within an engine cylinder.

Strut   See *MacPherson strut*.

Suspension   The group of parts (springs, shock absorbers, and so on) that suspends the car's frame and body above the wheels.

Thermostat   A heat-controlled valve that regulates the flow of coolant in an engine based on a preset minimum temperature.

Tie rod   A jointed rod that ties the steering gear to the wheels.

Timing gears   The gears that keep the camshaft (valves) in time with the crankshaft (pistons) using a timing chain or timing belt. See also *Camshaft* and *Crankshaft*.

Torque Converter   An automatic clutch on an automatic transmission. See also *Differential* and *Transmission*.

Transaxle   A transmission and differential axle combined into one unit. See also *Automatic transmission* and *Clutch*.

Transmission   A component that transmits the engine's power to the wheels using gears.

Tune-up   A periodic adjustment and replacement of parts as recommended by the car's manufacturer.

Turbocharger   Uses a turbine to force more air into the cylinders to increase power.

Universal joint   A joint in a car's driveshaft that allows the shaft to pivot.

Valve   A part of an engine that opens and closes to control the flow of a liquid, gas, or vacuum. Most commonly, the intake valve lets fuel/air into, and the exhaust valve lets combusted gases out of, an engine's cylinder.

Voltage regulator   A device that regulates or controls the voltage output of an alternator or generator. See also *Alternator* and *Generator*.

Wheel cylinder   A hydraulic cylinder at each wheel that magnifies the master cylinder's pressure to evenly operate the wheel's brake system.

Wiring diagram   A drawing depicting the electrical wiring and devices in a car—useful for troubleshooting electrical problems.

Zerk fitting   A nipple-fitting installed to allow pressurized lubricating grease to be forced into a component.

Index